Andrei Codrescu
and the Myth of America

Andrei Codrescu and the Myth of America

KIRBY OLSON

Foreword by Andrei Codrescu

McFarland & Company, Inc., Publishers
Jefferson, North Carolina, and London

LIBRARY OF CONGRESS CATALOGUING-IN-PUBLICATION DATA

Olson, Kirby, 1956–
    Andrei Codrescu and the myth of America / Kirby Olson ;
foreword by Andrei Codrescu.
      p.   cm.
    Includes bibliographical references and index.

    ISBN 0-7864-2137-1 (softcover : 50# alkaline paper) ∞

    1. Codrescu, Andrei, 1946– —Criticism and interpretation.
2. National characteristics, American, in literature.   3. Emigration
and immigration in literature.   4. Surrealism (Literature)—
United States.   5. Romanian Americans—Intellectual life.
6. Myth in literature.   I. Title.
PS3553.O3Z83   2005
811'.54—dc22   2005002560

British Library cataloguing data are available

Cover photograph of Andrei Codrescu by Chris Felver.

Manufactured in the United States of America

McFarland & Company, Inc., Publishers
  Box 611, Jefferson, North Carolina 28640
  www.mcfarlandpub.com

Acknowledgments

I would like to thank Andrei Codrescu, who was amenable to question and answer via e-mail at short notice for many years and who provided funny and inspiring correspondence. I would also like to thank Calin-Andrei Mihailescu, an ingenious and patient Romanian critic, who offered valuable criticism at both early and late stages of the writing of this book.

Thanks as well to Julian Semilian, a brilliant translator of Romanian poetry and poetics, for his encouragement and insights into the Jewish culture surrounding Dadaism in Romania. The Romanian Jewish literary scholar Raimonda Modiano discussed with me at length what it was like to grow up as a Jewish woman in Bucharest. Mihai Spariosu provided encouragement and inspiration. These Romanian writers and critics offered living insight into the continuing relevance of the Romanian avant-garde.

Thanks to Pastor Richard Niebanck for many conversations regarding postmodernism and other things. I would also like to thank my colleagues at SUNY-Delhi (Tony Markham, Bill and Andrea Campbell, Kathryn Dezur, Mike McKenna, John Sandman, Lynn Domina, John Nader, Rob Russell, Dennis Callas, Candace Vancko, and others) for giving me an agreeable place to finish this book. I would like to thank Steven Shaviro, the chair of my doctoral committee, whose conversation has continued to inspire me. Thanks go also to Mark Lester, for his Urmuzian sense of humor, and to theologian Robert Benne.

I am especially grateful to my wife, Riikka, for the being of my daughter, Lola, and sons Tristan and Julian, all of whom were born while I wrote this book.

Kitinoja, Finland–Delhi, New York
1998–2005

Contents

Acknowledgments   v

Mirror, Mirror: A Foreword by Andrei Codrescu   1

Preface   3

Introduction: Codrescu/Benjamin: Surreal Urbanism   7

  1. Communes/Suburbs: The '60s   23

  2. Postmodernism/The State: Nietzsche   26

  3. Poetry/Politics: Codrescu as Surrealist Citizen?   35

  4. Paradoxes/Linearity: Codrescu's Ars Vita   44

  5. Fun/Work: Fourier's City   51

  6. Variety/Uniformity: Detroit's Demise   56

  7. Paris/Las Vegas: Road Scholar   64

  8. Joy/Philosophy: Nietzsche in Detroit   78

  9. Outside/Inside: Polis/Police   90

10. Poetry/Oedipus: The Investigative Poets   100

11. Edward Sanders/Charles Manson: The Family   121

12. Good/Evil: Ceausescu   125

13. Surrealism/Protestantism: The Blood Countess   139

14. Messiah/Messiah: The Return of Paganism   145

15. Codrescu/Codrescu: Conclusion   152

Appendix A: Andrei Codrescu from a Romanian
  Viewpoint, by Roxana Maria Crisan   159

Appendix B: Five Interviews with Codrescu   170

Appendix C: Works by Codrescu   189

General Bibliography   195

Index   203

Mirror, Mirror: A Foreword
by Andrei Codrescu

A book whose subject I am would preferably be a magic mirror held by a beautiful naked woman. Failing that, the scribbles of a Boswell. Few subjects are so lucky. If the book is literally by a wife or mistress, you can be sure that the subject, even if dead, will not be pleased. Living authors are rarely accorded the attention they think they deserve because they overestimate in public what they know in private to be a lot less. Books whose subject one is may not be biographies, and Professor Olson's certainly isn't, but even essays about one's work will meet the idealized expectations of the discussee like a mirror meets a rock. Of biographies, the less said the better. Most biographies, even friendly ones, are *a priori* crap because the biographer has the unfair advantages of knowing how things turn out. The subject, in the process of leading a life, had no such perspectives. Besides, most biographies are not friendly, tending toward a genre the poet Edward Sanders called "the Poe job." Poe wasn't even cold in his grave when the first hostile biographies began appearing. In our hasty time, biographers no longer even wait for the subject's demise, they do their "Poe job" on people not yet half through with their lives. Essays on one's work are not as egregious as biographies, and are mitigated by interpretive layers, but, in the end, they deal with something far more sensitive than one's mere life. They deal with one's work, which is a writer's heroic effort to transform the dross of facts into something

1

closer to "real life." Creative work is already an interpretive attempt to revise the facts, even reverse them, in order to tease out a (hopefully) universal meaning of use to others. But in all honesty, that's usually an afterthought. The facts, such as they are, are under scrutiny and assault for psychological, not altruistic, reasons. The critic thus has the difficult job of mediating someone's work through the subject's reworking of biography, placing in context the actual elements of the "real" biography, and meeting the subject's inevitable resistance to a reading that cannot help but be less original and certainly not "authorized." And then there is vanity, from which no public performer (and all artists are public performers) is exempt, a vanity that keeps hoping for the naked woman holding the mirror. Kirby Olson's mirror flatters even less by reflecting the subject in a group. Of course, there is no escaping the group portrait if the subject lived in society, had peers, and referenced a context. In Kirby's book, the group flanking the image is various and distinguished and presented as the zeitgeist of an age. That's not at all bad and it makes for fascinating reading, especially since I do indeed admire many of my Olson-ordained club members. In all fairness, the guy has read a lot and brought home to me people whose work I will now reread, just as they (hopefully) will reread me when Dr. Olson's mirror comes calling. Kirby Olson has done in part what my inspiration always has, which is to make me aware of just how necessary my partners in crime always were to me. Has he also touched the deeper chords that I myself have often failed to understand? Here and there, yes. For readers of my work who are not me, i.e., everybody else, Kirby Olson shines a light that bounces off the mirror to good effect. Me, I'm thrilled to be thought about by a smart man.

July 25, 2004

Preface

In 1983, I was browsing in an English bookstore in Paris and came across a tall thin literary gazette by the name of *Exquisite Corpse*. I was delirious, as it said that the editor was Andrei Codrescu. I was 27, and had graduated from a progressive college (Evergreen) in Washington State, where I had spent months in the library reading everything I could find by this author. Unlike the deep image pietism of Robert Bly or the inwardly turned Sylvia Plaths of the era that were published in most journals, I liked Codrescu's outrageous humor, his iconoclasm, and above all his reverence for the stinging truth of surrealism. As I looked through *Exquisite Corpse* in the months to come, I noticed that these qualities were present in nearly every piece printed in the journal, and I was determined to become a contributor. It was the first literary journal I actually enjoyed as it was turned towards the outside rather than a narrow coterie of insiders, and turned to the outside again, as it was about reality, rather than literary conceits.

Months later, I sent Codrescu a letter about a set of experiences in Paris, which he published, and some poems that were not about places, which he didn't. Over the next fifteen years, I became one of the top contributors to *Exquisite Corpse*. Codrescu's journal had become my central focus, and so I studied it carefully and also spent two decades tracking down the many writers he had mentioned in his essays and poems. When I returned to graduate school I intended to write my dissertation on Codrescu's work but instead was carried off by literary theory, which became a full-time occupation and eventually the focus of my Ph.D. work.

It is now some 25 years after I had first encountered Codrescu's work as an undergraduate. I have met Codrescu on many occasions and corresponded with him at great length. During this time, I went to graduate school, I published a book on comic postmodernism and another book on the Beat poet Gregory Corso. I taught in Finland for several years, and then in one flash, I realized that I need to write a book about Codrescu as he was carrying on a great tradition of Bohemian fascination with the underside of cities.

I wanted to write the book in order to discuss the nature of an open society but also to bring to bear continental theory and see how Codrescu was carrying forward the surrealist project which had been much admired by important theorists such as Walter Benjamin as well as more recent theorists. Codrescu is constantly open to new ideas, to new formulations, and to new people, and especially to the idea that in every society there are people who are living their own lives outside the norms imposed by the government. At the center of every town and every city is a mystery, and it is to this mystery that Codrescu as urbanist is attuned.

Psychogeographical surrealism, from Walter Benjamin on forward, has had Andrei Codrescu as more or less the leader and top theorist of the North American branch.

But it was not only urbanism that captured my interest in the Codrescu project. It was an interest in the myth of America as well. America as a shining city. To what extent does Codrescu embody American optimism, to what extent does he embody Eastern European cynicism? These twin formations seem to speak to one another across his work.

As the project began to form in my mind I realized I would need to begin by grounding my ideas with an immense conversation with the poet and novelist himself. Immediately I contacted Codrescu through the Internet (I was living in Finland at the time) and told him I was setting out to write a book about him. He was on sabbatical and so answered my questions via e-mail on an almost daily basis for nearly three months. His never-ending brilliance and fun made the first draft of the book seem almost to write itself. But then I was stuck. I wished to write also about the foundation of Christian America, and to have it dialogue with Codrescu's Romanian Dadaism and European surrealist heritage.

I tried to find other American writers working in Codrescu's surrealist urbanist heritage who were more explicitly Christian in order to compare them. Charles Olson seemed likely. Olson was not a Christian, although his father was Swedish, and the son may have picked up the Lutheran ethos from that culture. There remains an intense interest in church and denominational history throughout Olson's poetry and essays. In Tom Clark's biography of Olson, he made it clear that Olson's mother was a devout Catholic but that Olson did not wish to adhere to the faith. However, Olson was a good citizen and wrote intensely about his chosen city of Gloucester with a remarkable insistence on saving its better qualities, and he often defended the Portuguese and their Catholic faith in his great sequence *The Maximus Poems*. Olson opens his 600-page poem with an invocation to "my lady of good voyage" (*Maximus* 6).

George Butterick, in his *Guide to the Maximus Poems of Charles Olson*, writes in reference to these lines, "On top of the Church of Our Lady of Good Voyage on Prospect Street in the Portuguese community of Gloucester, overlooking the harbor, is an eighteen-foot statue of Our Lady holding a schooner as described.... She is the invoked muse of the poem, and, as Olson has said (conversation with the author, June 1968), 'the poem is a voyage, and I want a good voyage'" (11).

Indeed, Olson was willing to allow his son to register in a Catholic school, and as he studied cosmic gods through his Jungian phase, he came more and more to accept the Catholic God of his upbringing (Clark 319). Olson's mother's faith was Catholic, although he had a "clear preference for [his] father" (Clark 5). The distance between Christianity and the avant-garde is not as great as commonly thought. Throughout Olson's works are references to myriad deities, as well as to the Savior. Going back one step further, Olson's mentors William Carlos Williams and Ezra Pound had a Catholic upbringing. Perhaps Christ could be seen as the common avant-garde figure to both the surrealists (who concentrated on the marvelous) and to America at its foundation (which concentrated on creating a locus of justice). While many of the important surrealists denied Christianity any influence on their movement, it is evident throughout that Christianity and its churches have profoundly influenced the French surrealists. There are so many references to religious icons and to churches and angels throughout their texts that it would require a very significant book to catalogue them all.

Several of the central Beats had a strong religious upbringing and were also central to Codrescu. Allen Ginsberg was raised in the Jewish faith, and Jack Kerouac and Gregory Corso in the Catholic. On the other side of Codrescu's lineage, the surrealist leader André Breton had a devout Catholic mother, and many of the other surrealists had a powerful religious heritage to draw upon. It is this sense of a God outside and above humanity that separates these schools from the Marxist or materialistic poets and philosophers around them. In Codrescu's immediate circle, Tom Clark grew up Catholic, Anselm Hollo Lutheran, Ed Dorn in a Protestant culture, Robert Creeley as a Baptist, and Codrescu himself as a Jew. I have been unable to locate the precise denominational upbringing of Edward Sanders, but he cites St. Augustine in *The Z-D Generation* without any kind of irony. Sanders has also written that his mother was "very religious" and that she taught "Sunday school" (e-mail of February 19, 2002). My contention is that Codrescu's circle, which I have called the Investigative Poets, have kept a sense of the puniness of humankind in relationship to the universe, and that their investigations of reality have therefore a humility before the human enterprise that materialists have not. The religious background of the Beat writers served that circle in a similar way.

Throughout this book therefore there is a dialogical conversation regarding the foundational myths of America, of modernism, of Eastern Europe and of the West. The West did not begin with Christianity but was prefaced by centuries of paganism that have never completely died and recently have flourished once again. In Codrescu's work and in the work of what I have called the Investigative Poets (Codrescu, Clark, Sanders, Creeley, Hollo, among others) there is a continual dialogue between these traditions. It has seemed to me that Codrescu's work is already a conversation about Christianity versus various kinds of paganism (this is increasingly the central subject of his novels) and that it would be well to follow this argument and to play up this theme in order to clarify it. It is a theme that has come increasingly into focus in regards to recent national elections with the red state (often orthodox Christian in inspiration) versus the blue state (often unorthodox and pluralist in inspiration). This conversation is amplified playfully in Codrescu's writings. He comes out of a deep heritage and brings to bear odd and paradoxical insights which often illuminate what is at stake in our changing mythos.

Introduction.
Codrescu/Benjamin:
Surreal Urbanism

Andrei Codrescu is known to a wide public as a radio commentator whose work seems offhand but is deeply affecting as he investigates specific places and ideas. He has been on National Public Radio with broadcasts to the nation for over twenty years. His broadcasts are heard by truck drivers, secretaries, millworkers on their coffee breaks, the unemployed, in nearly every community from Alaska to Florida, from Maine to Texas, from Hawaii to Washington, D.C., and every point in-between. The commentaries are not mere entertainment, but poetry smuggled into a new form, and made relevant to the nation. Codrescu, in this sense, is a public poet along the lines of Allen Ginsberg or Walt Whitman, although he is not so much singing as talking in a witty Transylvanian accent, with what he calls "alien candor" (the title of a book of his poems). He talks on almost any topic, from punk music to selling hot tamales. The voice is one of charmed provocation, but the themes are classic surrealist investigations of urban life from a meta-viewpoint, exploring issues of sexuality, transgression, and repression. Many of Codrescu's radio works are dedicated to the investigation of a specific city, using humor and poetry to open up and psychoanalyze a given place.

A useful comparison can be made with Walter Benjamin, who like

Codrescu, had a deep interest in the strategies of surrealism. Susan Buck-Morss, in her work on Benjamin's arcades project, *The Dialectics of Seeing*, sketches out further possible parallels, one of which was Benjamin's early use of the radio as a vehicle for the exploration and dissemination of ideas. "Even more innovative [than his weekly journalism] was Benjamin's work in the new medium of radio. In the years from 1927 to 1933, radio stations in Frankfurt and Berlin broadcast 84 programs written and delivered by Benjamin. These included a regular program for Berlin youth that drew on the common experience of the city, much as the novels of Aragon and Breton had drawn on their readers' common experience of Paris, as the context as well as the content of the story. While entertaining and often humorous, they had a pedagogic purpose, to teach their young audiences to read both the urban landscape and the literary texts generated within it as expressions of social history" (34-35).

Like Codrescu, Benjamin was not heavy-handed in his pedagogy, as Buck-Morss writes, "The didactic message emerges effortlessly and disarmingly out of historical anecdotes, adventure stories, and biographies of literary figures. As storyteller, Benjamin seems to be in complicity with children — and also with the lower classes for whom education has traditionally been a lesson in intellectual humiliation.... These programs affirm the intrinsically progressive, anti-elitist potential of radio as a medium of communication, capable of establishing a new form of folk culture" (35).

While Codrescu sometimes sounds like a travel writer interested in conveying the surface beauties and marvels of a city, and although he is in fact, quite entertaining, he is also a reformer. He wants to pour extra caffeine into the minds of Americans, providing them with curiosity towards their own culture, to look at their urban landscape with a critical eye, and to stimulate desire. He is a vortex of paradox, aiding and abetting like-minded individuals in his journal of more than a decade, the *Exquisite Corpse*, to reach a larger audience. He is working towards the creation of a more aesthetically conscious community. What overall themes can be discovered in his work? Rarely laying out a clear agenda, Codrescu is open-ended, and it can be difficult to draw a prescription from his work. As he looks for a new and sustainable polis, he has worked under a variety of voices, the best known of which is the Transylvanian humorist on National Public Radio. Simultaneously, he has developed the voice of a ludic surrealist poet in his many volumes of poetry, and the voice of a serious academic writer in his nonfiction philosophical essays, such as *The Disappearance of the Outside*. He is also a novelist whose fiction combines his essayistic gift with poetry and storytelling while attempting an escape from the surrealist project into a different dimension.

Benjamin and Codrescu share a common interest in surrealism as the most exciting of the modernist movements. Like the surrealists, Walter Benjamin found a theoretical ancestor in the early French socialist Charles Fourier — who had been deeply appreciated by Marx (Buck-Morss 470). To awaken the magical realm of objects through recourse to childhood memory was Benjamin's prescription. As Buck-Morss writes, "When the child's fantasy is cathected onto the products of modern production, it reactivates the original promise of industrialism, now slumbering in the lap of capitalism, to deliver a humane society of material abundance. Thus, in terms of socialist, revolutionary politics, the rediscovery of these ur-symbols in the most modern technological products has an absolutely contemporary relevance — and a politically explosive potential" (274).

Benjamin writes that play, rather than labor as such, was the model of Fourier's utopia:

> Human labor will then proceed in accord with the model of children's play, which in Fourier is the basis of the [passionate labor] of the [dwellers in his utopian communities]. To have situated play as the canon of a form of labor that is no longer exploitative is one of the greatest merits of Fourier. Labor thus animated by play aims not at the production of value, but at an improved nature. And Fourier's utopia presents a model for it, one that can in fact be found realized in children's play.... All places are cultivated by human beings, made useful and beautiful by them; all, however, stand like a roadside inn, open to everyone. An earth ordered according to such an image would cease to be part "Of a world where action is not the sister of dream" [Baudelaire]. In it, action would be the sister of the dream [cited in Buck-Morss 276].

It is through this theorization of places as "cultivated by human beings" that we must look at Codrescu's work in radio and in other formats. To render a potential flexibility back into a neurotic place is Benjamin's project, through remembering the childhood of a place, and thus its capacity for being reformed. Codrescu's tactics are similar, using surrealist humor as one of his primary weapons for refreshing the sense of place. When time gets too rigid, and a place no longer has the feeling of a fresh beginning, to remind a place of its childhood will simultaneously reinvigorate it.

Much of surrealism, according to Margaret Cohen in *Profane Illumination: Walter Benjamin and the Paris of Surrealist Revolution*, is an attack on Marxism. Breton had briefly joined the communist party only to find himself unable to agree with its leading precepts.

> Rather, against the Marxist interest in mobilizing the proletariat, Breton stresses the need for individual, tactical disruptions of reigning social orders in what he calls "unchaining." In doing so Breton disqualifies the class from which orthodox Marxism expects revolution, for he suggests as precondition to praxis the subject's being freed from the material conditions of industrial production. Socially transformative activity becomes instead the province of subjects who no longer define themselves according to their work [Cohen 107].

André Breton, in his *Anthology of Black Humor*, understood the use of humor as a method of blasting away at rigid mental states, and rigid states in general, but he saw this as an individual rather than a class revolt. Jacqueline Chénieux-Gendron writes, in her volume *Surrealism*, that in Breton's *Anthologie de l'Humour Noir*, "Humor is perceived as a powerful force for revolt, as the origin of an avalanche the political repercussions of which could go on indefinitely" (93).

Cohen writes that Walter Benjamin saw his great inspiration not so much in Marx's proletarian revolution as is commonly believed, but rather in Bretonian surrealism. Moreover, Cohen goes on to place Jacques Lacan (12), Louis Althusser (153), Gilles Deleuze (113), and even Hélène Cixous (113), under the sign of surrealism, all using humor as a kind of conceptual unchaining that creates "the aporias of revolutionary unchaining" (113) in twentieth-century Bohemian radicalism. It was Breton who turned against the materialism of Marx in order to recuperate Freud as a major aspect of the revolutionary project. Many later figures, fearful of the great influence that Breton had in twentieth-century France, tried to distance themselves from Breton by writing of minor surrealists, or renegade surrealists such as Georges Bataille or Antonin Artaud, but the central principles of Bohemian revolution were all penned by Breton. Cohen writes:

My concern in this book will be to reconstruct early attempts to theorize Gothic Marxism: the first efforts to appropriate Freud's seminal twentieth-century exploration of the irrational for Marxist thought. In France these efforts were initiated by surrealism, that avant-garde movement generally responsible for introducing psychoanalysis into French intellectual circles. They were most extensively elaborated by the movement's leader, André Breton [2].

Cohen shows convincingly that Benjamin's arcades project was heavily influenced by Bretonian surrealism. "Uncanny landscapes, ghosts and sorcerers, strange stones and constructions, *illuminati*: to these will be added such surrealist concepts as objective chance, intersubjective desire, the lucky find, the encounter, the dream, bohemian resistance, the social unconscious, and the capillary tissue connecting the communicating vessels of psychic and material life" (3).

Benjamin took Breton's powerful themes and made them even more powerful. "'Profane illumination' was how Walter Benjamin formulated the kernel of surrealist Marxism in an essay that remains arguably the most important assessment of the political and theoretical objectives of the movement to date" (3). One aspect of this thought that Benjamin did not extend was the surrealist interest in humor. To return this as a central aspect of Bretonian surrealism we must return to Freud.

Sigmund Freud wrote in his late essay "Humor" that "Humor is not resigned; it is rebellious" (cited in Morreall 113). "We obtain a dynamic explanation of the humorous attitude, therefore, if we conclude that it consists in the subject's removing the accent from his own ego and transferring it on to his super-ego" (Morreall 114). This displacement of the ego into the superego changes the locus of authority and has the rebellious citizen suddenly speaking in the name of authority. Andrei Codrescu, as we will see, himself uses the voice of a Transylvanian Dracula, one which is his own accent, of course, but which is also the voice of a count.

Walter Benjamin felt that we had to go back to our childhoods in order to look upon the mythic realms of that time through an adult excavation, which would in turn set up a dialectical process. Codrescu's dialectical process is enhanced by his having had a childhood in Romania under repressive conditions of one kind, and an adulthood in America under more liberal conditions. To double up this dialectic, he often uses the viewpoint of an ordinary American, pretending to know much less than he actually does, in order to seem as nonrebellious as possible, smuggling himself into the character of a responsible taxpayer (superego) in order to speak in the name of the People. Humor, according to Freud, is subversive in that the voice of the child takes on the voice of the parent and orders a holiday. This topsy-turvy state of events is inherently anarchic, as the principles of order are denied. According to Chénieux-Gendron, Breton called it the *Anthology of BLACK Humor* because such humor refers to anarchism. "Black is ultimately, for Breton, the color of exaltation: it is the color of the flag of Anarchy" (91).

Conceptual unchaining, spreading anarchy, and reversing hierarchies characterizes the work of the surrealists. Once this is done, however, there does not seem to be a constructive aspect. Puns that reverse the order of meaning, double meanings, cross-talking, Codrescu's humor is a machine partially fabricated from a surrealist sensibility. Codrescu wrote in his book *The Disappearance of the Outside* that "The surrealist antimachine produced two antidotes to the march of formulas: the Marvelous and its companion, Laughter, solidarity-building laughter, laughter that cut the Gordian knot, paradox-solving and paradox-making laughter.... Surrealist Humor would cause a liberating rippling of the Scale of Mirth, from the slight grin of Huysmans' Des esseintes to the rippling proletarian guffaws of Fantomas, and Surrealist Wonder would create a new human being and a community based on inspiration, not ideology" (135).

In the collection *Raised by Puppets Only to Be Killed by Research*, all of the pieces are short, about one page. In the piece "Fish Out Your Window," Codrescu writes, "There is a hotel in Seattle, the Edgewater, where they let you fish out your window. In fact, they encourage you. They say FISH OUT YOUR WINDOW! right in front. The evening I checked in, a horrifying scene was unfolding in the room immediately below mine: a puffing couple was wrestling with a small shark. They at last let it go, and off it went, hook in cheek into the cold water of the Puget Sound" (174).

Characteristically, Codrescu then gallivants off in several directions, talking about the small earthquake that beset Seattle the next morning and how the shark incident and the earthquake mirrored his violent dream life of late. "Yes, I was in a place where nature seemed to mimic my dreams" (174). He links the scene to animal torture, environmental danger, and his own child's fears of being kidnapped like the children on the sides of milk cartons. "At night, the sharks swim right up to the window, and you go fishing" (175).

This link between life and dreams, and the humorous but serious connections to environmental politics, is a typical example of Codrescu's mind, where he links seemingly random details in a larger rhizomatic landscape, apparently without any effort whatsoever. Where he differs from the surrealists is that his dreams are realistic ones in which children are kidnapped and sharks glide beneath the romantic waters of Puget Sound. In André Breton's *Les Vases Communicants*, he says that the role of the poet is "d'assurer l'échange constant qui doit se produire dans la pensée entre le monde exterieure and le monde interieure, échange qui nécessite l'interpénétration continue de l'activité de veille et de l'activité de sommeil [to assure the constant exchange in the production of mental life between the outer world and the inner world, an exchange which necessitates the interpenetration of the activities of waking and the activities of sleep"] (161). In Codrescu's short and seemingly merely entertaining piece quoted just previous to this, he manages to make these links between waking and sleep, but also to show how they already interpenetrate.

For Breton, the activity of sleep was a neglected aspect of human existence. Freud had posited the centrality of dreams and sought to bring them back to a valued place. Dreams were a condensation of that which was missing in our lives. Breton wanted to use Freudian dream-theory as a guide to reorient our lives towards the great destiny that awaits us. Even Napoleon, he writes, asked Hegel during one of his university lectures whether dream or waking life were the more important (cited in Breton's *Vases Communicants* 152-154). Napoleon, who had overrun Europe with his army and had gone far into Russia, didn't know how to make a value judgment on whether his dream life was more important than his waking. He was similarly confused as to whether his love life with Josephine was more important than his military career. He dreamed more often of her than he did of military conquest.

Breton wants to foreground this confusion of values between diurnal and lunar thought because he felt that Freud had not gone far enough in his analysis of dreams. Breton felt that dreams were prophetic, not merely something by which we could understand the traumas of childhood. Dreams were central to life — they were in fact the very center —

and the desires that they enunciated ought to be the real life of humankind. To make a bridge between waking life and sleep was the surrealist project, to empty the riches of the unconscious into the dreary world of material reality was the Bretonian project to create a world of marvelous humor, and it is this project which animates Walter Benjamin's reconstruction of the Arcades, and his excavation of the city as an aspect of the unconscious. To a great extent this is Codrescu's project, too.

Contemporary Nietzschean Gilles Deleuze uses the concept of the rhizome, plants that connect horizontally instead of vertically, in order to create a new paradigm of community. Potatoes throw out shoots to all sides, instead of aiming for the sky like trees. Codrescu writes of one of his poet friends, "Ted [Berrigan] was a rhizome (Deleuze), a potato that connected with whatever would connect with it. He even assumed the *shape* of a potato" (180). This image of the underground poets who connect and create a subterranean universe of connections becomes a central image for Codrescu as he negotiates his way through the vast commercial enterprise of American life, moving from one city to another on planes, ostensibly to give talks, and to sell his work, but always to meet other poets and underground writers, and to contribute to their inspiration, as well, becoming rhizomatic himself. The rhizome is the very image of Andrei Codrescu's densely clustered poetry and life, where new connections are always being made in the name of poetry, his central value. While Nietzscheans, revolutionary communists, and surrealists use poetry as a unifying metaphor, they also present ludic poetic revolution as their *telos*.

Walter Benjamin wrote, "Only when in technology body and image so interpenetrate that all revolutionary tension becomes bodily collective innervation, and all the bodily innervations of the collective become revolutionary discharge, has reality transcended itself to the extent demanded by the *Communist Manifesto*. For the moment, only the surrealists have understood its present commands" (*Reflections* 192).

In Walter Benjamin's arcades project, he collected hundreds of quotations, rubble of debris about the nineteenth-century Parisian shopping malls known as the arcades, from which he would attempt to reconstruct a superstructure. Benjamin was hoping to collect this debris into an elaborate history of consciousness that centered on the arcades as a symbol of bourgeois life during the period. In the arcades, which were a series of shops connected beneath a glass roof, the pedestrian was free to go into any of myriad elegant little boutiques which were laid into labyrinthine networks of corridors, all organized in order to titillate the flâneur. Benjamin wants us to look at photographs and quotations of these objects, in order to psychoanalyze the city as a crystallization of our own unconscious, and then to throw over false consciousness and to adopt instead a truer reality that would be continuously poetic.

Marcel Proust and many others of Benjamin's generation were all equally excavating the past, as was the philosopher Henri Bergson, in his works on memory. Benjamin writes, "Bergson emphasized the antagonism between the *vita activa* and the specific *vita contemplativa* which arises from memory" (*Illuminations* 154). This distinction between contemplation and action, first presented in Thomas Aquinas' *Summa Theologica*, was meant in Aquinas to separate a life devoted to the contemplation of God and a life devoted to political activity, which Aquinas relegated to the animal realm. Aquinas was a dualist, and unlike most Marxists, Benjamin was also a dualist. Benjamin separates the superstructure of the city from the dreams that it produces, such that the excavation of memory leads only indirectly to action in the political realm. For Codrescu, as well as for the surrealists, the city and its dreams are linked through poetry, but for the surrealists in general, dream and action are not so powerfully or enthusiastically linked. Because of Codrescu's background in Stalinist Romania, the two are quite seriously separate, but they are never completely severed.

While Marxists believe only in materialist revolution and the distribution of goods, surrealists have not abandoned the realm of the spirit. Poetry links the contemplative and the divine to the active and the mundane and it was the essence of the surrealist revolution, but in Codrescu's surrealism, imagination and dream tend to intertwine in unpredictable and sometimes critical ways. Surrealists want to break up static mental structures with their revolution, and to do so they try to create art that will sweep through the commonwealth and change the realm of thought.

The radio offers a new format for poetry, and as Codrescu has reconnected the word to a voice he has reinvented an audience. His is not a messianic voice, but one of paradoxes and zigzags, and he never rises to the fevered pitch of the great political reformers.

What Codrescu does on the radio, in these short pieces, is to offer listeners a chance to enter a lyric frame of consciousness. He offers new methods of perception.

While many rigorous thinkers have had us learn to think like trees, from a principled base out to many constituent parts, Gilles Deleuze has argued for a rhizomatic approach to thinking. "A point is always a point of origin. But a line of becoming has neither beginning nor end, departure nor arrival, origin nor destination; to speak of the absence of an origin, to make the absence of an origin the origin, is a bad play on words. A line of becoming has only a middle. The middle is not an average; it is fast motion, it is the absolute speed of movement. A becoming is always in the middle; one can only get it by the middle. A becoming is neither one nor two, nor the relation of the two; it is the in-between" (*A Thousand Plateaus* 293).

To think in terms of flow patterns instead of in terms of beginning and ends, to think in terms of rhizomes, in which one may be walking on a street and see a sign for an elephant and suddenly think about the problems of sub-Saharan Africa, is the way the surrealist's mind works. It is a-illogical, switching reference points and showing odd new pathways, insights. To achieve this, the surrealist poet has to find living forms of communication. Codrescu's voice comes from an older world where there was a different notion of time, and he presents this as an entertaining change of scenery and thus creates a niche through which to articulate his desire in the voice of a Transylvanian count while simultaneously wishing to give his vast audience the revolutionary perspective of the spiritual aristocrat.

The aristocratic Charles Baudelaire, a precursor to surrealism, wanted to communicate with the common man, from the first poem in his great cycle. Walter Benjamin writes, "Baudelaire envisaged readers to whom the reading of lyric poetry would present difficulties. The introductory poem of the *Fleurs du mal* is addressed to these readers. Will power and the ability to concentrate are not their strong points" (*Illuminations* 152).

The radio is connected to the human voice. Secretaries and fishermen and warehouse workers and others in solitary occupations just let it play all day to give them a connection to the human race. It is comforting. It didn't exist in Baudelaire's day. Codrescu's medium is the radio, and he has gotten famous through it. His voice, more than his words, or his ideas, is known. It is the voice of a contemporary Dracula. "I was conversing with a friend on the Greyhound, when the lady in front of us whipped around and said, '*I know your voice!*'" (*Raised* 14). His voice is one of relaxed humor, but behind this congenial voice is a legacy of surrealist revolution.

Perceptual changes take place ever so slowly, and radio still has a small audience compared to television. In the short essay "My Brush with Hollywood," a big producer says, after mulling over putting Codrescu on a syndicated program, "I'm sorry but your material is too elevated for TV" (*Raised* 112).

In the essay "The Mind Circus Is in Town," Codrescu wouldn't complain, on the other hand, that he has to compete with bodybuilders and beauty queens at a bookstore convention in New Orleans. He parties, he listens to jazz, he goes dancing. The humorist and surrealist in Codrescu wants to reaffirm the connection between not only the realm of sleep and waking, but also the realm of sexuality with that of thinking, the realm of the sensuous with the realm of the emotional. To throw a bridge between the idiotic and the intelligent is an aspect of his work. This is where the American public intellectual has thrown off the role of the European intellectual, exchanging a smoking pipe and thick glasses for a skateboard and boogie-woogie music, and where Codrescu departs from Walter Benjamin. Codrescu writes, "The moon is full, the velvety air of romantic old New Orleans caresses the exposed arms and legs of the swaying couples under the banana trees. The siren song of Café Brazil throws erotic shivers through the throng. Reading is the farthest thing from our minds" (131).

An emphasis on the aesthetic (the emotional and physical) aspects of life is something recovered in Codrescu's texts. Walter Benjamin wanted us to understand the historical context of consciousness through the arcades, but through direct experience. To paraphrase and turn Marx upside down in his "Theses on Feuerbach" is what Codrescu wants: The point is not to understand the world, or to change it. The point is to *experience* it.

Walter Benjamin writes, "This is not the place to give an exact definition of Surrealist experience. But anyone who has perceived that the writings of this circle are not literature but something else — demonstrations, watchwords, documents, bluffs, forgeries if you will, but at any rate not literature — will also know, for the same reason, that the writings are concerned literally with experiences, not with theories and still less with phantasms" (*Reflections* 179).

In the short essay on shark fishing from the window of his hotel in

Seattle, Codrescu writes this sentence: "They at last let it [the shark] go, and off it went, into the cold water of Puget Sound" (174). The word "cold" has both sensual and emotional connotations, which give the text another layer of meaning. The word "cold" has the sense of indifference, of cruelty, as well as the physical pain involved. Sharks may not feel the pain of a hook, but we do. The poet, not merely exploring places from an intellectual viewpoint, is more than a historian of consciousness. Codrescu elevates sensuous experience to a realm of poetic importance as he tries to create what Benjamin called in his essay on surrealism "profane illuminations" (*Reflections* 180). Codrescu actually invokes religion in the name of pleasure and said once in an e-mail: "Hedonism is hard work, and only a means to investigate the mind of God" (e-mail of November 25, 1998). Putting hedonism into the religious category, and the religious category into the category of hedonism, unites two fields. But Codrescu is not forcing them to stay together, he is just playing with them, rather than trying to create a revolution with a single new order in mind.

Like the surrealists, Codrescu chose a place to live for its poetic qualities. He was looking to maximize his dreaming pleasures in actual experience. "New Orleans was once home to William Faulkner, Sherwood Anderson, F. Scott Fitzgerald, Tennessee Williams, William Burroughs, and others, who found its genteel decrepitude well suited to dreaming" (*Raised* 131).

To use the resources of the mind for pleasure in a community devoted to sensation is Codrescu's project in a nutshell. New Orleans is one of the oldest cities in America. If the surrealist goal is to abolish time, why is surrealism so attracted to older cities, and why is it virtually impossible to imagine in new cities like Minneapolis, or Cincinnati? Playfulness is best established when there is a contrast, a loss of continuity between two separate realities. Urban theorist Kevin Lynch writes, "Ancient things seem most impressive in one of two contexts: either quite isolated, in some wild and lonely place, hidden or high, or in intimate contact with contemporary life, embedded at the center.... The partial destruction of the old center of Buda in Hungary in World War II revealed its medieval bones. Luckily, there was no attempt to rebuild it either as a medieval town or as a baroque city" (*What Time Is This Place?* 170). Lynch argues that the layering of time through placing the new next to the ancient produces a richness in the city that evokes continuity and change and offers endless themes for aesthetic meditation. "By temporal collage, we visibly accumulate the rich traces of past time. By episodic design, we can create contrasting states that resound against our personal memories and expectations and help us organize time into discontinuous, recurrent patterns.... While adding directly to our enjoyment of the world, they could also serve to vivify and make coherent our image of time" (189). Collapsing the artificial dichotomy between time and place, Lynch argues that time is one of our richest pleasures in a city, that time provides memories, and as long as those memories do not become rigid and ossified, allow for a precious interplay between elasticity and continuity, between the rigidity of the old and worn out and the young and playful. The foreign by itself can be piquant, and older frameworks of time bursting up through the newer can have this effect. Codrescu himself comes from the Old World, and his bursting into the literary realm of the New World offers a pleasure that he always makes veer into the ludicrous. This sense of two different kinds of time can be linked to humor in that it is a disruption of a metanarrative.

A cityscape with reference to different forms of time also causes time to curl into spirals. Codrescu's finest descriptions are often set in older cities such as Budapest, Paris, and Prague. He is uncomfortable in suburbs and more recent buildings, as they are perhaps too reminiscent of logical values and too far from the area of humor.

Mardi Gras is described in Codrescu's "Indecent Exposure," a work in *Raised by Puppets*, as a time in which strangers can exhibit flesh. The power of the flesh, and emotions, breaks through the tight domination of the superego. This is what Freud describes as the attitude behind tendentious jokes. An entire community coming together in a festival overriding the superego and the rational mind's attempts to clamp down on other aspects of human being is exactly the kind of community surrealists seek. I want to bear this in mind as I look at the criteria for successful communities in Codrescu's various book-length travel writings on utopian and other communities in America. Codrescu often looks away from the clock. In Codrescu's writings, the time of a whole relationship and many different kinds of gender curls into a ball during sex, and many times together are held in the mind during orgasm.

Codrescu writes in his surrealist vein, "This is one of those times, a time choked in the weeds of academic and civilian formalism. To put it mildly, most of what we see in print in North America is unbearably trivial and singularly devoid of courage. 'Eroticize the proletariat!' Says Gherasim Luca" (*Disappearance* 183). The insistence on a massive upheaval of erotic potential as a cardinal aspect of the marvelous is Codrescu's chief criterion for the new city. As we see him go around America, eros is what he's seeking, but he does so within older structures, communities reaching back into previous centuries, in other words, in places that have been tended by guilds and groups of citizens, rather than merely by the solitary flâneur. This is ironically what Baudelaire had sought in the arcades: rhizomatic pleasures, where the imagination could take flight into erotic reality and spread in a thousand different directions, unimpeded by laws, by censors, by Calvinistic attitudes that would valorize the modes of restriction and depth, as opposed to promiscuous openendedness. But to eroticize the proletariat means first finding a means of electricity that can jolt through the heavy barriers of logic and boredom that have been imposed on the masses by education, the mass media, the routines of a bureaucratic business-oriented community, and by history. How to turn the dreams of a population inside out so that we can see them? How to make people see again in risible terms? Is it only possible to do this within older cities that have dreams stretching back for centuries? How to make the straight streets of American cities, and the straight lives, into circuitous, paradoxical, fun lives, doubled over into laughter? In the paradigmatic suburban pleasure of the 1950s, the game of bowling, we have a straight lane that a ball is thrown down. The straighter the ball is thrown, the more points gained. In the 1960s the SuperBall was introduced — a ball that seemingly ricocheted in every direction at once. The SuperBall could be Codrescu.

Victor Burgin writes of Benjamin's project, "The transgressional magic of the *flâneur* is to make the interior appear on the 'wrong side' of its bounding wall, the wrong side of the façade" (38). The flâneur, by using his or her imagination, can create the notion of a dream world outside the phantasmagoria of a shopping space simply by walking a turtle or a lobster and dying the hair green, as Baudelaire did. In America, Codrescu brings in not the new, or the shocking, but the timeless, as he takes up the voice of Dracula, speaking with "Alien Candor," rendering public space dreamlike. Codrescu's goal is to attack authoritarianism under its Marxist, Christian, or capitalist guises, bringing authority down from its pedestal. The pleasure of the ludicrous is his principle weapon. Codrescu never downgrades suburban pleasures, but he tends to expand upon those cosmopolitan dreamscapes that were first celebrated by the surrealists and Walter Benjamin in his passages on baseball, egg-tossing contests, and picnics as the milder forms of play in American life. Perhaps it is too much to demand of a humorist that they present us with a social program, but insofar as Codrescu is also a reformer he offers playfulness as a value of its own. This book exists to examine whether there is some further prescription in his work, and whether surrealism can continue without a clearer prescription.

1

Communes/Suburbs: The '60s

Codrescu had lived through state communism in Stalinist Romania with clenched teeth but voluntarily lived again through small-scale "primitive communism" with less moral rage and something that swung from exasperation to amusement and back. North of San Francisco, in the 1970s hippie world of Monte Rio, Codrescu became a member of a bisexual orgiastic "overthetopia" (Codrescu e-mail of December 4, 1999) devoted to anomic experience, and found it just as appalling, finally, as the experience of everything being controlled by Stalinist politics. Codrescu charts the comings and goings of various small communal systems, and his friends who fell into these systems, giving up their individual sense of criteria to fit into a larger group, but he also charts his own experience of losing his sense of humor and passion in a sexual free-for-all.

Codrescu's brief affair with a member of a free-love commune is told with Ceausescu's communism as the dialectical backdrop to American commune-ism.

> The old demon jealousy started making tempestuous appearances.
> The abrupt flow and counter-flow of allegiances, gossip and
> changes in our extended family was exhausting.... A commune
> makes a din like a construction site. This is the noise, I said
> to myself, of a changing world. Individual love opens up into
> universal love: there is enough to go around forever. It was
> almost enough not to be jealous of food. I grew up in communal

23

kitchens in Romania where violence flared quickly over missing heads of cabbage. It was miracle enough to eat and share with people conscious of it.... It might be instructive to American Moscow-line Communists to stage an eye-gouging fight over a stick of salami for a look at the true nature of State-decreed utopia [*In America's Shoes* 145-146].

Towards the end of the 1970s, the experiment in free communal living is over for Codrescu. Exhausted, he and his wife tried to consolidate their things and get out of no-holds-barred California.

"In June of 1977, Alice decided she'd had enough of the endless bouts of drunkenness, moonlight madness and drought. We didn't sleep enough and our lives took on a strange tint of perpetual tiredness" (162). They sold their cabin in Monte Rio for $20,000 and decided to go to Europe.

The return to Europe, for Codrescu, marked a chance to analyze his values and evaluate his aesthetics.

"I had, in those ten years, become an American poet. I had published books of poetry, mastered the American language to the point where I could ask for a cheeseburger with the self-assurance of a cowboy. I had married a gorgeous woman and I had raised an intelligent, beautiful boy" (*America's* 174).

"It was in Italy, just after visiting Venice, that I began to get the odd feeling that perhaps I wasn't European any longer. A lot of the mannerisms of the French annoyed me and much of the café chatter got on my nerves.... I was irrevocably a man of the New World. I had become an American, no question about it" (*America's* 177).

How had this old world poet become a New World American? When he returns to America, the family rents a place near the Johns Hopkins University campus in Baltimore. "It was comfortable and the street was full of kids Lucian's age and toddlers too. When I thought back to the hostility of our San Francisco neighbors, I found myself enjoying the family feeling of the town more and more" (*America's* 192).

Desire is a trap, as Deleuze and Guattari have pointed out in *Anti-Oedipus* (170), just as duty can be, and if desire becomes a duty, heavily politicized? To totally undo the superego and let the id run rampant was possible in Monte Rio until it had become a carnival of the libido. This is the danger of deifying desire. San Francisco, meanwhile, was reterritorialized by ideology. Deleuze and Guattari write, "Psychoanalysis ought to be a song of life, or else be worth nothing at all.... Reich did not go wrong here, and was perhaps the only one to maintain that the product of analysis should be a free and joyous person, a carrier of the life flows, capable of carrying them all the way into the desert and decoding them — even if this idea necessarily took on the appearance of a crazy idea, given what has become of analysis" (*Anti-Oedipus* 331). Psychoanalysis began to posit the death instinct as greater than the sexual instinct, and thus obliterated the beauty of its own discovery, Deleuze and Guattari write (334-335). "Psychoanalysis is like the Russian Revolution; we don't know when it started going bad" (55).

In the relative quiet of Baltimore, Codrescu depicts the beauty of an unfashionable city without the hype of California. A doctor takes poetry in exchange for taking care of the baby. The crowd at the Baltimore Orioles' stadium boos and cheers, and while Codrescu is writing *In America's Shoes*, he pays heed to the populist call, and edits or admires what he has written accordingly. Far from the celebrated communes of hippie California and the elegant surrealist boutiques of Paris, a less stuffy, less crowded, less political city quietly devoted to a less radical idea of community — a place of stasis — where literature and a family are born, amidst friends. Time appears in a kinder light in this new setting, as history and tradition and common structural networks give pleasure through time. Urban theorist Kevin Lynch writes that, "Effective action and inner well-being depend on a strong image of time: a vivid sense of the present, well connected to future and past, perceptive of change, able to manage and enjoy it" (240).

In Paris, where surrealism flourished, there was already a very strong past. At the heart of Paris lies Notre Dame Cathedral, already eight hundred years old. In America, the sense of a past is much more recent. In Bucharest, the history was obliterated by urban planners under Ceausescu, bulldozing hundreds of years of history and destroying the deep connections in order to pave the way to a totalitarian future. Against Ceausescu, Codrescu posited surrealism; against capitalism, Codrescu posited the ancient device of storytelling and myth; against Christianity, he will posit the value of anomic experience. Against the anarchic commune of Monte Rio, Codrescu posited the pleasures of suburban Baltimore, the comforts of a family, and the bizarre structure of American baseball, a structure that allows for endless innovation within a firm set of rules judged by an umpire. Against the physical realm of America's favorite sport, Codrescu posits poetry.

2

Postmodernism/
The State: Nietzsche

Poetry is especially susceptible to successful breaks with tradition. Codrescu comments in the preface to *Alien Candor*:

> The last twenty years in American poetry have been the site of an epic battleground for competing claims about what poetry is, does, should do, can do. An anthology I edited, *American Poets Since 1970: Up Late*, takes up arms on behalf of certain poetries, namely New York School, East coast Zen & surrealism, and Performance poetry. As such, this is a moment in time marked, on the left, by Language poetry and on the right by the return of so-called academic "formalism." I am only bringing this up here to note that my own work has had its own lyric momentum and mysterious drive that has little to do with the quarrels in question [15–16].

Codrescu then goes on to lay his poems on the graves of nine writers and poets, four of whom are Romanian and five American: Ted Berrigan, Jeffrey Miller, Joe Cardarelli, E.M. Cioran, Mircea Eliade, Ioan Couliano, Gherasim Luca, Paul Blackburn, and Joel Oppenheimer (16). These nine male writers constitute a pantheon of those who died for values similar to those supported by Codrescu himself and thus constitute a tradition of iconoclastic poetry and philosophy and lifestyle. It is a strange legacy, because it is the legacy of those who seek to undermine tradition (excepting Eliade), and is mostly held together by its sense of revolutionary urgency.

Codrescu writes a longer piece about contemporary poetry wars in *The Disappearance of the Outside*:

> Poetry is an art of the Outside, where it best flourishes. In America now, poets have become marginally legitimate without having been illegitimate for very long. Our sojourn in the Outside hasn't been long enough. The new production rippling under the NEA/MFA/MLA umbrella is not benign. It is becoming imperative to restore both grandeur and honesty, always an impossible task. Current literary journals are, for the most part, tepid affairs [182].
>
> The poetry Whitman called for came and went in the 1960s, part of the adversary culture, classifiable with drugs and pacifism and free sex [174].

Charles Fourier posited the cabal, or the small group, as being in playful rivalry with other groups, in the society of Harmony. He wanted competition between inside and outside to remain a fundamental aspect of life, as it is in children's games. The game is now one of dry explication of the texts, as opposed to playful enjoyment without thought of the future. As Deleuze and Guattari write, "Interpretation is our modern way of believing and being pious" (*Anti-Oedipus* 171).

The outside is the school of what postmodern aesthete Steven Shaviro has called "passion and excess," a school of Dionysian beauty. What is inside is the Apollonian school of ethics, reason, balance, citizenship.

What is beauty? The philosopher Nietzsche, anti–Platonist par excellence, devoted most of his life rendering homage to Dionysian crushes, to bringing the frenzy of the outsider poet inside.

> Beauty is no accident. The beauty of a race or family, their grace and graciousness in all gestures, is won by work: like genius, it is the end result of the accumulated work of generations [*Nietzsche* 551].

The New York School of poets cultivated beauty, not intellect, not ethics, not politics. Nietzsche argued that this takes generations.

Codrescu's generation of poets begins with the surrealists in New York during World War II and the excitement they caused in the New York School and the Beats. Frank O'Hara's face gazing out over New York in the 1950s radiates confidence not in ideology, but in inspiration, in raw emotional feeling and the pleasure of sensation, not in understanding. In one very sharp essay, "Personism: A Manifesto," O'Hara reveals the brilliant critical intelligence lying just beneath the surrealist surface of his poetry. "It puts the poem squarely between the poet and the person, Lucky Pierre style, and the poem is correspondingly gratified. The poem is at last between two persons instead of two pages" (*Selected Poems of Frank O'Hara* 14). Evoking "love's life-giving vulgarity" O'Hara brings the poem out of the Platonic ether, into a real context between two individual persons, with an emphasis on eros. "But that's not why you fell in love in the first place, just to hang on to life, so you have to take your chances and try to avoid being logical. Pain always produces logic, which is very bad for you" (xiii). O'Hara is clearly not interested in pain here, but in pleasure, and his emphasis is not on thinking. When he writes, "I'm not saying that I don't have practically the most lofty ideas of anyone writing today, but what difference does that make? They're just ideas. The only good thing about it is that when I get lofty enough I've stopped thinking and that's when refreshment arrives" (xiii). This refusal to take ideas or meaning very seriously, and to concentrate on experience, and eros, is O'Hara's central thrust.

A poetics of effervescence rather than completion, Codrecu's work is unstable, and subject to immediate whims in its composition as well. "We must preserve the human nomad forms in all their *désuété* charm: gypsy scholars, misfits, politicos, truants, escapees, runaways, stewardesses, bus drivers, train porters, itinerants, night managers, self-bornagains, by themselves, hired guns, Kelly girls, corporate fixers, nurses, malcontents — the drifting globe" (*Disappearance* 165). How is it possible to maintain such professions, such picturesque vagrants? They can only maintain themselves, but they give a clue to Codrescu's values — impermanence, constant movement, preserving cracks in the political order so that strangers can get through the walls without a passport, as Codrescu got out of Romania in the trunk of a convertible, or on an airplane, depending on which story he tells, creating a membrane which hasn't broken, but which is permeable with cleverness and skill and luck. Marcel Cornis-Pope writes, "Codrescu's use of masks and personas seem akin to the surrealistic principle of *metamorphosis* and the game of 'one in the other.' But Codrescu ascribes to this kind of metamorphosis a more complex function: at once disruptive, 'unlacing' the rigid structure of language and reality; and constructive, filling the fissures created in the conventional order of things with a paradoxical, multidimensional life" (181). One way to put this is to say that Codrescu's work requires an understanding of the desperate measures to which Eastern European intellectuals have gone to preserve a space of aesthetic autonomy within totalitarian cultures in which anybody who didn't dance to the political metanarrative was murdered.

In the title poem of *Comrade Past & Mister Present*, many of the narrator's relatives want to get out of France and come to America. The people are working as waiters as they leave dysfunctional countries in which they were once members of the upper classes that have been devastated by revolutionary communism. What freedom is left? The freedom to destabilize is still a possibility in capitalist countries, whereas in communist countries almost no institution works well enough to destabilize. Perhaps only the censor is still functioning in many communist countries, as the ego of the state has destroyed all others, and so poetry is one last desperate act of freedom. "I'll write the poetry I always wanted to, or none at all./The conventions of my generation, life, teachers,/lovers, maps, cars, music, art, the things I've said,/fuck 'em all, ploys clearly of the anxious dead!" (*CP* 52). Codrescu strikes us as insane and yet opportunistic, as cold, and warm. He is a variety of opposites, and his poetry opens these varieties of individual within himself and lets them dance in the other worlds of cities, populating and proliferating new possible selves within the American language, but often within memory worlds that seem much like Romania.

In *America's Shoes*, he writes, "Conservative, progressive, nationalist, internationalist, populist, elitist, rural, cosmopolitan, pastoral, technocratic, hunter, hunted — I don't have to go to books for these notions. They are in me, watchful and violent" (183). Much larger than O'Hara in his opposites, Codrescu has also had to span larger gaps of time and place. To go from Stalinist Romania to American public radio commentator, by way of a passport in dadaism, is a leap larger than Frank O'Hara had to take.

This permanent place of exile between systems has become Codrescu's theme and what makes him so valuable to a vital critique of the postmodern situation. His aesthetics seem very close to those of Nietzsche, as they both depend on Dionysian energy, but Nietzsche always sneaks Apollo back in the back door, and with Apollo, the problem of judgment.

Nietzsche writes:

> Nothing is beautiful, except man alone: all aesthetics rests upon this naiveté, which is its *first* truth. Let us immediately add the second: nothing is ugly except the degenerating man — and with this the realm of aesthetic judgment is circumscribed. Physiologically, everything ugly weakens and saddens man.... One can measure the effect of ugliness with a dynamometer. Wherever man is depressed at all, he senses the proximity of something "ugly...." A hatred is aroused — but whom does man hate then? There is no doubt: the *decline of his type* [*Nietzsche* 527].

Coming from a nightmare country, Codrescu could have written books that presented himself as a victim of the Holocaust, of Stalinism, and so on. He stands against the ugliness of victimization and against the surrender of beauty now to a Platonic and perfect future. "Giving up the ideal for the real is our only job" (*Disappearance* 190). "Humans are more important than ideology; play is more important than duty" (64).

Nietzsche writes, "Culture and the state — one should not deceive oneself about this — are antagonists" (*Nietzsche* 509). Where many would have been destroyed, Codrescu found an opportunity. He writes, in *The Disappearance of the Outside*, that "In the 1960s, quite suddenly, censorship became the agent of an entire literature outside its edicts, a literature of exclusion. The excluded language found itself paradoxically helped into the outside by censorship, the guardian of the interior. This community outside the official community, the uncensored wilderness of samizdat, this breeding ground for exile, may be the twentieth century's most native phenomenon. My books came into being as products of my banishment" (100).

Where there is still exhilarating humor, there is still nomadism and safety from the appalling boredom of the closed society. When the inside is politicized, rather than given over to a private sphere, terrorism enters the picture, and humor is made to sit in the corner with an ax in its skull. Under totalitarianism, there is no humor, no shades of meaning, and no paradox. Humor, on the other hand, isn't "correct" and isn't "polite," as Freud indicated at the beginning of the century, and yes means guess. Humor is violent, trenchant, and explosive, as is the finest poetry, but it is also neighborly, or is a necessity of neighborliness. Without humor, it is impossible to imagine friendship. The totalitarian, by outlawing humor, also outlaws friendship and in imposing neighborliness ironically outlaws it, because it outlaws ambiguity and humor. Because we live in an imperfect world, we feel anxiety. To deal with this terror Codrescu reasserts both the values of humor at every level and yet also discourages the attempt by one dictator to rule over all others in the name of harmony. Even the censors must have censors, who are capable of blocking their desire to censor, but these censors in turn must have censors. Censors are those with a memory of certain standards, which all too often ossify, and attempt to hold a population in paralysis.

A poem, or a joke, for Codrescu, is a temporary revolution. It destroys the old order. "La Revolucion ... topples the orders & starts the bad news all over, with a different cast" (*Comrade Past* 86). In this case, the new guy in power is the joker or the poet, who wants you to remember his poem and joke and pay endless homage to him. Everyone wants to capture energy and have it turn into a statue of himself, which others in turn want to smash, so as to set up their own idolization within the polis. The police want the same thing. To see how Codrescu phrases this paradoxical need for self-beatification within the secular polis, by members of the Outside, we might cite an entire poem:

A Petite Histoire of Red Fascism

> All connections
> are made by energy.
> The inert masses
> know nobody & not
> themselves. Nobody &
> Not Self are well worth
> knowing but connecting
> them takes energy
> so they are known
> only by their masks
> of inert proletarian
> matter — Bolshevik
> statues. The people

with the most energy
employ themselves to
know the statues. The
statues are well-known
by the inert masses.
The people with just
a little less energy
are then employed
to interrogate the inert
proletariat. One energy
grade below, the police &
mental-health apparatus
employ themselves to
energize the inert mass
which is now for the
first time broken up
into individuals.
Breaking it up releases
energy — enough energy
to respond to questioning.
The police level then ex-
tracts a primitive narra-
tive from the recently
inert & this narrative
generates enough energy
& excitement to produce
a two-level discourse which
makes sense to the upper
energy level. New
energy is created & soon
the top echelons are
introduced to the dis-
courses of Nobody &
Not Self. Together,
the brass & the mass
envision the statues:
the energy of the mass
will henceforth be em-
ployed to make statues
of the brass.
[*Comrade Past & Mister Present* 102–103]

In the Nietzschean framework the publication of poetry doesn't heal, it is itself an illness, like all writing, and all publishing, and all attempt at law. It leads to sanctimoniousness, as it is a mark of capture by the inside. The biggest outsiders are thus turned into insiders, which reduces the pressure from the outside. As Deleuze and Guattari write, "Every writer is a sellout. The only literature is that which places an explosive device in its package, fabricating a counterfeit currency, causing the superego and its form of expression to explode, as well as the market value of its form of content" (*Anti-Oedipus* 134). Writing is the beginning of degeneration into fixity, of which publication is the completion.

Nietzsche writes: Was Socrates a Greek at all?... Was Socrates a typical criminal? (473).

Turning the inside out, turning the man who defined the polis into a typical criminal, is Nietzsche's operation here, and it is a skillful rhetorical twist. Whereas philosophers come and pretend to heal us, we must first ask, what ails them? Why are their lives lived for literature, even if it is supposedly revolutionary literature? Why is it that so few famous philosophers wrote poems for their lovers, or even had them? What was the matter with philosophers? Why do they prefer canonization in libraries and the complexities of verbalization to the simpler pleasures of sexual love?

What forces went into the creation of Andrei Codrescu? Is he truly a revolutionary force, a force of health? On what basis can I make the claim that he is one or the other? What criterion shall I use? Implicitly and explicitly, I am positing Codrescu as a new kind of worldly ideal (and yet by no means perfect): witty, generous, knowledgeable (and yet anti–Platonic), eccentric, hedonistic, fallen, risen, and above and beyond every other value: ludic, unlike Socrates. At the same time, he is a jogger, a tax-payer, one who cares about his family, a house-owner, a tenured professor, and a lover of holidays. How many figures of the avant-garde could be more paradoxical? "Dionysus, as Otto so clearly illustrates, is a god of paradox. Any study of him will inevitably lead to a statement of paradox and a realization that there will always be something beyond, which can never be explained adequately in any language other than the symbolic — and yet concrete — language of poetry or myth" (Palmer xix–xx).

More important than Codrescu himself, is how he resuscitates the job of the surrealist poet. Urban theorist Kevin Lynch writes, "We can change our minds so that we enjoy the dynamics of the world. We can also change the world to correspond more closely to the structure of our minds" (242). Using Codrescu as the image of the consummate insider changes the nature of the polis. Codrescu has been an outsider almost from birth, and yet his effervescence has triumphed over his would-be victimizers, and he can now move back and forth between inside and outside at will. The Outside disappeared in communist Romania thanks to Marxism, and the worker on a tractor became the model that it was dangerous to depart from. Codrescu writes in his poem "Model Work,"

> I model myself after someone I made up at ten walking
> The mazes of my medieval city's streets, a being
> So light, so bright, so generous and so complete
> He almost had no body, only a black hat. Furthermore
> He appeared only in the rain. To this day
> He cannot be mauled because he is both outside & in.
> When I think of him I feel the sorrow of my later models.
> ...
> Modeling is a warm march through grace without recourse.
> ....
> But there isn't a country where there are no models.
> [*Alien Candor* 175].

Codrescu's model is surrealist poetry. His poetry is a model of inventive uniqueness, and odd laughter.

3

Poetry/Politics:
Codrescu as Surrealist Citizen?

The literary critic Charles Altieri, in his epochal volume *Enlarging the Temple: New Directions in American Poetry during the 1960s,* writes that the creation of a model identity is necessary to the creation of the set of values that creates a community.

> History shows that man's efforts to build temples have little effect on the specific practices characterizing life in the city. Yet history also shows that without the temple, however it may be constructed, life seems at best vulgar and callous, at worst a demonic force driving man back on the woeful inadequacy of endless introspection. When [Robert] Lowell left Rome for Paris, the archetypal secular city, he found only the second alternative — forcing him to a more and more enervated self-consciousness and a desperate quest to locate all value in domestic experience.... Once identity has a fixed base, it is possible to endure the contradictions, restraints, and tentative projections of ideals that constitute the public moral life. As Hegel put it, the temple must exist before men can create in it the statue or image of the ideal man that will serve as the center for communal self-definition. Only then, he argues, can the subjective arts emerge to express the many ways that image can be reflected in the political and social organization of the community [239].

Codrescu's attempt to reformulate an identity for himself as he left Romania and entered America is an essential aspect in his building the community that came to exist in his journal *Exquisite Corpse*. He had to both fit into America on Immigration and Naturalization Service terms, and yet be an international surrealist poet with one foot in the unknown night.

When an FBI agent went to investigate Codrescu's background during the time he had applied for citizenship, "Hunce Voelcker explained to him that there was serious speculation in many circles that I might not be from Transylvania at all. Some said that I was born in Brooklyn and my accent is Berlitz fake. Harold Norse declared that I was the most American person he knew. 'He smokes Marlboros, drinks bourbon and if he knew how to drive, he'd probably drive a Datsun, so help me Buddha, pass the Doritos!'" (*Shoes* 13). Codrescu's FBI file, duplicated in *In America's Shoes*, is rather brief, a mere four or five pages of dry data, when Codrescu had hoped for a biographer of stature. "'The Boswells of the bureaucracy,' as Ed Sanders calls them, may have done OK this one time" (*Shoes* 11). The reports clarify a few details on Codrescu's father, and the nature of his departure from Romania (airplane), but nothing is said of the character of the individual, previously known as Andrei Perlmutter, aka Andrei Codrescu.

The insistence on the establishment of an identity through the accumulation of voluminous notes had to be done by hand, by Codrescu himself. Instead of having his own Boswell, or Balzac, doing field research and interviewing all the clerks who had passed him by in the streets, Codrescu had to elaborate a self out of language. "Nasty people always said that I wasn't from Transylvania really, but from Detroit or Chicago or Boston and that I'd been hypnotized by a Hungarian count at the age of 10 or that my accent was Berlitz fake" (*Shoes* 133). Crucial to understanding Codrescu is that he never allows himself to shrink to one identity. He is always playing different identities off of one another because his central value is the ludicrous.

> "I is another" [Je est un autre], said Rimbaud. "My mind grew too big for the Balkans" said Tzara. The mind is a rapacious beast whose appetites outgrow geography. Freedom is a greedy appetite of the mind.... This hunger is at the core of poetic exile, its need to establish an atemporal, a-special identity capable of taking on all the temporality and localities of its habitations. This identity

affirms whatever is true-in-motion, and is simultaneously an
"escape" and a "remaking," both religious metaphors [*Disappearance* 55].

Codrescu's exile from Transylvania fed readily into a poetic myth
that had long lay on the surface of America, like pimples on teenage vampires, the myth of Dracula. Codrescu saw that this would be useful to
him in terms of the creation of a public persona.

> Dracula was already a figure of some magnitude, having been
> deified to about the size of Satan's chief of staff. His main function was to bite maidens in their semi-sleep. Since then a relatively minor holiday, Halloween, has increased in importance to
> the point where it is now overtaking Christmas as the nation's
> greatest holiday. On Halloween, Dracula is *the* chief deity, and
> just as Halloween is displacing Christmas, Dracula is replacing
> Jesus Christ.... For me, Dracula was generative to the point of
> embarrassment. I did resist at first. I was a gloomy young poet for
> the longest time.... But what a gift! His bite ended being-in-
> time, reinstated aristocracy and difference, and what a way to
> meet girls! [*Disappearance* 43].

The consummate outsider, Dracula, combined with a surrealist
appeal, have turned Codrescu into a considerable cultural force, having
appropriated the images of dadaist, Count Dracula, and surrealist poet,
all virtuous within canons in which the celebration of desire has rapidly
become the central criterion, but precisely this acceptance in the surrealist canon came at the expense of his acceptance by the immigration
department. "My own battle with the Immigration and Naturalization
Bureau was prolonged and epic, but I had little taste for it. I tried to be
neither an 'ethnic' nor a 'minority,' but an aristocrat, a poet" (*Disappearance* 47).

These two images of self take center stage in Codrescu's epic battle
to create an identity that is acceptable to himself, his surrealist public,
as well as the INS.

> Tristan Tzara, the exiled Romanian Jew, is the founder of the
> Dada movement and the embodiment of the poetic exile.... Our
> century's artistic self begins in the antiauthoritarian Dada explosion.... Dada, by its exacerbation of individual freedom, lent a
> sudden vitality to the myth of exile. Word-weary and word-

profligate, Dada finished the dominion of words in the west [*Dis-appearance* 49–50].

Codrescu comments, "Being a homeless creature of hell, an outsider, and a nomad, I was in a magical position, attested to by the entire arsenal of human thought" (53).

In Codrescu's case, it is important to keep in mind his Romanian, and specifically Jewish Romanian, ancestry to reaffirm his authentic status as a scapegoat of a totalitarian regime. In order to fit into America, the Immigration and Naturalization Service at the time of Codrescu's immigration needed to see him as a genuine refugee from a communist society, but also one with an ability to contribute to American society. The Romanian Jews fit this double criteria perfectly. As Lya Benjamin writes of the Jewish population of Romania, they were an important part of the liberal intelligentsia into the 1930s.

> On the eve of the Second World War, 2,000 of the 8,000 doctors were Jews; some 3,000 lawyers were registered in the Bar Association, etc. Interwar Jews took part in political life, contributing to the strengthening of the Romanian unitary national state, to the development of democracy and political pluralism, siding with the democratic forces, fighting the extreme right wing led by the Iron Guardists and the Cuza group, [who were] promoters of an aggressive antisemitic policy of slandering and incriminating the Jewish population, often culminating in violent action and beatings, especially in institutions of higher education. ...A great many scientists, writers, actors, composers and musicians were Jews. They produced substantive works that have enriched the Romanian scientific, literary, cultural — spiritual and artistic repository. But creative activity in the midst of the Romanian society was suddenly interrupted by the dramatic events that preceded and continued during the Second World War [540–541].

When we think of the Romanian Jewish milieu, which produced Tristan Tzara, Benjamin Fondane, Paul Celan and Andrei Codrescu — and think of how it was almost exterminated or dislocated during the Second World War, and the conditions of repression, it is impossible to see Codrescu as simply masquerading as a libertarian outsider in this country. Instead, his creation of an identity was part of a long aesthetic search to find a personae that would act as a passport.

Codrescu has come a long way to get inside, from a small Jewish community in Sibiu, Romania, where he was one of the outsiders, in spite of speaking perfect Romanian, to America, where he has slowly become an insider (citizen). Codrescu's poetry, which is in the vein of the New York School's Frank O'Hara, has attained very little critical reputation inside academia. In the Modern Language Association data base (2004), there are two articles about Codrescu's poetry. These articles were both written by Romanians. Outside of his own national boundaries, Codrescu is extremely difficult to understand, being one of the most complex and contradictory writers in contemporary American literature.

If it were only for Codrescu's poetry, and not for the cultural commentary, Codrescu might have ceased to appear as a cultural force simply on account of this difficulty. As an outsider looking in, he has built a reputation that may eventually make him into a member of the American canon.

Surrealism, which is quite a different gatekeeper than the INS, has opened a conduit for new Nietzscheans, such that a constantly new set of outsiders can be let in to the center of cultural power, and especially those who get in should be those who are capable of retaining their incomprehensibility. At the same time, a sense of immortality must be carefully cultivated against the notions of impermanence these poets wish to circulate. In this way, we can have our institutions and yet feel alive within them, as the barbarians will not only be at the gates, they will be the guardians. Just as prisoners make the best wardens, so outsiders will make the best preservers of our traditions. Codrescu doesn't have much taste for creating canons and prefers the ephemeral, but even about this he has second thoughts.

Codrescu writes:

> The new cities-for-the-automobile have no centers: they are endless, circular periphery. Man's attempts at re-entering the shrinking, living Outside by regaining the center while escaping the marginal and constantly marginalizing interiors have been mostly sporadic, violent failures. The violence is inevitable, but as the policed interiors become seamless, the violence is increasingly against oneself.... The interior of body and society depends on stability, on reasonable rules [*Disappearance* 203–204].

Nevertheless, Romanians, since Dadaism, have excelled in getting rid of any kind of rules. Eugène Ionesco said that it was the Frenchman Paul Verlaine who had first given him the precept, "Take eloquence and wring its neck" (*Hugoliad* 7), but it was a Romanian who turned this into a life's work, as opposed to a marginal sentence in a larger career. Destroying the image of Victor Hugo, an insider, was Ionesco's work in this book. In a work simply titled *Nu (No)*, Ionesco leveled all the major Romanian literary giants and was awarded the top Romanian literary prize for it. Ionesco turned language into a brickbat with which to club himself and all of his contemporaries, and he was crowned with laughter and a literary prize. Nevertheless, as Ionesco admitted to E.M. Cioran on one occasion, toward the end of his life all he could stand to read were modern theatre histories, to see how he was being dealt with, to see if his position as an insider after the Theatre of the Absurd had become canonical, and would remain (Eliade *Journals* 20).

I asked Codrescu in an interview: "It seems that you come out of a tradition of crazy comic Romanian intellectuals. I'm thinking of Urmuz, Tristan Tzara, Eugene Ionesco, and E.M. Cioran, among others. Is there something that makes Romania a breeding ground for intellectual anarchism?"

"Yes," he responded. "In the Balkans we have a tradition of absurdist writing. It is a tactic for survival, like an underground shelter on wheels. The Balkan metaphysical methods of survival are becoming high currency now because human beings everywhere are powerless. The whole world is becoming Balkanized" (*Asylum* 35–36).

It was the Romanian poet Urmuz (1887–1921), widely regarded as a proto-dadaist, who is the master of this absurdist tradition. In his "A Little Metaphysics and Astronomy," he posits that at the beginning there was a mute alphabet, simply waiting for humans to arrive. It is in this two-page fragment that we get the beginnings of the reversal of the signifier and the signified, which lies at the heart of the Romanian avant-garde's sense of humor. Urmuz writes in complete sentences and tells the rudiments of stories in his "antiprose" (see Urmuz, *Weird Pages*). But there is also in these weird pages, such as in the story "Algazy and Grummer," a terror about the fact of eating, and a disturbing new understanding of the relationship of one human to another and to food without any overarching principles. The war of all against all found in Arthur Schopenhauer and Friedrich Nietzsche is brought to absurd new heights in the pages of Urmuz.

Famished and unable to find, in the dark, the ideal food they both needed, they took up fighting again with redoubled energies and, under the pretext of merely tasting each other to complete themselves, and to get to know each other, they began biting and devouring each other with ever-increasing fury until both got to the last bone.... Algazy finishing first" [63].

Tristan Tzara took a great deal from Urmuz, as did Ionesco. Isidor Isou, the Jewish Romanian leader of the Lettrists, reduces the legitimacy of beings to letters, transforming them back into a mute alphabet.

Urmuz's character Fuchs was thrown out of paradise for making art instead of love. When Venus is neglected after offering herself to Fuchs in the Fuchsiada,

Everybody was livid at the insult that clumsy mortal had leveled at Olympus.... One powerful hand, following the orders of Apollo and Mars, yanked Fuchs' fig leaf out, then tacked on the things to which he was really entitled. A stiff ordinance was passed that fig leaves from then on, would indeed be awarded, but only to statues.... A delicate hand, in the meantime, actually the Goddess's rosy-fingered hand, picked the artist by one ear and, with one noble motion, threw him out into Chaos" [Urmuz 87].

Taking the strange strands of his native alphabet, and absurdist philosophy, Urmuz created a sequence of stories that illustrate the diaspora of the avant-garde. The avant-garde is a tribe of ludic Dionysians who celebrate love over the preferred values of stability. For stable values, they substitute art and adventure and hilarity and sexual affairs. Venturing into a country that mostly thought of Romania as the original home of Dracula has caused Codrescu to play a kind of eternal Halloween game of drag, in which his accent is used to playfully dip in and out of a pagan cultural legacy that amuses Americans and has thus become part of the entertainment industry, the circus of American life, in which each person is a simulacrum of some other, everyone mimicking some other outsider, in order to merit their place inside. Whole industries are devoted to this mimickry: nose jobs, facial tucks, courses in how to achieve a midwestern accent are all meant to keep a person on the inside. By playing his role of outsider, Codrescu has become an insider. In his critical essays and in his role as editor, he is beginning to play the role of gatekeeper, putting a stress on ideals of flexibility and eroticism. When Codrescu turns to gatekeeping, he tends to privilege the liminal. What he chiefly desires is the monstrous, tempered by the saintly. In his poem "The New Gazette," Codrescu writes:

> I want to be the publisher of a vicious illuminated newspaper.
> All the viciousness in it will be gold-leafed, raised and colored-in
> By art students with medieval bodies....
> My writers will hate everything
> With passion, fervor and murderous disregard for their safety
> Which will take in writing the form of classical tragedy....
> Two persons, a man and a woman, called Tolerance and
> Intolerance,
> Will be in charge of love and lights"
> [*Alien Candor* 170].

Once desire for the strange becomes the criterion it is not only how to maintain strangeness but how to remain desirable, which is paramount in the postmodern critical pantheon in which hedonism is the central principle and oddness its litmus test. Deleuze and Guattari write, "In his recent works Klossowski indicates to us the only means of bypassing the sterile parallelism where we flounder between Freud and Marx: by discovering how social production and relations of production are an institution of desire, and how affects or drives form part of the infrastructure itself" (*Anti-Oedipus* 63). How to think against cultural desirability, and explode older notions of what is desirable, in order to replace them with something else: Laughter. But if there is nothing serious, no piety, then there also cannot be impiety. The superstructure requires an inside and an outside, or Tolerance and Intolerance.

By June 1977, in the hippie commune of Monte Rio, Codrescu writes in his memoir *In America's Shoes* "the truth is that I didn't remember laughter. Just then I couldn't. I tried enumerating the varieties I knew, out loud: 'Giggles, hysterics, pure, clean laugh, chuckles, chortles, guffaws, gales, the ha-has, suppressed laughter, nasal whine, the laugh-til-you-cry....' I was reminded of one of W.S. Merwin's poems about a man who stole laughter. There was nothing funny about Merwin's poem..." (163).

Laughter can only take place within restraints or within a sense of limits. This world is limited. To laugh is to be reminded of this disjunction. When desire becomes a duty, as it did for the hippies, there is no motivational force for it. Codrescu writes of the terror of his childhood:

> When the communists came to power after the war, the flow of books was stemmed, both from within and from without. State policy at the time of my birth in 1946 was a Dracula-like activity of cultural impalement. First, the authors were victimized [prison, murder, silence], then their books [burning, banning, oblivion].
>
> At the age of fourteen, four immense towers of time removed from Mioritza, I had become a reading monster, a master of the flashlight and of sleepwalking. I was also obsessed with all the books I wasn't supposed to read. I knew that they couldn't have all disappeared, because people winked when I brought them up. They were about me, hidden like swamp treasures, their nocturnal flickering full of mystery and promise [*Disappearance* 17].

Poetry is about the ambiguous realm, and it dies in contact with the certainties of the political realm if it is subsumed by it. But the political realm is also poisoned by the poetic. If the political realm tries to live up to the realm of poetry, it will collapse in vagaries. They must remain separate and yet always remain as if playing a game together.

> In modern times the myth of exile has conquered the West. If an image were to be invented as the proper icon of the beginning of these times, it would have to be a photograph of Lenin and Tristan Tzara playing chess in a Zurich café in 1916. The two exiles often met for that purpose, but there is no record of their conversations. One imagines two slightly bored onlookers watching over the shoulders of the two refugees with expressions of superior indulgence for the obviously amateurish quality of the game. But the snobbish spectators would be terribly wrong. It is a great game, this game between politics and poetics, and it goes on still [*Disappearance* 49].

4

Paradoxes/Linearity:
Codrescu's Ars Vita

Nietzsche traces the beginning of linear thought in logic as the beginning of the fall of Socrates. The need to make sense of the world, to make this stand for that, is the beginning of the nonacceptance of the circular nature of seasons, orbits, the curved nature of space and time. Nature doesn't make linear sense. Logic is hard pressed to figure out where the universe ends and where it began. None of the big questions make any sense within the strict realm of logic, with its straight lines. Nature is circular, paradoxical. Life and death, love and hate, being and becoming, creativity and censorship, faith and doubt, insider and outsider, all seem related on a continuum which circles back on itself. Politics requires an inside and an outside, while poetry must play on the line between them.

Nietzsche writes, "I mistrust all systematizers and I avoid them. The will to a system is a lack of integrity" (*Nietzsche* 470). Against logic, Nietzsche positions music, and poetry, as the principles of a sound philosophy. "Without music, life would be an error" (471). "I, the last disciple of Dionysus" (563). To follow nature, with all its curved inner and exterior space, is Nietzsche's philosophy. "Here is the most profound instinct of life, that directed toward the future of life, the eternity of life, is experienced religiously — and the way to life, procreation, as the *holy* way" (562).

Codrescu uses paradoxes and antinomies throughout his writing to create a state of mental ambiguity in the reader. Codrescu has as many identities as Imelda Marcos had shoes, and he dances in them, performing travesties of the ephemeral fictions of identity. Life-enhancing writing isn't propaganda that aims to brainwash, but rather that which opens the mind to new possibilities of beauty. What a person is, is not what he can dream.

In the volume *Coldness and Cruelty*, Gilles Deleuze writes that logic is a form of cruelty for the Marquis de Sade.

> The libertine may put on an act of trying to convince and persuade; he may even proselytize and gain new recruits.... But the intention to convince is merely apparent, for nothing is in fact more alien to the sadist than the wish to convince, to persuade, in short to educate. He is interested in something quite different, namely to demonstrate that reasoning itself is a form of violence, and that he is on the side of violence, however calm and logical he may be [18–19].

Against this violence perpetrated against victims, Codrescu is looking to inculcate a masochistic language, which bends, which forms pacts with the reader. Deleuze comments in another context: "Possession is the sadist's particular form of madness just as the pact is the masochist's" (21).

In Codrescu's poem "Dear Masoch," he writes, "Dear Masoch doodling with his contracts/ pens Venus in Furs on the margin of the document" (*Comrade Past & Mister Present* 1). Using the female lead of the poem as international cover girl, Codrescu writes, "'They imagine they think,' she says./'I can get around reason as easily as Nietzsche/gets around his house to meet his fate'" (2).

"'In all this,' she says separately, to someone apart,/ 'Reason looms separate and voluntary like a fruit/ in a rabbinical garden, or braces on the teeth/ of Mormon belles.'" (4). Twice Codrescu links reason to religions, in which he no longer believes. He believes in a paradoxical rapport with physical pleasure, fooling around with the tamed sadist of masochism by pretending to be serious and coming upon her in surprise. In the masochistic contract, a woman is assigned the role of state torturer. She must not relish the position, but rather perform it reluctantly, becoming the evil father only in order, paradoxically, to parody and humiliate him by portraying him in her weakness, and thus confirming the masochist's supreme power over the dictator. Deleuze writes:

> The masoschistic ego is only apparently crushed by the superego. What insolence and humor, what irrepressible defiance and ultimate triumph lie hidden behind an ego that claims to be so weak.... In projecting the superego onto the beating woman, the masochist appears to externalize it merely in order to emphasize its derisory nature and make it serve the ends of the triumphant ego.... Humor is the triumph of the ego over the superego, to which it seems to say: "You see, whatever you do, you are already dead; you only exist as a caricature; the woman who beats me supposedly stands for you, and yet it is in fact you yourself who are being beaten in me.... I disavow you since you negate yourself'" [124–126].

In similar fashion, Codrescu closes his poem letter to Masoch, "The State is a terminal cancer, it sucks/ the lollipops of our souls, it sits on our skulls./ She does not exist./ Oh, but I do" (8–9).

The state, linked here to the superego and its fascistic Sadean intentions, is denied its very existence, as the soul supremely announces its own existence in defiance. Nietzsche writes, "All great ages of culture are ages of political decline: what is great culturally has always been unpolitical, even *anti-political*" (*Nietzsche* 509). What Deleuze is arguing is that without the superego, or Nietzsche saying when he speaks against the state, is that there will be a new age of cultural freedom when the superego or the state disappears. However, when the state or the superego disappear, there can no longer be anything coherent whatsoever. The masochist needs the attention of the superego, his own father, in the guise of his girlfriend, in order to produce a defiant orgasm. Similarly, as Nietzsche admits at the end of his formulation, culture is not unentranced by the political, but flies against the political, it is *anti*-political. Without this political there would be no animus, no line for the anti- to draw itself up against, there would be no tension, like playing tennis against the wind. Without rules, no game can be played. Masochism is a game of power in which the power over rules is the goal. Codrescu uses Stalinist Romania to great effect, playing against the grim conditions of his early youth even when those conditions are no longer in existence. It is his departure from that state, however, which made his work genuinely possible. Had he remained in Romania, and continued his line of thinking, he would almost certainly be in an unmarked cemetery somewhere in the Balkans. Nazis, hardline Stalinists, grim corporate monsters, these are the superegos against which Codrescu's ego defiantly defines itself, but this is only possible within a liberal state. Without these external-ized monsters, there could be no heroic ego to laugh and to sustain its pleasures above the harsh strictures that seek to abolish it. It must not be forgotten that the great majority of like-minded individuals were either smashed into mediocrity, or actually lost their lives in arguing with the censors. But some degree of tension between the culture and the writer is necessary, or there would be no reason for oppositional writing, some degree of difference, some differend with the duties imposed on one by others is seemingly necessary. Hegel's temple does not fix identity — it provides a maypole for citizens to dance around in mock laughter.

R.M. Sainsbury defines a paradox: "This is what I understand by a paradox: an apparently unacceptable conclusion derived by apparently acceptable reasoning from apparently acceptable premises. Appearances have to deceive, since the acceptance cannot lead by acceptable steps to the unacceptable. So, generally, we have a choice: either the conclusion is not really unacceptable, or else the starting point, or the reasoning, has some non-obvious flaw" (1). The bias of Sainsbury's definition is that he doesn't accept that a paradox can be more truthful than a logically valid proposition. This need to make clear, logical sense of the world can be traced back to the origins of Western civilization, to Plato's fear of humor and poetry, and to the twin banishing of the poet and comedian from the polis.

The surrealist poet tries to bring the elements of confusion back into the polis within elegant verses, within the realm of art, as a mod-ern-day Dionysus. As our knowledge has expanded, it has met the outer walls of reason and begun to curve. Poetry, and art alone, can respond to this place where logic turns back and the circle (circus) amuses itself. Life is in orbit.

Stephen Hawking writes in *A Brief History of Time* that "Aristotle thought that the earth was stationary" (2). It would make sense, if the earth were stationary, and stars were fixed points in space, that straight lines would make sense, and that the earth could be defined in terms of static givens. Because we now know that life is in motion, and subject to so many laws that we can't keep track of them all, our descriptions must bend with the flow, just as space and time bend at the speed of light.

Although the natural world abounds in such paradox, the realm of reason, and mathematics, so recently invented, argues for eternal verities, for straight lines, and laws. The poets, as early as Ovid's *Metamorphosis*, argued for change, for becoming, as against static being, but inside of this they imposed forms. They tried to make a compromise between the powers of the state and the beautiful sensations of the libido. Ovid, banished to what was later to become Romania, is the poet laureate of that state, the first Romanian poet. Codrescu writes:

> The myth of exile was imbedded archetypally in our culture. I belong to a country whose main export is geniuses. The most famous exile of antiquity, Ovid, was exiled among the ancient Romanians and founded their literature. Since then, in misguided reciprocity, Romanians have been exiling their poets with a single-minded devotion to their beginnings [*Disappearance* 38].

Poets flow from the east to the west. In the west, poetry is a weak force because the governments are so liberal, and capital is the only realm of meaning. In the east, at least until recently, the Stalinist-style governments formed two poets every time they threw somebody in prison. The poetry of the east, under poets like Joseph Brodsky, Vladimir Mayakovsky, and Wislawa Szymborska, has the potent cry of freedom in it because it was formulated under the worst possible conditions of tyranny. Codrescu writes, "The East remains, for me, the totalitarian place where I grew up slanted, the place that defines the terms of my adolescent rebellion, and that of the 1960s. Psychologically, every system of restraint-artistically-resisted is the East" (*Disappearance* 97). With the removal of the restraints, it is felt, poetry and art will come to the fore. However, without the restraints, the paradox is that there will be no felt need for the freedom of poetry. There is a need for poetry in the West, as a countervalance to the demand that everything be useful, everything be economic, as money is our maypole, and there is the demand that everything we do be able to be turned into money, but it is not explicitly taboo to write poetry. It doesn't have the glamour of the illegal. We don't have to be explicit prisoners in order to feel the thirst for freedom. In the West, Codrescu's poetry is only known within rarefied Bohemian pockets, whereas in Romania, for many years, it was forbidden to mention his name, even in crossword puzzles. Just because his name was taboo, however, does not mean it was not on everyone's mind. Only since the liberalization of 1989 has Codrescu's name become well-known within Romania (personal conversation with Julian Semilian February 2003).

In the black and white world of Stalinism, poetry had a mission and could easily be distinguished from the linear propaganda that surrounded it. Against the grim malevolence of the control freaks in charge of the political utopia could be posited the aesthetic values of joy, light, intelligence, wisdom, humor, and fun. The architect of perestroika, Alexander Yakovlev, writes in his volume *The Fate of Marxism in Russia*, "We cannot expect that the great sobering that has begun will continue automatically" (5). "The tragedy of Marxist teaching," Yakovlev writes, "is that it is alien to any dialogue" (8). Always assuming it was right, the political leadership assumed the role of dictator. "Ivan Pavlov called freedom the innate reflex of any being. All the movements of a trapped bird or an insect are aimed at reacquiring freedom. And a person bound by ideological, economic, or political chains never forgets freedom" (50).

Against the hard, ruthless logic of a utopian state, poetry not only exults, but begins to crow. The wild bird trapped in a cage bites at the wire and seeks escape. Codrescu writes: "The real job: to make all ye hear again that metarooster crowing!" (*Comrade Past* 110).

Marx posited a conflict of classes that would work itself out in the eventual victory of the proletariat followed by universal peace. Yakovlev comments: "The idea of the inevitability of, or even usefulness of, violence, hostility, and the physical confrontation of opposing sides has outlived itself" (86).

Can we have a society that is based on playful thinking? Perhaps we can do so if we constitute the ideal of our culture as a maypole rather than a Procrustean image of the divine judge. They both constitute a center around which to dance. It seems more and more that this is the new utopia that was outlined by surrealism, one perhaps more in keeping with the work of utopian Charles Fourier, than Karl Marx. Fourier saw attraction as what kept a society together, not adherence through hatred of a scapegoated class. Fourier wanted to bring people together in a party based on mutual fun and enjoyment, rather than a party based on exclusion of some other group.

Codrescu writes of Fourier and surrealism in reference to America:

> America is de facto surrealist. There is no need to upset "reality" here. "Reality" is manufactured continually. The incongruous

meeting of different realities is a routine matter. People inhabit
the landscape at angles so odd they would surely fall if a continually evolving projection machinery weren't constantly correcting
the perspective.... America was the projection of European
utopias, a heaven on earth very much like that of Charles Fourier,
who believed that the pear was the most noble fruit and whom
the surrealists adopted as an adequate counterweight to Christian
futurism and fatalism [*Disappearance* 139].

That paragraph was published in 1990. Three years later, Codrescu
published the book version of his documentary film *Road Scholar*. In that
newer volume, Codrescu travels across and up and down the country
looking for vestiges of European utopias and beatnik utopias and looking at the wreckage of the inner cities, investigating them for what they
have become, and what they have yet to offer to a scholar in search of
functioning Fourierist phalansteries and capitalist punneries, and Quaker
oatmeal fruitcake asylums. Is it possible that art can be made within
communities in which polarization and judgment is not a strong factor?
Codrescu's utopia has certain criteria, which we will seek in his words as
he seeks in his mind and imagination for a place that has successfully
remained playful, and yet earned its right to make a living within a larger
capitalist society. This is Codrescu's mission, after all, to make a better
community. From communist Romania, to hippie San Francisco, to suburban Baltimore, to the nightly riot of New Orleans, there is a constant
seeking for an America which was born in the Eastern European imagination. Where is the place where opposites are reconciled, and the result
is hilarity and joy and light and poetry, and where dictators are ruthlessly tickled into giving up their authoritarian pretensions? In America
at its inception, Yakovlev writes, "This was perestroika in an almost pure
form, without the need first to break down the colossal resistance of what
had outlived itself" (176).

5

Fun/Work: Fourier's City

Whether Codrescu's Romanian possesses the word "fun" is something I asked him in the several-years-long e-mail interview I conducted while writing this book. (He writes that American fun is different from the sleepy Romanian fun that has to do with Turkish coffee, small talk, and relaxation between wars. This turned into a piece on NPR but has yet to be collected.) Fun is different for every person, and for Codrescu it is an art form, a science, a deep philosophical belief system, a spiritual system, an obsession, a role as deep as certain religious traditions of prayer. What crosses are to the profoundly religious dreaming of other worlds, fun is to Codrescu. Toys are his crosses, and everything is a toy, even cities.

In 1990, he got a call from Roger Weisberg, a documentary filmmaker, who asked him if he wanted to learn to drive in a documentary and go around America, offering insightful statements. Codrescu comments:

> Here was a chance for me to transform myself once more, to begin again. I love being born again, and I practice it. It's my passion, also my métier, my specialty. Changing names, places of residence, body shapes, opinions ... what endless delight. America was set up for this kind of thing, a vast stage for projecting images of self that Europe had made impossible [*Road Scholar* xiv].

When Codrescu met Weisberg, he met a good planner.

> Roger made documentary films about the health-care crisis, clear-
> cut statements filled with moral outrage calculated to induce a
> change in public policy. [They did.] I admired this sort of thing.
> On my planet, however, the twilight of ambiguity reigned. My
> landscapes were paradoxical, my motives obscure until examined,
> my expectations nonexistent, my outlook ironic and pessimistic
> [until proven otherwise], and my hatred of the seeming sturdiness
> of facts a lifelong struggle [xiv].

Codrescu was approached at the same time by another bunch of people who wanted him to commute around America on public transport
and make a movie with them. Here, he makes a value distinction. "There
would be little new for me in seeing America from buses, trains, and
planes" (xvii). He had already been all over America in cars, as a passenger, in trains, in planes. "I have taken Amtrak from coast to coast,
and I fly more planes than I care to think about. I know the people who
drive the buses well, and one day I would love to write about them. The
train is but a nostalgic throwback. Air travelers are busy, distracted, and
uniformly depressing" (xvii). He wanted something new, a precious criterion in Codrescu's terms, a term that links him to the avant-gardes of
the twentieth century, and to their ceaseless quest for what art critic
Robert Hughes has called "the shock of the new."

There is another criterion that came into the equation: independence. As a passenger, he had to rely on others. And being a pedestrian
was good, but inconvenient. He opens his book with this:

> All my life I had two claims to fame: I was born in Transylvania
> and I didn't drive a car.
>   The first fact made people naturally assume that I didn't *need* to
> drive because I could always use bats. I can, but it's a hassle to
> harness the bats every time you need a quart of milk. Try parking
> bats outside the Safeway! My life would have been much simpler,
> I think, if I had learned how to drive when I came to America....
> A careless person is a stationary object, a prisoner, not really a
> grownup. A homeless person, by contrast, may be an adventurer,
> a vagabond, a lover of the open sky [3].

Read closely, Codrescu's values come through in this short paragraph. Movement, adventure, and independence, are counterbalanced

by a certain desire to avoid the responsibility of owning a car. Having spent nearly three decades as a passenger, he was now moving into the driver's seat and at last assuming some responsibility. He had driven a few times before, moments of extreme power accompanied by an accident. Driving into a hat shop in Romania in his father's big black Packard, driving into a stream in California. Getting the car, driving to New York to visit the Statue of Liberty, Codrescu's commentary on various before him, men like F.T. Marinetti, place him in a historical tradition of lovers of speed, men who loved adventure, especially if it was accompanied by power. He even ironically questions himself whether he is not now similar to the Nazis who unleashed the Blitzkrieg, the Anschluss, the drive on Moscow. He buys a red '68 Cadillac convertible — '68 for the year of student riots, and a link to the past of revolution, Cadillac for its link to the American dream, and to the classic dream of American life, in its glorious rush to get nowhere fast and in style. With the past beneath him, he goes off in search of the new:

"I like cities that start with 'New': New York, New Orleans, New Rochelle, New Haven…. There are hundreds of them in the New World. Every one of them was set up to be the New Jerusalem, the place where the sins of the old were cleansed, without losing the amenities of their origins" (27). And yet his first stop is to see the elder Allen Ginsberg, the member of the older generation of Beat poets who Codrescu felt should pass the torch on to his generation, and bless this televised and doubly ironic version of Kerouac's *On the Road*. Then stretching even further back, he visits Walt Whitman's grave, to give us a historical background, with the Statue of Liberty as one more raving speed freak standing in the harbor like a fan at a Formula One race. All along, as Codrescu inspects and mostly dismisses the various utopian communities he meets along the way, it is speed of change, the ability to fit in, and then move on, which animate him. It's a charming ability to find the weird in every circumstance, extracting it like a Dracula goes about searching for blood. To entertain with these strange delights, and then reflect on them, is his niche in American public life.

What Codrescu is looking for is what Ezra Pound described as poetry. "News that STAYS news" (Pound 29). This has a long tradition in aesthetics. Immanuel Kant denounced Marsden's view ([1790] 1951, 80) that it is novelty alone that produces beauty.

All stiff irregularity [such as approximates to mathematical regu-
larity] has something in it repugnant to taste; for our entertainment in the contemplation of it lasts for no length of time, but it
rather, in so far as it has not expressly in view cognition or a
definite practical purpose, produces weariness. On the other
hand, that with which imagination can play in an unstudied and
purposive manner is always new to us, and one does not get tired
of looking at it" [(1790) 1951, 80].

Codrescu visits the old people at the Oneida Community, over 90
and still a sparkle in their eyes. "And yet she exudes a childlike happiness,
the mysterious certainty of an age completely out of reach to my cynical,
quickly disappointed contemporaries. I think of other joyous old people
I know, the poets James Broughton, Carl Rakosi…. They all have it. Perhaps the dream of community, the love of beauty, interest in others instead
of oneself is the secret of longevity" (62). This contradiction of youth and
age implies continuity, a generous link between the elderly and the children. It is aimed at communal fun, in a life of beauty and hedonism. At
the Bruderhof community, a Spartan group in upstate New York, Codrescu
wonders what these people would have felt about his own experiment in
communal living in Monte Rio, California. "I wondered what these good
Christians would have thought of our commune in northern California
and the curry-laced bowls of luscious vegetables that we ate with our bare
fingers in delicious anticipation of erotomaniac postprandial *frissons*" (57).
The utopians Codrescu first meets he describes as cousins to his
own countercultural movement.

Americans in the latter part of the nineteenth century were like
us — in many ways. Jacksonian prosperity — achieved in part by
ruthless dispossession of Native Americans, was followed by the
Civil War, and then by an accelerated technological revolution.
Like us, they felt keenly the passing of nature, the breakdown of
families and familiar values, and the alienation of workers in the
cities. Millennial fervor swept among them, bringing them news
of the end of the world and the coming of Christ.
Things are in the saddle,
And ride mankind. [Emerson] [59].

Shot through Codrescu's book is disapproval of racists, sexists,
money-grubbers, Spartan ascetics, dead corporate men, communist

tyrants, authoritarian schemers, and those who are blind to history. His book is meant as a remedy to these spiritual diseases. As he speeds into the west, through the great hinterlands of industrial capital, his vengeance tends to deepen as his sense of the pleasure of place is overcome by the meaning of time. Always, fun has a counterbalance, morality. And morality must be there to steady the fun, or else one has no discipline, no art, no need to reconcile opposites. In himself, there is a hungry, angry reformer, whose anger and reformation are not steeped in traditional religions or in traditional politics, but who uses them as a handrail as he goes down and down into the middle of surrealist America. Codrescu's morality goes deeper than orthodoxy or tradition. It is neither Christian nor Jewish, but it is a spiritual quest nevertheless that Codrescu is on as he travels across America, informed by an ancient aesthetic practice that goes back at least indirectly to Dionysus. What is his spirit hungry for? Why is he so bitterly disappointed at so much of what he sees, and when is he most contented? Detroit presents Codrescu at his most disappointed, and deserves a small chapter of its own, as it presents Codrescu in the role of a messiah, a new framer of law, an odd situation for a surrealist poet to find himself in.

6

Variety/Uniformity: Detroit's Demise

When Codrescu drives into Detroit, the first American city he lived in, he has nothing but ashes in his mouth. Detroit in the 1960s functioned quite well until the riots of 1967, which brought the city to a standstill. Businesses moved out, convenience stores started to close at 4 P.M., and restaurants today are heavily guarded, making customers pass through two or three locked doors, under the surveillance of video monitors, before one can sit down and have a slice of pizza. At the Renaissance Center, in the rebuilt center of the city, the remnants of the old order have placed some artifacts of the former regime on display. The Detroit Institute of Arts, one of the most magnificent collections of art in North America, was then open only a few hours a day, as it didn't have the money for guards to stay open any longer. At night, the only sound one hears are police sirens and gunshots.

Codrescu writes:

> Motown wasn't the only bright light to abandon Detroit. The Pistons left Cobo Arena for the greener hoops of the suburbs. The science museum closed; public libraries shut down; Amtrak trains don't stop at the station anymore; even Rodin's "Thinker" wonders what happened to the Detroit Institute of Art, which can only afford to stay open a few hours a day. Between 1950 and 1987 Detroit lost 40 percent of its population. During the decade

> after the riots of 1967, the city lost one third of its jobs.... On
> Devil's Night before Halloween the rabble rages through the
> streets, setting fire to whatever is left. "Motor City" is now
> known as "Murder City" [*Road Scholar* 70–71].

Revolutionaries must have some resistance. When the resistance
crumbles and relocates to the suburbs and to Mexico, the revolutionaries are left with the task of having to rebuild.

> When Mr. Henry Ford introduced the assembly line to his fac-
> tory and invented the modern world, diverse people cheered.
> Even the Communists thought that the workers' paradise was
> now at hand. Among the Communists who paid homage to this
> capitalist panacea was Diego Rivera. His mural stands on a wall
> at the (mostly closed now) Detroit Museum of Art, testifying to a
> gentler, kinder time. His workers are clean, his bosses look
> human, the coming world of the industrial utopia is hopeful.
> Nothing was going to stop the march to safe labor and full
> employment! [*RS* 73].

In reality, meat factories churn out guts and are operated by former
Eastern European fascists.

> The manager pulls a scared Romanian refugee from under a
> boiler in the underground room, which is lined wall to wall with
> huge freezers. The man, a short, stocky peasant with sweaty hair
> glued to his pocked narrow forehead, salutes me shyly and cow-
> ers. He begs me in whispers not to take his picture.... He tells
> me that he left just as "the butchers" had begun hunting people
> after the death of Ceausescu. I'm not quite sure I understand, and
> then I do. The only men hunted in Romania after the execution
> of Ceausescu were the worst members of Securitate, the secret
> police. Only those charged with killing unarmed civilians were
> pursued at all [*RS* 88].

The revision of this city, Codrescu says, "broke my heart" (89). It
is an earnest chapter, where a feeling close to panic surges to the fore in
the prose.

> In Romania before World War II the Iron Guard pulled thou-
> sands of Jews out of their beds in the middle of the night. They
> transported them in trucks to the stockyards in Bucharest. There

they shot them and hung them from meathooks. They carved
KOSHER into the flesh of their bodies [88].

It is only after he goes to Chicago and leaves for the great spaces of
the West that Codrescu can manage anything like a moral statement, so
overwhelmed is he in Detroit by the disaster that the city, and all those
who live in it, have become: his former poet friends falling drunken off
of stages, the city closed for business, and only the ripping of guts and
turning animals into food remains as a livelihood in this savage, carnal
place. Finally, somewhere near Denver, Codrescu manages a working
definition of the difference between art and trash. He has been discussing
the case of a woman artist who buried a car in her front lawn in Detroit
and called it art. The city government made her remove it. Codrescu tries
to come up with a criterion that would establish justice in the case.

> Working definitions: If it leaves behind nothing that will cause
> animals to choke to death, or humans to die a slow, lingering
> death, it's art. If not, it's garbage. Seeing God in a rocky butte
> out of your car window is art. The exhaust of your God-viewing
> contraption, however, is garbage [102].

Jane Jacobs, in *The Death and Life of Great American Cities*, discusses
succinctly the problem of Detroit. "Virtually all of urban Detroit is as
weak on vitality and diversity as the Bronx. It is ring superimposed upon
ring of failed gray belts. Even Detroit's downtown itself cannot produce
a respectable amount of diversity. It is dispirited and dull, and almost
deserted by seven o'clock of an evening" (150). Jacobs argues for diversity, and overlapping utility, for short blocks, and mingled old and new,
with heavy concentrations of people, and a vast range of activities, but
her view remains one of reconciling the material with the spiritual. "The
range may not stretch to African sculpture or schools of drama or Ruman-
ian tea houses, but such as the possibilities are, whether for grocery stores,
pottery schools, movies, candy stores, florists, art shows, immigrants'
clubs, hardware stores, eating places, or whatever, they will get their best
chance. And along with them, city life will get its best chances" (151).
Diversity, multiple use, density, and the need for small blocks, Jacobs
argues, are what is needed in a vital city. "Detroit is largely composed,
today, of seemingly endless square miles of low-density failure," Jacobs
writes (204).

As Codrescu motors through the Motor City, the ghosts of the automotive industry, with their main mission being to keep cars circulating, to spread the myth of the power and fun of cars, is questioned, or interrogated. The car, in Codrescu's work, is an evil, enchanting beast. His best friend Jeffrey Miller is killed in a car in the early autobiography, *In America's Shoes*. Codrescu prefers to walk and has an unholy alliance with cars. The most he's willing to do is get in the passenger's side until he's nearly 50. Is a car art or is it deadly, is it life itself, and the very meaning of life?

Jane Jacobs comments, "Nineteenth century Utopians, with their rejection of urbanized society, and with their inheritance of eighteenth-century romanticism about the nobility and simplicity of 'natural' or primitive man, were much attracted to the idea of simple environments that were works of art by harmonious consensus.... This futile (and deeply reactionary) hope tinctured the Utopianism of the Garden City planning movement too and, at least ideologically, somewhat gentled its more dominant theme of harmony and order imposed and frozen by authoritarian planning" (374). In communist Romania, whole sections of old Bucharest were knocked down to make room for a city center that would be a garden city monument to Ceausescu. Small villages were erased and ferroconcrete apartments thrown up in their place. What Jacobs seems to imply is that the city should have the density of an aesthetic object, that it be neither too mechanically straight nor too heavily planned, but that there be constant room for surprise, as in a poem.

Turning art into life, turning life into art, was an aspect of the modernist project. Leaving nothing for anybody else to do but go along passively with somebody else's vision. In a sense, this is what Codrescu objects to in all the communities he finds. The control function has been seized by a small group of individuals and exercised at the expense of other individuals. In Detroit, an authoritarian mentality prevents even his own visual curiosity from random foreplay as he walks into automobile headquarters. The car appears in Codrescu's work as Dionysian, however, and he refuses to condemn it. It is a male that only has a mother.

> The Cadillac assembly plant isn't yet closed, however, so I decide to take my Caddy back to *his mommy* for a visit [my emphasis]. Security precautions at the plant make the prisons of New Jersey look like a piece of cake. There are metal detectors, armed guards, a big white line that can't be crossed, special badges, bulletproof control booths. After what seems like several days, I am

cleared to enter the Caddy sanctum, provided that I stay on the right side of the painted line, do not speak with the workers, and look only in the direction approved by the guide. The Gestapo-like guide has already classified me as a dangerous pinko liberal on account of my involuntary irreverence.... We enter a construc-tivist hell of rail lines, overhead trains, revolving compartments, drawers, subdrawers, screws, and twisting appendages, from which hang the workers — mere appendages themselves in a vast, clanking geometry of boredom. An enormous American flag hangs over the assembly room. The guide proudly tells me that only a few days ago, General Colin Powell, fresh from the Gulf, and his Soviet counterpart, fresh from hell, addressed thousands of workers at the plant. "About what?" I ask her. She looks at me astonished and peeved. "What do you think?" She says sourly. "About these poor workers who look like parts of parts of parts fitting holes into holes into holes?" I try, tentatively. She pierces me with a gaze of pure GM alloy. "About the New World Order" [*RS* 72–73].

There should be worker control of the means of production. And yet, in the communist countries this was achieved, but to no good effect. Whereas the auto factory may have seemed like hell to Codrescu, its cen-tral function was to be efficient, and to bring out cars at a profitable rate. If the factory was one where every worker was getting a Swedish mas-sage, and every worker was distracted by a football game on TV, and there was no order, the place would have been much less safe, much more open to industrial sabotage, and to the loss of profits.

Codrescu's ideal is to assert total ludic utopia in the workplace. Workers who scream for two-hour coffee breaks and Swedish massages on the hour may not like it if they are only paid half of what they would otherwise get, and thus have no money for the weekends. But Codrescu's job as a surrealist poet is to question the fascism of the logic of top-down aesthetics. An office where no input or creativity is permitted and the work is the wind-up toy of the management is equally atrocious to him. In this regard, Codrescu agrees with Breton that the workers engaged in industrial production are not those who will create the surrealist revolu-tion. For the surrealist revolution to take place everyone must first become an aristocrat.

How to make everyone into an odd, wealthy eccentric? Surrealism privileges instead the constant riot of revolution. This is not the climate sought by the leaders of industry. The business climate of Detroit was made unsafe during the 1967 riots and the businesses decamped. Codrescu writes, "When I lived here people sat on their porches and talked. The descendents of Polish, Ukrainian, Romanian, German and Irish immigrants who came here to work in the car factories lived noisily in their neighborhoods. The black sections of the town teemed with life" (71–72). After the riots of 1967, when Codrescu left, tanks moved into place, but it was already too late. "There are no tanks now: only unemployment, poverty and fear stalk these streets.... There are no people — only sculptures of people" (72). Once a city, like a society, goes bad, the rebuilding process might take generations, or even centuries.

Jane Jacobs writes, "lively, diverse, intense cities contain the seeds of their own regeneration, with energy enough to carry over for problems and needs outside themselves" (448). What went wrong with Detroit? What goes right in a good city? Jacobs summarizes: A mixture of order and disorder, of planning and of life, of top-down control combined with the ability of pedestrians and residents to change the intention of the planners rather than to merely carry out those intentions. This is central to her aesthetics. Jacobs writes, "I think this is what European visitors are getting at when they remark, as they often do, that the ugliness of our cities is owing to our gridiron street systems" (379). Too much logic can kill the poetry of a city, which is dependent on diversity, paradox, and surprise, but too little logic, too little safety, too little sense of the planned can do the same. When neighborhoods become convulsive, the upper class does not stick around to exploit the workers. What is interesting in our dreams and in our poetry is not necessarily interesting in our cities. There is a necessary disjunction between the superstructure and the dream. When the superstructure crumbles, those who have most invested in it get their luggage.

Somewhere between the overplanned company town and the continuous insurrection of the surrealists is the city of capitalist democracy with a deeply felt ethos of neighborliness. Few American cities have attained anything like this. Perhaps this is because this takes at least ten centuries to achieve, and our cities haven't had the time to grow into themselves.

Codrescu writes in *The Disappearance of the Outside* that

> Eugene Sue's *Mysteries of Paris* discovered that one did not need
> to travel in order to find strange and mysterious things but could

do so right at home in one's own city. But: [1] not every city is Paris, and [2] our *fin de siècle* is infinitely better guarded against such reversal. The only mystery of most twentieth-century cities is how one can endure living in them. Particularly in those made-for-the-automobile urban wastelands of shopping mall America where human beings are mere accessories of engines, textiles, and electronics. Statistics show that youth violence is endemic to many of these places, a natural response to the institutionalized dehumanization of the surroundings [203].

The malls are owned, every inch of them, by the management company. It is forbidden to pass out political leaflets, and one can be arrested for doing so, as if you were passing out leaflets in somebody else's bedroom. The malls are owned, and controlled by their owners, and they do not function as older cities used to as democratic centers. In Seattle, a leafleting campaign at a mall by the activist John Runnings led to confrontations with the mall owners, who told him he could not pass out leaflets on their property. There is no longer an outside in Mall Land. Every inch belongs to management. Capital has seized every inch and belligerently defends its rights. You can shop and give us your money, but you can't speak. In Russia, just handing out pages of blank paper during the Stalinist period made a citizen subject to arrest. There was to be no circulation of ideas that wasn't granted beforehand by the owners of the society.

The thoughts of Jacobs and Codrescu dovetail here, creating a critique of overly planned Utopian communities that force people to act like passive consumers rather than as living beings with minds and intentions of their own.

Jacobs writes:

> "City air makes free," was the medieval saying, when city air literally did make free the runaway serf. City air still makes free the runaways from company towns, from plantations, from factory-farms, from subsistence farms, from migrant picker routes, from mining villages, from one-class suburbs [444].

Against uniformity, Jacobs and Codrescu rail. For diversity, openness, intensity, density, freedom, and mystery, but also for safety and stability, they yearn. "As in all utopias, the right to have plans of any significance belonged only to the planners in charge" (Jacobs 17).

Poets and artistic radicals and theologians are vital in such instances, in terms of rebuilding a sense of hope, even if many of them are put in prison or thrown into gulags in fascist countries, or are overlooked in capitalist societies. Any situation which keeps people apart, alienates them, and encourages them not to pass information on to each other, as the University Shopping Mall in Seattle obstructed the passing of leaflets by John Runnings, should be considered a dead space, a place of dead people, where statues, as envisioned by the planners, have replaced people, creating the conditions of a miniature Detroit. The increasing polarization of the proletariat and the upper classes in such instances can lead to deadness, but the continuous insurrection of revolution can lead to the flight of business interests and a downturn. The point in such cases is to get in the car and move on, as Codrescu does in his Cadillac, or as 40 percent of Detroit has done since 1950. A great city is about as rare as a great poem — it needs a solid structure but endless invention within it. The individual words must be able to breathe, but to do so within a set of flexible rules that have a universally understood form.

7

Paris/Las Vegas: Road Scholar

Hannah Arendt writes, "To this day Paris is the only one among the large cities which can be comfortably covered on foot, and more than any other city it is dependent for its liveliness on people who pass by in the streets, so that the modern automobile traffic endangers its very existence not only for technical reasons. The wasteland of an American suburb, or the residential districts of many towns ... where one can walk on the sidewalks, for miles without encountering a human being, is the very opposite of Paris. What all other cities seem to permit only reluctantly to the dregs of society — strolling, idling, flânerie — Paris streets actually invite everyone to do. Thus, ever since the Second Empire the city has been the paradise of all those who need to chase after no livelihood, pursue no career, reach no goal — the paradise, then, of bohemians" (*Introduction to Walter Benjamin*, 27).

The New York School of poets, from which Codrescu drew inspiration, saw the French as their model. Frank O'Hara's poetry is based on, and often cites, French counterparts. Guillaume Apollinaire, Robert Desnos, François Villon, and others are frequently cited in his poetry. Codrescu spent time in Paris. John Ashbery spent a decade in Paris. Ashbery has translated a great deal of French poetry into English. Kenneth Koch, likewise, the third in stature among the New York school of poets, has often based his writings on French models. All of these writers were much more familiar with the verse of the French surrealists than they were with the work of the English: Aldous Huxley, or Rudyard Kipling. Faint echoes of Coleridge, fainter echoes of Shakespeare, maybe, but the writers to whom they felt a true kinship and rivalry were specifically the French. Those writers that the New York School accepted from among the American canon were the ones that the French first canonized. It is Whitman and Poe that the French adored. The English have been sidelined in this matter of canonization within the New York School. And all of these French writers, in turn, were inspired by their beautiful capital: Paris.

In the same way, it is the café life of Paris that is idealized by American bohemians. When we think of England, we think (often unfairly) of lifeless snobs having no fun. French philosophers are the ones to whom Americans instinctively turn, often elevating them to the level of a deity, for which there are no English equivalents.

Simultaneously with this adoration of French culture, however, is an intense rivalry. The French are friends and enemies at the same time — a paradoxical relationship, in which many American poets feel called upon to specifically reject French culture, in a way that they don't feel called upon to reject British culture. Codrescu stands in a weird relationship to this American fascination with the French, because he, too, is fascinated, but it is not a strict dichotomy for him.

Towards the end of *In America's Shoes*, the Codrescus got money from their California cabin and parlayed it into an extended trip to Europe. Codrescu went to a Parisian movie theatre with his son Lucian to see a Donald Duck film with subtitles. The theatre was in a historical quarter, and all the great names of the people who had lived in this area were written on the ceilings and walls.

> So while Lucian tried to ignore the French subtitles and listen to Donald Duck in the original English, I was making out in the semi-darkness the names of Leon Trotsky, Picasso, Max Jacob, Apollinaire and so on. But the turning point came when we went to visit my friend Ron Sukenick, who was in Paris on a Guggenheim and lived right on Place St. Michel. We burst in on Ron while he was entertaining a few of his refined French friends with tea and petits-fours. The guest of honor was a French-Israeli novelist of great distinction, a distinguished, silver-haired man who reminded me a little of the chief warden at Folsom Prison.... Ron was glad enough to see us and from that moment on, the conversation, which had been conducted in polite and strained French,

switched to English ... the chief result of that visit was that Ron gave Lucian a skateboard somebody had left behind [175].

This conveyance of American fun was used by Lucian to deterritorialize French solemnity, as he did the Louvre, Luxembourg Gardens, and other places, as "part of the new phenomenon sweeping Paris" (175). Lucian wore a baseball cap backwards and "did things on the skateboard I was afraid to watch" (175). The French, in short, are always made to sound slightly boring and out of it, in Codrescu's chronicles, while also having an enviable past which can hardly be topped. In his short radio piece, "Paris, France," Codrescu contrasts the tired, anemic, historically based Parisians with the naive restless American mentality. He speaks with his Romanian compatriot E.M. Cioran.

> Pointing to the spires of Notre Dame in the sunset, he said, "In the year 2000, Notre Dame will be a Mosque." I laughed, but he didn't....
>
> American faith in the future is contagious. It makes one instantly young. But the young, as everyone knows, can be foolish as well as dangerous.
>
> I asked Cioran if he had ever been to America. "Oh, no," he replied. "I am a provincial of the Quarter" [the Latin Quarter of Paris]. Some other provincials of this place had been Voltaire, Sartre, and Trotsky. As I watched the life swirling about me, I tried to feel the lingering power of this cultural vortex. It was there even as the surface was made of signs from elsewhere. The young people in their touching American clothes did not perhaps want to be Americans. What they wanted was some of America's young energy, its optimism. Weary like Cioran of the bitter lessons of Europe, they merely wanted to be young [*Raised* 187–188].

Codrescu comments: "Bucharest and Paris have a lot more in common than San Francisco and Paris. I was irrevocably a man of the New World. I have become an American, no question about it. In a few years I will have lived in America exactly half of my life. That would and will be the turning point" (*In America's Shoes* 177). The forward-looking mentality of the Americans versus the historically based Europeans. If Paris provides a backdrop to the American scene, a kind of paradisical mecca that turns out to be a bore, Codrescu playfully tries to put American life one-up by citing guns. Guns are something we've got that Parisians don't.

Nevertheless, as Codrescu continued to explore America in *Road Scholar*, a disturbing ambiguity about guns comes to the fore. Codrescu's earliest book of poems, *License to Carry a Gun* (Big Table, 1970), seemingly celebrated the ultimate equalizer within a democratic and open-minded frame. "The license to carry a gun is a license to be," Codrescu writes in the poem of the same name in his *Selected Poems 1970–80* (6). And there is this poem, on the following page, untitled:

> there is an orange rotting on the table
> closer to freedom than I ever was.
> I'll throw it away soon, its smell
> gives me the same sweet hallucinations
> I had when I was holding a gun.
> orange of sun, my useless state of mind [7]

This fruity smell of being, of overripe tranquility, animated his early poetry of guns. In *America's Shoes*, there are several brief sequences in which Codrescu holds a gun or lavishes his attention upon a gun. During his second job as a poet-in-residence, at a small experimental high school, a big black girl is waiting for her cheating boyfriend. "Only then I saw that the girl had a gun in her hand. She lifted it and fired once. The boy fell, clutching his leg and the girl threw the gun down and ran out, crying. In a few minutes, the place filled with hysterical kids and then there was an ambulance and they took the lightly wounded lover away" (80).

The American love affair with guns goes back to the beginnings of the country, and to the Second Amendment, which guarantees the right to own a gun. The freedom that was won in the Revolution against the English has become fetishized as the gun has become a veritable symbol of freedom. It is an icon that kills. It is a form of expression of liberty, which the Bill of Rights made sacred. The First Amendment and the Second Amendment, the twin pillars of the American idea of liberation, are also its two greatest controversies, with citizens mouthing off about topics from birth control to euthanasia on talk radio, with presidents getting shot at intervals.

"I know only too well that these beastly things kill without rhyme or reason and that we are all victims of it," Codrescu writes. "Call it irrational boyish fascination, the immature nostalgia of a reader of Westerns (I was on a Louis L'Amour kick for a whole month), but I'm still not listening to myself. I'm in thrall to these shiny toys of death" (*Road Scholar* 109).

Codrescu visits a Romanian gold medalist marksman and his marksmen daughters in the golden West, and then joins up with a Playboy model named Bo who takes men on shooting expeditions in the nude near Las Vegas. Codrescu asks her what it feels like to shoot a gun, and she makes it sound like poetry:

AC: Tell me what it feels like to shoot a gun.

Bo: Exhilarating. Especially a machine gun. It's something that nobody does, that people think is taboo, so you're out there doing something that nobody else is doing and you just feel exhilarated [112].

Codrescu asks Bo's boyfriend, who runs the Survivalist Store that Bo works out of, about his ideology.

> I asked him if he believed in Armageddon. I told him that I had heard that survivalists all over the west were laying in supplies for the final confrontation with liberals, Jews, blacks, feminists, homosexuals, pro-choicers, and vegetarians. Chuck dodged these questions, which he wasn't about to answer on camera. He declared himself a simple American patriot like John Wayne. "When *it* comes," he said, "we'll be ready." I asked him what "it" was but he gazed absent-mindedly at the Nevada hill I'd been pumping full of bullets. I had the distinct feeling that *I* was *it* [*Road Scholar* 114–115].
>
> The contradictory impulses of the American spirit flourish in the West: shooting and transcending. We shoot our way across the land while simultaneously raising our arms to the sky and trying to be better and bigger than we are. And then there is Bo, urging us on like Delacroix's Liberty to shoot and transcend some more [115].

Driving through the kitsch of Vegas, the new age of Santa Fe and Taos, Codrescu has various orgasmic states and pseudo-orgasmic states, none of which seem quite satisfying. At the end, he goes back to San Francisco, and the Café Trieste, a European symbol, which, he writes, connects him "with all the cafés of my adolescence and youth, café Maria in Sibiu, the Capsa in Bucharest, the Figaro in New York" (*Road Scholar* 186). After all the trickery and weirdness of the American West, with its fake glitz, Codrescu feels at home here, poet's quarters, the cafés of the world, which connect through the rhizomatic underground to Europe. Here it all ends, only to begin again. Codrescu interviews Lawrence Ferlinghetti, who waves away the road and argues instead for a settled place, San Francisco, as the end, as a separate state which he hopes can separate itself from the horror of America — after the sea rises a few feet and turns San Francisco into an island again. This radical wish to separate from the rest of America is simultaneously reinscribed by Codrescu, as he says that the Café Trieste is linked to all the cafés of Europe and America. Against Ferlinghetti's wish to secede is Codrescu's globalizing, at least of café society.

Codrescu's road trip, underwritten by a documentary filmmaker, is in itself a simulacrum of Kerouac's road trip, and Henry Miller's road trips, and John Steinbeck's, and Jack London's. Ferlinghetti says, "Jack London was on the road, and what about Henry Miller's The Air Conditioned Nightmare? I mean, Henry Miller drove across the country during the Second World War, when he had to leave France, and he went from New York to the West Coast in an old car and wrote The Air-Conditioned Nightmare. That was the beginning of the vision which Kerouac really elaborated on, and it was much more potent in Henry Miller as far as I'm concerned. Miller was more focused on the reality of America whereas Kerouac was off in his Catholic consciousness more. When you read On The Road closely, you see he really wasn't observing the reality in front of him" (186). The paradox is that nobody can observe the reality in front of him except through religious and philosophical mental maps which were provided by previous writers, previous thinkers. Ferlinghetti himself reterritorializes deconstruction in his little speech as "a pure anarchist idea" (184), but Ferlinghetti's heritage is anarchist. Codrescu's road trip across America is structured by his Romanian, surrealist, New York School, Beatnik mental maps, as much as it is structured by Rand McNally's.

All across America, he is looking for and reveling in paradoxes, which takes us back to Urmuz, and Cioran, and Tristan Tzara, as well as to Paris, and its school of paradoxical Catholic philosophy stretching back to St. Thomas and the Middle Ages, and before that back to Dionysus. As Gilles Deleuze writes, "Philosophy is revealed not by good sense but by paradox. Paradox is the pathos or the passion of [Dionysian?] philosophy. There are several kinds of paradox, all of which are opposed to the complementary forms of orthodoxy — namely, good sense and common sense" (*Difference and Repetition* 227).

Unlike Henry Miller's road trip or Jack Kerouac's, Codrescu's is lit with contradiction, irony, and humor. Is Codrescu a simulator of these prior road scholars, who sailed across the west driven by misery and need? Is Codrescu a sophist, in a land of sophists? Is this why many seek to call him a fake Romanian with a Berlitz accent? Deleuze writes in another context that:

> The function of the notion of the model is not to oppose the world of images in its entirety but to select the good images, the icons which resemble from within, and eliminate the bad images of simulacra. Platonism as a whole is erected on the basis of this wish to hunt down the phantasms or simulacra which are identified with the Sophist himself, that devil, that insinuator or simulator, that always disguised and displaced false pretender.... It is as though there were a strange *double* which dogs Socrates' footsteps and haunts even Plato's style, inserting itself into the repetitions and variations of that style [*Difference and Repetition* 127].

Codrescu as the philosopher who can differentiate between false and true image, between the image of those who bear an internal resemblance to the truth, and those who merely mimic it, is relentlessly disturbed in the latter parts of the book, in a way that it never is in Kerouac's vision, or in Henry Miller's version, since they never doubted themselves, or introduced self-irony. What is Paris or café society but a myth? Is Paris the real and everything else a poor copy? Is Paris only a myth? Hannah Arendt writes:

> In Paris a stranger feels at home because he can inhabit the city the way he lives in his own four walls. And just as one inhabits an apartment, and makes it comfortable, by living in it instead of just using it for sleeping, eating, and working, so one inhabits a city by strolling through it without aim or purpose, with one's stay secured by the countless cafés which line the streets and past which the life of the city, the flow of pedestrians, moves along [*Introduction to Walter Benjamin* 26].

Codrescu writes:

> Drive through the desert. Avoid the speed traps. The insane
> prospectors with beards to the ground and crazed eyes. Charlie
> Manson's tenth tribe still driving dune buggies through ghost
> towns built by Hollywood. Rattlesnakes on every cactus waiting
> for sunset. Emaciated wild horses. Carcasses of everything ani-
> mal, mechanical, and from space — human skeletons, coyote
> skulls, car bodies, wrecked UFOs. Nuclear tests underground.
> America everywhere you look [178].

The task of separation of the false from the true, which started the
book, has unraveled by the time he gets to Santa Fe. Romanian freedom
seekers turn out to be former members of Securitate in Detroit. But he
isn't sure. By the time he gets to Santa Fe, there is amused hysteria, as he
visits one faith healer after another, all of whom have their own facts
wrong and freely admit they understand nothing of what they are doing.
Middle-class Sikhs, middle-class channelers.

> Shiela left her old life behind and came to Santa Fe, where she
> met a man [now her husband] who understood the reality of her
> extrasensorial experience. And the business potential. Now Shiela
> channels Theo for people who need answers to their questions.
> Theo is a corporate entity, several spirits which have merged for
> the purpose of warning and advising humanity…. Unfortunately,
> Theo uses the royal "we" [or perhaps only the corporate "we"]
> and speaks with a ponderous German accent…. The spirit world,
> just like ours [only more so] must abound in the untalented,
> ungifted, pretentious, and ambitious…. According to the Bud-
> dhists, assholes stay assholes for myriads of incarnations before
> their assholeness starts to give a little. My dead friends Jeffrey
> Miller, Ted Berrigan, Darrel Gray, and Glen Knudsen wouldn't
> sit with Theo for a second — just because they're dead doesn't
> mean they've lost their senses. It amazes me, Theo, the effrontery
> of presumed intimacy! [151].

But Codrescu isn't quite sure of all these quacks. He undergoes genuinely weird experiences with Cherokee, a crystal healer, and something
that seems like a huge orgasm with Chris Griscom, who has a Light Institute. "My inner journey mirrored in a funny way my outer one, only
instead of a Cadillac, I was driving a sliver of blue light across snow"

(147), and afterwards, after experiencing a past life, "I experienced great peace. I walked about on unsteady new legs and felt, how shall I say? great understanding and love" (148). If experience is the great separator of the false from the true, how do we know what part the mental state of the participant has to do with the experience?

In Vegas, Codrescu meets Elvis impersonators, beauty queens, and Marilyn Monroes, all strange simulations of what was already once a fabrication. His instinct is to separate the wheat from the chaff and to put it all down as a conspiracy of Mormon bankers. Ultimately, Codrescu collapses these distinctions.

> A rich man may be eating an individually wrapped tomato that's an imitation of a real tomato while the poor man may be eating an infinitely tastier home-grown tomato. There is no system of values in place to validate which is the original and which is the copy. America is a democracy, which means that it's rude to value the original over the copy. But the opposite is not true; Americans value the copy over the original. Elvis is dead [when he died very few people cared any longer whether he was alive or dead] but the Elvis industry lives on. Marilyn Monroe is gone but her look lives forever. Real people are an encumbrance, actually, to the joyful use of the image. The hollo-deck is nice, TV obliterates those pesky differences of personality [178].

Deleuze writes on this distinction of copy and model that

> Plato attempted to discipline the eternal return by making it an effect of the Ideas — in other words, making it copy a model. However, in the infinite movement of degraded likeness from copy to copy, we reach a point at which copies themselves flip over into simulacra and at which, finally, resemblance or spiritual imitation gives way to repetition [*Difference* 128].

What then, is thinking, if it is not a matter of straightening out paradoxes and determining the true from the false? Deleuze writes that it is thinking without a prior model. "The thought which is born in thought, the act of thinking which is neither given by innateness nor presupposed by reminiscence but engendered in its genitality, is a thought without image. But what is such a thought, and how does it operate in the world?" (*Difference* 167).

Codrescu's journey is as much in the mind as it is in space. His journey is a paradigmatic excursion into self-creation without prior model, it is a becoming without a father principle, a sense of being born out of oneself, as if one were Athena born out of one's own forehead. Codrescu's entire life is a matter of self-creation, of being born again, endlessly, creating a new model after every new model, and trying to avoid the traps of logic that try to reterritorialize him. This is the new game of the poet and the surrealist philosopher — to avoid the traps of Platonists, logicians, state senators, and school board administrators and outdated academics. How to live and think afresh. "We passed Hoover Dam, a monstrous structure set for no good reason in the middle of the desert, and then backed up to it for bodily functions. We peed and some of us puked in the black marble bathrooms that were like devil's mirrors" (168). The fear of going to Las Vegas, and being trapped within the so-called good time, which is set like a snare so that one can relive the adventures of others, is also a fearless leap into the possible act of recreation, watching dice tumble and hoping the magical seven will appear within the dance of difference and repetition such that money will appear from cabinets, setting one free on the material plane, which is always a greater trap for those who wish to be free on the spiritual plane. "Three raises later everybody's looking at us. The camera's rolling. I spread out my cards. I did it, once again. Jean is disgusted. He stops shooting, and then, of course, I lose the next three games. Everything goes. Well, at least the movie's on my side. Kodak be with you" (177). With the film no longer being shot, and the act of repetition deliberately revoked by the French cameraman, Codrescu loses, loses everything, and goes on to a drive-through wedding chapel, where mechanical repetition rather than pious vows takes the cake. "Here, at the Little White Chapel, is the assembly line of sentiment, Vegas style. Charlotte, the Henry Ford of the heart, is the owner and claims she's the minister, too" (174). Ministers of the eternal return, each copy threatening the model, and threatening to break out into a simulacra which will overwhelm its original. Could such a simulated marriage ceremony create a real marriage? Why not? "Barbara, Charlotte's receptionist, whispers to me that she's a Polish writer working here for her book on America. She's undercover, like everyone else, it seems to me. In America we are all aliens with very obvious accents working undercover for the American Dream, in whatever shape — whether the great Polish American novel or the Romanian American search for utopias" (176).

All caught in the image fabulation machine of America, all trying to maintain difference, all a matter of repetition, Codrescu's journey from the grave of Walt Whitman and his champion, Allen Ginsberg, through the machinic factories of Detroit, replicating lives and parts, lives and parts, through the false surrealistic authenticity of Santa Fe's new age religions through the Las Vegas of dreams and to the new world's version of European society cafés at Café Trieste is a journey through a mental landscape with questions and terrors about identity going full blast on every page, with references to the past intended to disguise the fact that everything is new. It is a metaphysical journey rather than a true road odyssey, one that leaves one physically frightened by the narrator's close calls with the demons of authenticity parading within the American Dream. Thinking is essentially problematic, and the problem with it is that one doesn't ever know if one is thinking, or simply living out somebody else's thinking script. Identity is always at risk. To be original, not to be a copy, is to be a new model, a new image, which is always of course a simulacrum — Dracula, American, poet, Kerouac, Rimbaud, joker, Codrescu animates all these images and stirs them into a stew of hilarity while seemingly writing a simple travelogue with commentary. Deleuze writes, "The ego is a mask for other masks, a disguise under other disguises. Indistinguishable from other disguises. Indistinguishable from its own clowns, it walks with a limp on one green and one red leg" (*DR* 110).

The question of what is an American is tried throughout the volume, and is left satisfactorily unresolved by book's end. Codrescu says go ahead and remain yourself to the other immigrants, but let go of your hatreds based on old identity formations. "You can be born again here, but like a baby you must cancel the pain that brought you here. America was set up as a place to get away from the murderous sentimentalities of the old worlds" (192). To think in terms of paradoxes, a land of freedom in which guns signify that freedom, but also cancel it in seconds flat; a world of new hopes in which members of older countries forget and hope to renew their cultures. How do we measure America in contrast to Europe, or a Romanian American in contrast to a Romanian?

This difficult mental map shows the terror in even trying to construe a map of multicultural America, which Codrescu has been trying to depict in his book. In the final chapter, he writes,

I parked the car at the end of Golden Gate park and walked on the beach. It was a gray day, the color of thought.... Hugely incompatible ingredients were thrown into the boiling cauldron of this continent — and very little, thank God, has actually melted in this vast melting pot: languages, people, habits, cuisines, mores, customs, manners, and beliefs continue undaunted side by side. What keeps us together is precisely the awed awareness of our differences.... Paradoxically, the most materialistic country in the world is also the most spiritual.... "The land is an Indian thing." I believe that. But it's also a Romanian thing [193].

Distrustful of his own project, and armed with misophy, a hatred of knowledge, Codrescu goes across America in a car that was the symbol of big American style capitalism in order to find its spirit and finds a paradoxical country of schizophrenia that manages to cohere. A country that is both spiritual and materialistic, and spiritual because materialistic. It is the materialist base that allows time for spiritual reflection. Neither knowledge, nor nostalgia, nor understanding is acquired and transmitted to the reader. What is given is an arduous peek through the hilarious lapses in identity which America has offered, a philosophical space where a new chess game is being played out against the demonic rigidity practiced by European society, which American thought tried to alleviate with the Bill of Rights (freedom to speak and own guns), and the simulation factories of Las Vegas. It's a dizzying journey through the process of evaluation. Is everything finally equal? Are Detroit and Las Vegas, San Francisco and New York, one univocal being, known as America? Must we measure them against Paris, the ultimate inside? Are the Chinese and the Indians and the Sikhs and the Jews all separate but equal? Are they equal to the French? Are American poets as valid as French poets, who remain in some sense Codrescu's model? Having once identified as Americans, Codrescu seemingly says that they are equal or even superior to their European counterparts, even superior to the selves they have left behind, united by an imaginative hope which was the beginning, the origin of the country, the original dice throw. This adventure in equality harkens back to the adventure posited by Stalinism, in which, too, everyone was equal. But in the American case, the situation is reversed in that so many are fleeing to get into this opportunity to be equal, whereas in the Stalinist case many were fleeing the forced demand to be equal.

Codrescu writes:

> The secret of capitalist happiness is that everyone lives exactly like everyone else. The only difference is that whereas the rich consume expensive items, the poor consume the imitation of those items. The difference between an Armani suit clad man wearing a real Rolex and his poorer image in an Armani clone with a fake Rolex is visible only to tailors, watchmakers, and thieves. What's more, the expensive items that guarantee the rich man's authenticity are often inferior in quality to the poor man's [177–178].

The paradox is that absolute difference, without the criterion of a model American, equals absolute sameness. Same difference. But there is one thing left out of this equation. In communist society, everyone begins and ends with an identity, determined in advance by the state. This identity is unchangeable. In America, there is the chance for a radical becoming: sex changes, race changes, place changes, occupational changes, a change of heart. For Codrescu, this is the small difference between Ceausescu's communism as he knew it, and America.

The possibility of liberty opens the prison of being, into the endless wonder of creation. Deleuze and Guattari write:

> The issue is not at all anarchy versus organization, nor even centralization versus decentralization, but a calculus or conception of the problems of nondenumerable sets, against the axiomatic of denumerable sets. Such a calculus may have its own compositions, organizations, even centralizations; nevertheless, it proceeds not via the States or the axiomatic process but via a pure becoming of minorities [*A Thousand Plateaus* 471].

To create new possibilities of nomadic movement, just like dancing in a new way across the hopscotch grid, as each participant goes through the center, and shows a different way to get through; this is the way in which to see Codrescu going across America, not using Kerouac or Miller or London as models, but as other copies of the great migration which preceded it, and its potential for liberty, while not forgetting its actual violence. To see in Codrescu a participator in the Great American Road Novel is not to see him necessarily as a plagiarist, or as an imitator, but rather in the light of difference and repetition, in which the fraudulent and the true, the sophist and philosopher, are irrevocably mixed, as both create not only beauty, but also exhaust, and exhaustion, as well as inspiration. As Codrescu says to the new immigrants in his speech before them at the INS, "It's your turn" (193).

It's the turn of many as they enter the Las Vegas of postmodernism or what's left of Catholic Paris with its Notre Dame and bridges left over from the Middle Ages. But it's not just our turn to move through them. We must also evaluate them and decide which is to remain. And what kinds of cities we are to design and build, based on what values? Las Vegas with its endless deferral of origins, or Catholic Paris, with Notre Dame Cathedral at its center, and at the center of that, a convulsive deity that hurtled Western civilization through two millennia of becoming? Codrescu clearly prefers Vegas, but only if he has Paris as a solemn contrast.

8

Joy/Philosophy:
Nietzsche in Detroit

In the endless rerun of the classic car chase across the United States. we have countless waves making the heroic journey. The original explorers, Lewis and Clark, and the other great adventurers of the 1800s; Jack London; the Henry Miller and John Steinbeck sagas; the Kerouac and Neil Cassady saga; the Codrescu saga. Of these, the most postmodern, in that it is the most self-conscious, is Codrescu's, along with perhaps that of Jean Baudrillard in his epic journey, which he recounts in *America*. The emphasis on the earlier journeys is conquest through discovery, the emphasis on the latter journeys is performance, from Kerouac forward. The idea of experience, rather than settlement, takes center stage. What exactly is the experience sought in such a journey?

I asked Codrescu how planned his trip across the United States had been. He answered:

> I had a pile of clippings about interesting people. My producer took an advance trip [a "dry run"] to set up interviews, and most people agreed because they liked me from NPR. The Sikhs, who hate journalists, are all middle-class and listen to NPR. Other misticos think they hear in my pieces the distant strain of a metacall. But when I got on the road with the camera, all sorts of unexpected things happened. Some of the best:

the Haitian squatters in New York, the women in front of the prison across the street from Walt Whitman's house. The voice-overs were written by me after the shooting when I looked at the rushes. I also kept a journal on the road, the basis for the book Road Scholar. The photographer for the book, David Graham, revisited all the places after we edited the film. He photographed in the spring, whereas we shot in the winter, so I had to readjust seasonally some of my descriptions to match the photos [e-mail of November 13, 1998].

What we need is a criterion, or a backdrop, against which to measure the various trips across the United States. Codrescu's trip, unlike that of many others, was planned with an itinerary, but there was room to improvise, and discover, along the way. Magnus Bernd discusses Karl Löwith's understanding of the problem in the introduction to *Nietzsche's Eternal Recurrence of the Same.*

As the reader will see, Löwith surfaces with enormous clarity the paradox he believes he finds latent within Nietzsche's doctrine of eternal recurrence itself. On the one hand, argues Löwith, eternal recurrence is a cosmological theory replete with a history he traces back at least to Heraclitus. In all of its formulations, however, it suggests that, roughly, a finite number of states of the world is destined to unfold in time—which is infinite, not finite. Hence, given the finite number of possible states of the world and the infinity of time, any single state of the world must recur. More than that, it must recur eternally: the eternal recurrence of the same. At the same time, however, Nietzsche's aphorisms also exhort an imperative, namely the injunction to live in such a way that you will gladly will the eternal recurrence of your life—without change or emendation—over and over again [xv].

The assumption that states are finite, while time is infinite, ought to be examined. First, there are only 50 American states at present, with Alaska and Hawaii outside the possible hopscotch route. If time is infinite, and the number of states finite, then the movement through any of those states will ultimately yield repetition. But since time moves forward, and the states themselves change in time, then it would theoretically be impossible to do the same trip twice. As Heraclitus said, "It is impossible to step in the same river twice." Therefore, the same trip across America is impossible, using Nietzsche's own terms. Space might be vast, but it is finite, at least in terms of what a car can traverse (with rockets, and spaceships, the flâneur can dérive through solar systems until eternity, or until her oxygen is exhausted), but time is infinite (unless we believe in an alpha and an omega), and changes within time are infinite, and cannot be returned, so this means that space, too, is infinite, in that it partakes in time, if we accept the Nietzschean viewpoint.

The dichotomy of space and time has been deconstructed by contemporary science and also in contemporary arts. Urban theorist Kevin Lynch writes that while Immanuel Kant separated the arts into those of time and those of space, in order to privilege music and poetry, the "plastic arts are rich in temporal themes" (166), and that the temporal dimension of place offers a poetics of its own, as "old gardens have a peculiar charm that comes with maturity," (167), and "The great cathedrals, in particular, are repositories of time. Canterbury is not so much beautiful as it is awesome" (168).

Kant's attempt to turn back David Hume's positivist dismantling of time and space resulted in his theory of the category of *synthetic a priori*. In Donald Palmer's *Looking at Philosophy*, he neatly summarizes the problem:

> David Hume had consistently and vigorously followed the program of empiricism to its logical conclusion. The results were disastrous for the philosophical enterprise. The sphere of rationality was found to be very small indeed, reduced as it was to verbal truths and descriptions of the sense data; yet nearly everything that interested people as philosophers or non-philosophers fell beyond those limits.... Kant's solution was to demonstrate that space and time are the synthetic a priori foundations of the faculty of perception. An a posteriori sentence like "The cat is on the mat" *presupposes* the truth of the sentence "Objects exist in space and time." According to Kant, we sometimes know the first sentence to be true, yet it cannot be true unless the second is also true" [Palmer 209].

Although Kant admitted that we could have no sense data concerning space and time, we nevertheless understand them, and understand them in common, and therefore they have a valid existence, and can be considered to be true.

Driving through American states one sees erosion over millions of years in the Arizona canyons, and trees that have taken a thousand years to grow to their present girth in the California redwood forests. Places are suffused with time, whether they are natural, or man-made, and time has an aesthetic dimension that is a "fashionable though rather illegible" concept, in the words of Kevin Lynch (241). Each person who drives across America receives different impressions. Baudrillard rarely gets out of his car and has a rather merrily lugubrious attitude to begin with. Miller has a similarly lugubrious attitude. Neither of them expect to meet much. Kerouac has a better attitude, but he is locked in a depression, and only Neil Cassady can get him into the necessary state of fun. Codrescu has both a philosophical background and an immigrant background (but he's not going back to Romania, as Baudrillard will go back to France). Each of these fellows is doing the trip for different motives, with a different mental map of what they will discover. Codrescu is going through old hunting grounds, from New York, where he once lived, on to Detroit, where he once lived, to Chicago, where he once lived, through Santa Fe and Las Vegas and on to San Francisco. At each place, he meets former friends, mostly poets, and a sprinkling of Romanian immigrants. His contact points, his points of reference, are different than they would be for Henry Miller, or John Steinbeck, or for Kerouac or Baudrillard. Codrescu is interested in religious sites and is more or less disgusted by factories. Also, he is traveling with a camera crew. He has a certain timetable and probably can't depart too much from that timetable. How much of the trip was planned, was there a script written in advance? Was there a rough sketch? The travelers couldn't just go around in circles. They had to go west, and they had to write ahead for hotels, motels, and to get in touch with people to interview, as Codrescu has already roughly sketched out above. Exactly how tight their script was is not scrupulously defined, and yet there was at least a rough schedule, which was tighter than Kerouac's trips.

Codrescu's journey was a collaborative project between a documentary filmmaker, a crew of about six people, an editor, a photographer (who went later), and all the people he met and documented along the route. Then, of course, the car, the red Cadillac, and the tires, and the roads that had been built by thousands of unidentified people, the towns, and the various religions, which had sprung up long long ago and whose ancestors were the ones to be interviewed by Codrescu for their versions of what it meant to be a Sikh or a Bruderhof, or a Las Vegas croupier. America is not the invention of one individual. It is the collective invention of millions of people. To travel across it is to get caught up in a game of hopscotch in which millions of changing faces take part in some way—walking along sidewalks in Chicago, or gambling at the tables in a Vegas casino, it is an aleatory event staged by literally everyone seen, as well as everyone who is in some way responsible for everything experienced: architects, bricklayers, roadworkers, litterbugs. Therefore, to choose one's experience is only partially possible. We are not alone in the world, and do not choose our experience, or our states. Our states are modified by the states already available, and which are changing as we go through them, just as the weather changes, and fashions change. For just as Nietzsche would imply that we are responsible for our choice, he recognizes just as clearly the antinomy of choice. We are not responsible.

> Wherever responsibilities are sought, it is usually the instinct of wanting to judge and punish which is at work. Becoming has been deprived of its innocence when any being-such-and-such is traced back to will, to purposes, to acts of responsibility; the doctrine of the will has been invented essentially for the purpose of punishment, that is, because one wanted to impute guilt. [*Portable Nietzsche* 499–500].

Are we responsible for our states? Can we choose the life we've led, born to certain parents in certain times, against our will? As it is understood in postmodernism, our fall into time is much like the fall onto a craps table of a pair of dice, and as we roll across the green expanse our fate is a matter of bumps, jumps, and thumps until we bang against the far edge, and come to a rest so that we can be read, and understood. Life is an experience of movement, which can barely be glimpsed, and is influenced by institutions, which are beyond our control, and phone calls, which are beyond our control. David Graham, the photographer for Codrescu's *In America's Shoes*, writes that "I should clearly and loudly state that, without Roger, this book would have never happened. The idea and execution of the project began with his idea and the resulting film was the wave upon which the book rode" (frontispiece).

Given all this, and the fact of our not being responsible for the universe, or cognizant of its ultimate design, if it even has one, we are nevertheless forced to orient our lives through certain criteria, whether they be safety or adventure, power or peace, religion or irreligion, following the rules or breaking them. These criteria allow certain groups to cohere and to form a rhizomatic structure based on a goal. To reduce all the qualities of an experience to the criteria that guided them is madness, and yet I want to get at the criteria Codrescu uses to practice and liberate joy.

Codrescu writes in an e-mail, when I'm asking the difference for him between morality and aesthetics, that "I am aware, at all times, that my 'fun' is taking place in a death camp called life and guarded by deeply rooted (and highly charged) ethics" which he goes on to compare to the electric barbed wire around concentration camps. Ethics and responsibility corral the prisoners in the death camp. "The esthetic of amusement is sharpened by ethics like story is sharpened by danger, or, if you prefer, the ethical is a frame around the esthetic" (e-mail of November 19, 1998).

Codrescu's approach to his trip is critical in the sense that Gilles Deleuze gives to Nietzsche. "Criticism is destruction as joy, the aggressivity of the creator. The creator of value is not separable from the destroyer, the criminal from the critic; he is a critic of established values, a critic of reactionary values" (*Nietzsche et la Philosophie* (99). As he tumbles across America, like a set of dice, Codrescu doesn't close his eyes. He is aware, like Christ, like Dionysus, like the men who were crucified with Christ, that the world they are going through has been designed by other men, other men with values not their own, and which they would like to challenge.

Art for Nietzsche consists in a tragic doubling back on itself, representing life so that the falseness of truth steps forth, laughing at its being hidden for so long. To invent new possibilities of life, one must invent new images of life, by cracking up the old ones. "Art is the highest power of falsehood, it 'magnifies the erroneous nature of life,' it sanctifies lies, it turns the willingness to play tricks into a superior ideal," Deleuze writes (*Nietzsche* 117). This reinvention through parody is exactly what Codrescu agrees to do as he goes across America, doubling the same performance on wagon wheels of 150 years previous, with a quick zip funded by public broadcasting, in the comfort of a Cadillac. Nevertheless, the trip is philosophically arduous and fraught with suffering. Art is tragic, and it is only when tragedy doubles over that laughter bursts out. In the suffering of Detroit, Codrescu meets his friend of youth, Jim Gustafson, and they reunite to stage a poetry reading, an example of an eternal recurrence in Codrescu's life.

> I had asked him to read his poem about Detroit, but when he took the stage at Alvin's, he threw his book away, and began what sounded like a choked lament and eulogy to his youth and mine. He'd had too much. Too much emotion from our reunion, too much poetry, too much Jack Daniel's. He pitched forward and fell off the stage with a thunderous sound like a bulldozed house. He crashed spectacularly, like Detroit [*Road Scholar* 78].

The tragedy of Gustafson's fall is described as if it were a performance in the middle of a performance in the midst of a reunion. Codrescu writes, "He hadn't planned it. To his credit, our great cameraman, Monsieur Jean de Segonzac, never stopped rolling" (79). Therefore, this unplanned act of drunken comic rage could be reseen by millions of others in the movie version. It could be replayed as art. Two kinds of suffering rolled into one, and then subdivided again, in the viewer's eye. Deleuze writes, "Dionysian madness and Christian madness are opposed: Dionysian drunkenness and Christian drunkenness; the Dionysian laceration to the crucifixion; Dionysian resurrection to the Christian resurrection ... two kinds of suffering and sufferers" (18). Gustafson's fall into time is tragic, heavy, and yet he gets up, and isn't seriously injured, so it's comic, and yet what has fallen isn't merely a body, it's a city, a past, youth. Was it entertainment, or personal tragedy? Codrescu comments: "He was, miraculously, unscathed. It was a poet's fall but it was not the fiery crash of Icarus: it was the dusty collapse of fin-de-siecle Midwest" (78).

This Dionysian fall has something of Judeo-Christian pity in it, the only moment in Codrescu's book where something of deep feeling penetrates through the Dracula-esque commentary, a commentary that in general seems to be by someone seemingly outside of time, outside of feeling, inside a wild experience, but seemingly untouched by it and in control. This isn't entertainment, but it is funny, tragedy doubling up, and releasing itself, in order to release the horror of life itself, which as Nietzsche says, we must still laugh at. The Greeks knew that life was tragic, as does Codrescu, but they still laughed. "I canonized laughter!" Nietzsche writes (cited in Deleuze on Nietzsche 196). Codrescu is in that canon, waiting to be shot out over the circus of America, like a midget waving to the crowd as he arcs to his death. Life is a catastrophe that overrides all of our attempts at law, goodness, truth; we must learn to laugh simply to remain sane, and seize what joy we can from it. This is Nietzsche's tragic message, one that his own sad life does much to contradict. Codrescu is a stronger individual, having come from a tragic state, and found himself in an even more tragic state, which by celebrating, he renders even more tragic, to the point of comedy. The fall of Gustafson off the stage into nostalgia is irrecuperable. Unlike the various deaths that mock Codrescu's gaiety, such as the death of his early friend Jeffrey Miller, who died like Icarus in a speeding car, this fall, while it was really only a short distance off the stage accompanied perhaps by embarrassment and momentary concern, is one of the great moments in Codrescu's narrative, and it orients the rest of the narrative the way the black plague orients the Middle Ages. It is a warning, and a song, but nothing that can be understood.

The experience shakes Codrescu and provides the emotional center of the book. Codrescu writes of Gustafson, "When at last Jim Gustafson's turn came, what was in his heart never made it to his lips" (81). His drunken suffering in some sense relieved the tragedy of Detroit. Feeling replaced understanding. Was Gustafson grieving over Detroit, and Detroit over Gustafson? Was his own loss of youth, sorrow over long distance from his friend, or something else responsible for his fall?

Deleuze writes of Nietzsche:

> The joyous message is tragic thought; because the tragic is not a matter of recrimination and resentment; in the conflicts of a bad conscience; nor in the contradictions of a will which feels guilty and responsible. The tragic is not even a battle against resentment, bad conscience or nihilism. We have never understood what tragedy was for Nietzsche: tragedy = joy. Another way of putting it: will = joy. We have never understood that tragedy was pure and simply positive, a dynamic gaiety. Tragedy is affirmation: because it affirms chance, and chance, necessity; because it affirms becoming, and becoming, being; because it

affirms multiplicity and multiplicity, unity. Tragedy is a dice throw. All the rest is nihilism, Christian dialectics and bathos, a caricature of tragedy, a comedy of bad conscience" [41].

Gustafson's fall shows the true risks involved in being a part of life, of being a part of death, of willing or not willing, as we see those who are part of us and yet not part of us rise and fall in the stock market of fate, as their dice throw comes up snake eyes.

A poetry reading, a commentary, is a risk, a dice throw, and it can always come up snake eyes, or sevens. The important thing is to be able to throw the dice, and to realize that that is what life is for Nietzsche, not a dialectic, not something thought out in advance. Gustafson had the guts to put away his text, and risk a fall.

This passage on poetry reading in the text is linked thematically to a short trip through Taos, New Mexico, and the World Heavyweight Poetry Championship. Here, poets risk the live creation of poems before live audiences, reminding one of the Greek festivities surrounding the presentation of plays at various holidays of the gods. Codrescu writes:

> The bout consists of ten rounds. Each round consists of one poem, and the last round is improvisational: the poets pick their subject out of a hat. I was World Heavyweight Poetry Champion in 1987, when I beat Lewis McAdams in front of the entire town of Taos, cheering, booing, and taking loud bets after each round. The mayor of Taos handed me the Max, a heavy cast-iron sculpture named after New Mexico's beloved poet Max Finstein. It set off every alarm at the airport. Some of the past heavyweights include Anne Waldman, Ntozake Shange, Gregory Corso, Victor Hernandez Cruz, Al Simmons. In past years, losers have been known to throw themselves into the Rio Grande, which is particularly ferocious in this area. The winners go to the Hot Springs at Ojo Caliente and sit in caves full of mineral steam [118].

The notion of chance introduced by the improvised poem strikes fear into the heart of those accustomed to living by a written text, which is why Codrescu attacks the fortune-tellers of New Mexico so viciously. He prefers a future open, where the unloaded dice can unroll one's fate freely, tragically, joyously. Against the logic of the fortune-teller, and his cash-in at the expense of the believer, the poet's gaiety is based on the drunken tragedy of existence, the Dionysian way, against those who think the world is unrolling according to a plan that they can read in advance, like fortune-tellers.

This is why writing is a dance, undiscoverable in advance, like a dice throw. There is no aesthetic that can guarantee success, there is only the suffering of the active creation of values, through falsehoods, and the risk of living, which no insurance company can guarantee. There are no ways to guarantee a poem, or a poet, or a success. Philosophy rather, should serve to sadden. "A philosophy which saddens no one and contradicts no one is not a philosophy" (Deleuze on Nietzsche 120). It is this paradoxical joy that arises from suffering, the nails in the feet of Christ, the drunken madness of Dionysus that leads to a greater sobriety. To begin with intelligence, and work towards an appreciation of life's experience, as traditional philosophers since Socrates have done, is to get everything backwards, and to arrive nowhere. As Pierre Klossowski writes in his book *Nietzsche and the Vicious Circle*, "Superior reason is the central symptom of decadence. Intelligence at its greatest is a species of madness" (192). What then is the criterion of value? "Intensity is the only criterion" (Klossowski on Nietzsche 142). The job of the poet since Nietzsche is to be as unusual as possible, to fight against the normativization of everyone and everything; against the rendering of everyone equal in socialism, Nietzsche argues that we should all become incommensurable (Klossowski 221).

Identity itself is questioned by Nietzsche, as it's only a sequence of intensities (Klossowski 314). The greatest intensity is by nature inarticulate, the greatest tragedy cannot be put into words. Against *Tel Quel* and the formulators of a new cultural revolution inside the West which would function through an overturning of signs through an ideology agreed upon in advance by a central committee, or for a similar program instantiated by a Nicolae Ceausescu or a Chairman Mao, Klossowski argues for a silence beyond language where emotion alone lives as we kneel among the pews of the church. When we are forced to turn ourselves into signs it kills the emotion and straitjackets us into articulable units of meaning, which are guaranteed to be uniform with that which others know. In contrast to this signification, Klossowski would argue that significance is beyond language, in silence, in Jim Gustafson's inarticulate tumble off the stage.

"That events, acts, and apparent decisions, that the entire world had an entirely different aspect from that which has fallen on us in the night of time in the sphere of language, that was always the obsessive thought of Nietzsche" (Klossowski 354). Against ideology, and for an emotional life which can only be farcically hinted at in words, a life of experiences for which words are the clown act which mimes them out, for a physical life for which words are a poor substitute, this is what Nietzsche is asking. It is this turning away from language into mutism that is the poet's turning away, turning language into an obscure function, a blocking of language's communicability in order to force feeling to be expressed within the body, rather than within the mind. It is the intensity of experiences that matter behind art.

Art tries only to free these intensities, by killing off the concept of a verifiable truth behind them, and opening up a new falsehood, behind which is the truth of experience. This is the fiery crash of Gustafson, of Detroit, which sounds like a bulldozer knocking down a house. It is the image being removed, so that ideology and false feeling can be reinaugurated with a crown of thorns, and a flood of voluptuous emotion, the tragic sense, which can give us the sense of feeling otherwise missing.

Poetry surfaces for most of us only when someone close dies, or in a near-death experience, when the proximity of life's tragic meaning is now so close that it can't be ignored. It is Detroit that causes Codrescu to write his only poem in the book, as nothing but poetry can address such an intensity.

Like the experience of Romania, the experience of a place like Detroit creates poets. Codrescu writes, "I have lived on both coasts and I always made friends there with refugees from the Midwest" (81). "Seeing you [Detroit] like this broke my heart" (89), Codrescu writes, and thus reawakened his poetry. Klossowski writes of Nietzsche, and the need for creation: "The phantasme is only produced when it is met with a restraint. A positive experience goes against the necessity of the creation of a phantasm" (283). That is, the necessity of the tragic, which blocks our sense of a delicious existence, calls forth the need to meet this experience with an image of equal intensity, creation is instantiated by an irritation, a frustration, in the matter of our freedom, of our happiness. Happiness creates nothing, because there is no need to create anything.

Klossowski writes of Nietzsche's unsuccessful affair with Lou Salomé:

> Nietzsche put into play, in his adventure with Lou, all the weight of his thought: if the whole thing had turned out "happily," perhaps Nietzsche would be reconciled with social necessities; Lou would have enabled him to do so. Thus life would have preserved the "center" of his nature...
>
> But, how many creations are not born from the experience of a restraint as if the restraint was the indispensable condition. It is so in more than one case.... Following the disaster with Lou, not only would the master remain without a disciple, but the virility of the man would be unquenched; this frustrated virility constituted in 1883 a profound wound, a hiatus, and the ego of Nietzsche broke apart, ruptured: the creation of Zarathrustra was thus an exterior compensation [283–284].

The original frustration of Romania is the reason we have all of Codrescu's writing, a heart broken by rigidity and fallen workers' states, reactivated momentarily by the fall of Jim Gustafson. Art redoubles this experience, recuperates its tragedy, turns it into comedy, and releases it, releasing the heart's ability to live once more, resocializing a private disaster, so that one can rejoin life. It takes a very strong person to continually get up and do this. What makes Codrescu so strong? What makes this guy keep getting up, after being floored by such experiences? The artist says yes to life, especially to that which is most terrible. This is what Nietzsche found in the Greeks. It is a philosophy of life that depends on art, which has been nourished in Romania since the time of Ovid, where the art of banishment was practiced long before Codrescu's banishment to the west. The Balkan antidote of poetry has been formulated in a crucible of suffering. Now, Romania has sent its banished artists out to the rest of us, to teach us how to live in a state of exile from perfection through laughter, and acceptance of the tragedy of life, as the rest of the world is slowly Balkanized.

Philosophy, or an ideological critique, doesn't help at a funeral. It would be out of place. Only poetry has that place because it can speak of love and forgiveness, an acceptance of the *experience* of life, which is beyond that of understanding, in a place of silent grace.

9

Outside/Inside: Polis/Police

In Bill Readings' *Introducing Lyotard: Art and Politics,* he writes,

> To be blunt, theory in the literary academy has become a cloak
> for the political policing of literary texts, in that the ultimate
> meaning of all theoretical insights is held to be political. This is
> hardly surprising, since it shares absolute continuity with the long
> tradition of literary humanism — except that now the "ultimate
> significance" of a text is named as a "political" rather than "tran-
> scendental" or "essentially human" truth. It is in this light that
> the justification and relevance of literary theory has been as an
> interpretive tool to allow us to decode accurately the literal politi-
> cal meaning of texts. Thus, deconstruction has been welcomed
> insofar as it offers a sophisticated analytical mode that awakens us
> to the "hidden" political meanings of binary oppositions in cul-
> tural texts, dismissed if it tends to undermine our assurance of
> the decidable reality, the non-rhetorical nature, of political mean-
> ing.
>   The importance of Lyotard's work is not that it gives post-
> structuralism a decidable political dimension that it had other-
> wise lacked. Rather, Lyotard's refusal to think the political as a
> determining or determinate metalanguage, as the sphere in which
> the true meaning of false metalanguages [such as "aesthetic
> value"] is revealed as "political effects," pushes him towards a
> deconstruction of the representational space of the political....
> Just as the aesthetic cannot provide the legitimating grounds of

the political, so the political cannot legitimate the aesthetic. Rather, the analogy between the aesthetic and the political is that their grounds of legitimacy remain always to be decided [86–87].

The reason I've given such a long quote is because I believe that Bill Readings puts his finger on the differend Codrescu shares with the American academic community. The work of Gilles Deleuze is also oriented in precisely this direction. The main point Lyotard and Deleuze make in common is that there is no blueprint, no Platonic form, no Hegelian map of history, which can decide the political or the aesthetic in advance.

Because of his background in Stalinist Romania and his membership and familiarity with the European surrealist avant-gardes, Codrescu has been able to hold onto some crucial distinctions, distinctions that align his thought with Deleuze and Lyotard. The most crucial distinction for Codrescu is the separation of the inside and the outside. This distinction, which he makes throughout his book *The Disappearance of the Outside,* is the central line that must be held against a totalitarian political system.

Codrescu opens *Disappearance* with a short foreword written just after the Romanian revolution in 1989. Codrescu was there as a reporter for NPR.

> I am writing this literally in the ruins of the Communist world, in my hometown of Sibiu, Romania. This beautiful Gothic city in the heart of Europe has been badly damaged by fighting.... The greatest fight for liberty in Romanian history took place in these parts in what seems like only moments ago. That is the great secret: only a few moments, only a *single* moment separate life from death, liberty from tyranny, the Outside from the inside. The people of the East — as I sometimes call this region and its mind in my book — have come Outside at long last after painful dark decades in the repressive interiors of police states. I have been waiting twenty years for this moment.... This euphoric Outside will not, I believe, be long-lived.... The thesis of this book, which is both personal and merely reflected, is that the two former oppositions of East and West will join together in a new electronic globe that is not a good thing for human beings. I attempt to show from two sides how this future is coming about, and I propose a number of escapes from it [vii–viii].

Lyotard writes in *Discours, Figur* that "It is necessary to see that the act of vision is a dance" (14–15). Against the Tel Quel school founded on Saussure, Lyotard writes, "A language doesn't speak, we speak it" (32). This is obvious, and yet it is taken for granted with the disappearance of the author, and hence the subject itself, that we are passive beings who speak in the name of mysterious corporate entities, such as whole languages, which speak through us, denying individual responsibility to a degree that renders independent action impossible as we are supposedly all ideology, and zero individuality. Lyotard writes, "Every act of speaking is a means of presenting something which is not language.... This would seem to exclude that the order of discourse could be a closed system; ... the use that the subject makes in the act of speech ... is motivated *from the outside* by a perception of the object.... The order of discourse does not have its reason for being from behind, that is to say in its structure, but rather in the intentionality of the speaker, who is no other than the subject who is designating" (74). Language, according to Lyotard, presumes something outside of language. This flies in the face of the Tel Quel school, who constantly reduce everything to language and permit nothing to escape it. In Jacques Derrida's famous phrase, which operates throughout *Marges de la Philosophie*, "Il n'y a pas de hors-texte" [There is nothing outside the text].

An author is outside of his or her own text. Also outside of a text is the elusive truth of the historical context of any text. It is one pole of reading to state that everything is inside the text, and nothing lies outside. Lyotard quite explicitly seems to contradict this. "Mais il ne faut pas, à partir d'elle, faire ce contresens qui consiste à conclure: il n'y a que du texte" (83). [But it is not necessary, stemming from that, to verify the opposite by concluding that there is only text.] "Our idea is not to discuss a *word* when we say MOON, but to discuss the THING" (107). "Discourse is always speaking of SOME THING" (120).

That the real world exists, and that language speaks of it, is Lyotard's point. Tel Quel sought to make the world into language, and to make everything recuperable within language, including fashion, food, and race. The intention of professional wrestling, or the wearers of clothes may be staunchly against Tel Quel's interpretations, but were forced into a closed circuit of meanings. The forced marriage of inside and outside, in Platonic thought, where what is outside should be subordinate to the divine forms which are divined through logic and dialectics on the inside, are replaced in Lyotard's thought with the stipulation that the outside exists on its own, it is not subordinate to our interior reflections, but instead resists our reflections and our judgments, which are rarely if ever adequate to our interior reflections. This is the reason for Lyotard's mysterious phrase at the end of his famous essay, "What is the Postmodern?"

"The answer is: let us wage a war on totality; let us be witnesses to the unpresentable; let us activate the differences and save the honor of the name" (*The Postmodern Condition* 82). Why would the honor of the name need to be saved? The writers of Tel Quel took it for granted that the world was language. Bishop Berkeley took up a similarly solipsistic position, but he sweated over it, and his proofs elegantly disprove themselves, making us inordinately aware of the outside world. Tel Quel, and the psychiatric movement stemming from Jacques Lacan that has been replicated in many factions of the Cultural Studies movement that uses psychiatric thinking as a basis of authority, *shrink* the external world to a tiny fraction of human understanding through language. The name "postmodern" stands against this shrinkage, and that is its honor. Postmodernism is not political thought, with a prior blueprint. It is aesthetic thought, based on improvisation.

Lyotard's use of Gottlob Frege as a reference point is crucial here because Frege resists just this move to reduce the outside world to psychology. Lyotard cites Frege in *Discours, Figur*. Even in an epic poem, Frege says, we want to think about the truth value of it. "Ce qui nous pousse à progresser de la signification vers le désignation, c'est l'aspiration à la verité" (108). [That which progressively pushes us from signification towards designation, is the aspiration towards truth.] Truth, or the sense that the outside exists, can never be adequately recaptured by language. Truth is always beyond us, in an objective space much contemplated, but never adequately seized. Our minds are too weak to understand infinity, but we know it is there, or something like this. To forget it is to live in a claustrophobic man-made space, a world composed entirely of symbols without any outside referents.

In contrast to this humility before the vast infinity of space and time, the Tel Quel school sought to reduce the external world and humiliate it before our powers of interpretation. This leads to self-righteousness on the part of the readers, as they take up the position of God. Roland Barthes' humiliation of the writer, an abolition of the pole of the author in favor of the new imperialism of the reader, was followed by

Foucault's claim that the author is merely an institution, with no independent reality. This is a destruction of the outside, of the independent and objective, in favor of an inside that was monopolized by Tel Quel. Felix Guattari remarks in regard to Jacques Lacan that they had a good rapport "until it was ruined by the appearance of Jacques-Alain Miller, whom I'd rather not characterize more precisely, and of his group at the Rue d'Ulm, which established a monstrous symbiosis between Maoism and Lacanism" (*Chaosophy* 8).

What is needed are two things: One, a remembrance that there is an outside, and two, a sense that history has not been prewritten. Lyotard writes, "In a dualist philosophy there is an in-between, but in a philosophy of mediation EVERYTHING is in-between" (*Discours* 43). In short, this means that we have the opportunity to ruse with meanings, because meanings are not tied down. There is a space outside meaning, vast and irrrecuperable, which we must save, in order to save the honor of naming ourselves, in order to save our own subjectivity in terms of choosing, and rusing. We do not have the power to do this without laughter from others. What is crucial in Lyotard is that he preserves the possibility of an outside. A totalitarian revolution would like to prohibit satirical laughter directed at itself, would like to close off the possibility of a counter-critique through seizing the image-making centers: universities, television studios, publishing houses, and assuming the position of authority. In Wittgenstein's philosophy of language games, there is a similar denial that one narration can or should be dominant. This seizure of history is exactly what Lyotard warns against and is why another realm must be maintained as separate, and yet interpenetrating. Freedom is not a given, and is not the result of a gradual unfolding of History. It is a matter of vigilance, and it is always provisional. It is a matter of preserving the room for spontaneity. Lyotard writes in *Just Gaming*, "I don't happen to think that to be pagan is the essence of human being, nor do I think that in the dialectic of history a pagan moment is now necessary after the era of religions and totalitarian sects. Neither essence nor necessity uphold this prescription. At most, it is regulated by an Idea" (18). Like Codrescu, Lyotard does not believe that human freedom is the default. What is the criterion of freedom? Lyotard says in *Just Gaming*, "I have a criterion (the absence of criteria) to classify various sorts of discourse here and there. I have a rudimentary notion of paganism, and indeed I rely upon it in deciding. But this operation of classification belongs to a language game that has nothing to do with prescriptions" (18).

Lyotard positions something that he calls heteronomy as his model of discourse. "Heteronomy implies that the marked pole is not the pole of the author, which explains why narratives are anonymous.... Why do we find it natural — and we always seem to find it natural — that the first narratives, that the oldest narratives we know, are anonymous? ...Which means, as the content of the narratives makes abundantly clear anyway, that human beings are not the authors of what they tell, that is, of what they do, and that, in point of fact, there never are authors. Which does not mean they have nothing to do. On the contrary, they have a thousand things to do, and they must constantly match wits with the fate they have been given, as well as with the fate they are being given in being made the addressee of any given speech act, such as an oracle, or a dream for instance. It is precisely because they are not the authors of meaning that they must always rely on their wits. We are never in the autonomy of power" (36).

Rusing with the authorities, with the gods, with the public, with various spoken texts and with various enunciations, with wives and husbands, with paramours, implies that meaning is always created between speakers, and that we can change that meaning, and play with it, but not to the degree of abolishing it, as in the Tel Quel school, where the imagination of the reader can abolish all independence of the author. In a sense both poles are authors, and both are readers. Both poles are active. There are no masters of the world in Lyotard's shifting formulation. "A narrative that has been handed down is picked up and will be passed on in such a way as to remain recognizable. But it will undergo a metamorphosis in the way that it will be given. It will not be a matter of conquering the narrative, that is, of putting oneself forward as the utterer, and putting one's name on it" (*Just Gaming* 41).

Codrescu is always rusing with speech that has been handed down to him, retelling jokes, for instance, from a particular angle. He opens *The Disappearance of the Outside* with a Romanian folktale told by a mythical figure.

> One August evening in 1956, when I was ten years old, I heard a thousand-year-old shepherd wrapped in a cloak of smoke tell a story around a Carpathian campfire. He said that a long time ago,

when time was an idea whose time hadn't come, when the pear
tree made peaches, and when fleas jumped into the sky wearing
iron shoes weighing ninety-nine pounds each, there lived in these
parts a sheep called Mioritiza [1].

The sheep Mioritza overhears two older brothers saying they will
kill the youngest at dawn, and Mioritza warns the young brother, but he
says to go out and retell the story, saying to everybody that instead of
murder it had been a story of his wedding to the moon. Mioritza wan-
ders throughout Romania telling the story. "Mioritza herself is the moving border of the nation, a storytelling border whose story is borderless
and cosmic. She calls into being a place and a people that she circum-
scribes with narrative. She causes geography to spring from myth, she
contains within her space-bound body the infinity of the cosmos" (2).

Here there is a valorization of the spoken over the written word
because the borderline is moving. Books were already too mechanical,
too rigid. "Something was not well with books. They were sick in a way;
they had been made in time and they were of it" (12). They were fixed
and had rules attached to them. One could not play with them, and one
was not free to retell them or else there would be charges of plagiarism,
whereas with the Mioritza tale there was an injunction to retell the story,
pay tribute to it, or ruse with it, as here there was something outside the
fixed meanings of History.

In Codrescu's Romania there was the official history, to be picked
up at the Russian bookstore. "The Russian bookstore at the center of
Sibiu was a curious place: no one frequented it. It was cold, empty, and
frightening.... No self-respecting Romanian would have been caught
dead in this place, but I was curious and I liked to go there in the summer, both because it was cool and because I was intrigued by the mystery of a place of books that nobody read in a strange language that
everybody despised" (20). "I also became aware that hidden everywhere
among us were people feeding on forbidden books. To pick the secret
readers out of the crowd became the great game. I studied strangers like
maps to try to discover the surreptitious reader in them.... The Cam-
bodian communists learned to read for 'intellectuals' in much the same
way in the 1970s. Everyone wearing eyeglasses was murdered" (22).

> I could conjure invisible books from the air and absorb them
> through my skin into myself. I experienced thousands of books

by this process of psycho-osmosis, books that came into being via my imagination, and that would one day demand to be written.... Where else but in a country where books are viewed this way will people line up at five in the morning outside a bookstore when there is a rumor that a new book of poems by a daring young poet will go on sale that day? People also line up at that early hour for cheese, fruit, and chicken, but spiritual hunger is felt every bit as keenly [22].

Throughout my adolescence we watched censorship like the weather: cloudy today, rainy tomorrow.... The names of Romanian writers in exile, for instance, were never mentioned. A law had been secretly passed that certain writers' names could never be used in print, *not even in crossword puzzles*. Until December 21, 1989, I was one of these writers. It amuses me very much to think that somewhere in the gloom and misery in daily life in yesterday's Romania, some desperate soul might have attempted to attack the regime by inscribing my name in a crossword puzzle [25].

Inside this world of controlled language, authors were literally killed, so that the state philosopher, who brooked no rivals, could determine the meaning of every word. No one could argue with him. To remain inside meant getting along with him. With the disappearance of the state philosopher, a single meaning collapses, but in that space can now be a tension between competing meaning makers as the notion of factional democracy emerges.

In Codrescu's childhood, he writes that when he was bad, he was banished from the house and forced to go outside. If he was bad outside, he was forced to stay inside. His mother acted as authority, to decide whether he was to go in or out, and later the state philosopher acted as state mother, banishing some, and sending others into internal exile. The child needs this authority, until he or she can grow up and be reasonably trusted to act on his or her own authority.

In the most vulgar Christian and Marxist arrangements, the state makes everyone outside of the party faithful into a child and makes every moment of individual thought into the act of a rebel. What Charles Fourier wanted was a culture in which the beauty of childhood was present, but within an adult framework, in which adults could make their own rules, but even he assumed that he alone understood the form of the society to come and wanted to regulate it from the top down.

That which is outside of language, the referentiality of the universe, must be maintained, if we are to have democracy, as an outside humbles language. To allow everything to become language, without a speaker and without a listener, without some sense of bodies exchanging ideas, without any kind of accountability, in which only one can determine what is the truth and everything else is false consciousness, or backwards ideology, is the world of the totalitarian who has all the power of the adult over children.

Somewhere between the inside of a police state, and the outside of an unpoliceable state, lies both freedom and meaningfulness. The Marxism of Codrescu's childhood was an attempt to control all language and discourse from the inside. L-A-N-G-U-A-G-E poets, with their self-referential worlds of poetry, are the logical outcome of this collapse of heterogeneous language into a monologue without a speaker. Codrescu comments, "Practitioners of the 'language' school, Marxist neo–Dadaists, are likewise involved in the effort of destabilizing the extralinguistic claims of poetry" (*Disappearance* 184–185). He adds, "The poetic must make clear the thinking that connects it to the world" (185). "All that has been gained by modernism in its exploration of the world through language, since the last decades of the nineteenth century, is now being made innocuous by the new interior" (185).

It is in this sense that Codrescu's one-sentence manifesto must be understood. "Giving up the ideal for the real is our only job" (190). The writer must make maps of the real, while understanding that the maps are not reality. Codrescu finishes his argument in the book with the statement that

> Until the recent revolutions in the East, the distinctions were clear: the Censor ruled that World, TV ruled ours. The Censor and the TV were the neat Couple in whose suffocating embrace the human slowly gave up the ghost. It now appears that the Old Censor has dissolved into the illusionary liberty of our image-making machine. What happens from here on out is no longer a question of ideological oppositions, but a struggle for global reality. There are two global realities, resembling in a nonrepresentational way the old programmatic realities of East and West: the imaginary electronic globe, and the poetic-specific-eco-community.
>
> The poet's job is to short-circuit the imaginary globe [207].

To destroy the imaginary, the term of Lacan's which is meant to indicate that we are between the real and the symbolic, is short-circuited by Codrescu in order to play up once more the value of the real, the poet's world, of ecology and community in space, more so than in future time, in an evolving world which is unpredictable, instead of shrinking off into the closed circuits of TV or language or psychiatry. To verify that the outside exists, that is the poet's job. Codrescu's move is explicitly one of deterritorialization not only of Romania through its recent revolution, or America, but also the recent dead end of L-A-N-G-U-A-G-E poetry. Codrescu is always taking us back outside, demolishing systems of thought with humor and grace, the way psychoanalysis should be ridding us of neurosis. But like the Russian revolution, at some point psychoanalysis went bad. Deleuze and Guattari write of psychiatrists, "We dream of entering their offices, opening the windows and saying, 'It smells stuffy in here — some relation with the outside, if you please'" (*Anti-Oedipus* 357).

10

Poetry/Oedipus: The Investigative Poets

Codrescu's inner circle of poet friends includes the Finnish poet Anselm Hollo, who also publishes his work at Coffee House Press in Minneapolis. Like Codrescu, Hollo is a poet who has come from another European language culture and is one of the few outsider poets in the history of English to reach something like insider status.

Hollo's family lineage is purely Baltic. His Swedish-Finnish father was a famous translator of Russian and English texts into Finnish, and his mother was a German speaker from Riga, Latvia. Hollo has made his niche in the American poetry world alongside of Codrescu. His poetry is also a reference to the outside and maintains the distinction between inside and outside as a central theme. Codrescu has written a blurb to one of Hollo's books, *Outlying Districts*: "I await Anselm's new poems with more eagerness than those of any other living poet. His work is 'news that stays news,' a poetic gazette that is one of our times most accurate neural readouts. If you can't remember your way to your heart, Anselm's poems will show you."

In the poem "On the Occasion of & as an introduction to Robert Creeley's reading at Kultuuritalo ('The House of Culture') in Helsinki, Finland on Valentine's Day '89" we can see that some of Hollo's concerns are also Codrescu's:

time & again when I falter & half believe
those always articulate dogmatics
who say our words can never be our own
but are merely signs
devised by controllers
(the controllers being the other dogmatics
on top of the heap)
thus
they say
anything one might say
is merely a reflection
of those historico-socio-economic conditions
that make one this deluded
miserable
little pile of shit
that presumes to have thoughts
feelings
epiphanies *recognitions*
of use to others as species fellows
I think of the way a hawk's
or a gopher's days are an investigation
of its world
the way the days & words
of Robert Creeley's poems are
an investigation
of our human universe
se on saatanen hyvä runoilija
se panee psyyken lepattelemaan
a bloody great poet/ he makes the psyche flutter
like the little white curtain
in the candle-lit window
at the end of the booby-trapped garden path
[from *Outlying Districts* 27]

Like Codrescu, Hollo is multilingual. He speaks Finnish, Swedish, German, and English fluently. He moves between cultural worlds in a way that very few American poets have ever done. He is prolific and yet has a very limited critical audience. In the Modern Language Association bibliography, there is not a single article consecrated to his work, after some 30 volumes of poetry.

In the poem just cited, Hollo is arguing that poetry should not be a matter of language closed in on itself, in the L-A-N-G-U-A-G-E school vein, but rather turned outwards towards life, in an investigation of the outside world, in the manner of a hawk or a gopher. Many of Hollo's poems reiterate this theme, in a soft, and not very aggressive voice, which is always lit with humor. His is a nomadic poetry, describing places and the life in them with a precision that lies always close to the American vernacular. In the poem "and Today's Credo is..." he writes:

> Don't feel like hiding in the archetypes
> Don't trust the stuff that's supposed to give you
> The Grand Shivers
> [take top off head, etc.]
> But what about melodious?
> Melodious
> I have trouble with
> So I guess this avuncular
> vernacular
> will have to do
> [from *Outlying Districts* 27]

In the opening line, Hollo dismisses the deep image school of Robert Bly, founded on a Jungian dream analysis paradigm for poetry. He doesn't go in for the big emotions, nor for melodiousness, but rather goes for an "avuncular vernacular," which describes his poetry — friendly, generous. His major theme is the breaking up of the artistic act. His art is an art of artistic self-disruption, letting in the incidental, and keeping art from closing out life.

Always nomadic, obsessed with a certain kind of perennial marginality, Hollo's poems, like Codrescu's, are often composed on the run and composed circumstantially, that is to say, in honor of certain almost nonoccasions, in which incidents are put together into a poem, providing a seemingly incidental snapshot. His poem "The tenth of May (1988)," for instance, praises the quotidian qualities of a life without great events. "Jane is out being a delegate/ when she comes home/ we'll light the candle & have some spinach spaghetti/ with Mr. Paul Newman his sauce/ his good cause sauce & smiling face on the label ... oh Eros we thank thee for thy gifts/ this day the day/ of the great book burnings in Deutschland/ fifty-five years ago" (*Outlying Districts* 18). "Letter to

Uncle O., for Andrei Codrescu," is an homage to Ovid, and pays tribute to this solitary genius in a land of barbarians. Like Codrescu, Hollo is a poet who in some sense is an outsider and in a more limited sense an insider. A European in America, he writes in an American vernacular, about American subjects. He is not writing in a Finnish vein, but in a peculiarly American vein of the picturesque inflected by a certain Finnish love of nature, exploring the country in the manner of a hawk or a gopher, neither of the two being overly glamorous creatures, his central metaphor being an investigation of the poetics of community. Unlike Codrescu, he is not a Hapsburg, but from a Baltic nation, with a different history, a different religion, a different language of origin, which occasionally asserts itself within his poetry. Like Codrescu, there are no hard and set criteria in Hollo's poetry. He doesn't categorize. Everything can find its way into his poetry, and there is a sense that both everything and nothing matters.

A poet they both reference is Robert Creeley, a member of many communities, who spent a year in Helsinki on a Fulbright. His poetry is also a poetry of ordinary human experience, also an exploration of place, and of the vagaries of going through space in time and taking little notes. Creeley's book *Hello: A Journal,* is an account of a trip from Fiji to New Zealand to Australia to Singapore and the Phillipines, Hong Kong, Japan, and Korea. He comments on what drove him to write this book, to live this book, in the brief forward: "I went because I wanted to — to look, to see, even so briefly, how people in those parts of the world made a reality, to talk of being American, of the past war, of power, of usual life in this country, of my fellow and sister poets, of my neighbors on Fargo Street in Buffalo, New York. I wanted, at last, to be *human*, however simplistic that wish. I took thus my own chances, and remarkably found a company" (*Hello: A Journal,* n.p.).

This poetry of movement, on buses, trains, airplanes, and through various communities, is a poetry of daily life, in which daily life is enough. It has obvious similarities with the poetry that Codrescu writes in his NPR commentaries, in which life itself is enough, and has a lineage in the dictum of William Carlos Williams' "Only connect." Perhaps more appropriately for this school would be another dictum, "Only cathect." This group of poets seemingly cathects, or gives emotional investment, to just anything, the way Williams himself would cathect a cat walking across a table, or a smashed soda bottle in a parking lot. The point is to connect poetry to the outside world. What does Creeley mean by the word "human"? He doesn't define it. This is a school of description without meaning.

In his poem, "Pocatello, Idaho," Hollo writes:

> thin man whacking
> away at tire with a mattock
> in 7-11 parking lot
> 9 P.M.
> Saturday night
> we
> saw
> that
> sight
> [*Outlying Districts* 11]

In this short poem an obscure individual performing an obscure action in an obscure parking lot in an obscure town is given his own poem, which is a celebration of just anything, an incidental poem along the lines of Williams' "This Is Just to Say," a celebration of something as seemingly fleeting as eating cold plums. This love of the ordinary, a turning away from the great topics of love and death towards the zone of the familiar, is an important lineage in the poetry of Codrescu and Hollo. However, whereas in Williams' poem there is a clear assertion of a belief in marriage and its domestic delicacies, it is hard to pin down a clear assertion of any kind in Hollo's or Codrescu's work.

The poetry of Tom Clark (as well as his nonfiction investigations of poetic community such as *Charles Olson: The Allegory of a Poet's Life*) and the poetry and fiction of Edward Dorn and Edward Sanders share a certain lineage with Codrescu's work, or at least a certain set of affinities. They form an assemblage, a group, a discourse community, a school of poets by default. What to call them? Can we say that Codrescu is the chef d'école? Or is it another? As Codrescu is one of the youngest members of this group, to argue that he has had a retrospective influence on these poets would be fun, but obviously untrue. Each of the members of this group have worked hard to make his own distinctive body of work, with each other as constant reference points. What is Codrescu's contribution to the group? To a certain extent he is emerging as the best known, if not as a poet then as a cultural figure, the most active, and probably the most publicly articulate about the poetic practice. They are all prolific, and although they get prizes, they are not valued in the university setting, because they work against the prevailing standards of ethical statement, and in Codrescu's case, this differend with those who do is argued quite strenuously in his nonfiction work. Loosely connected by their affiliation with the postmodern poetics of Charles Olson and with the '60s peace movements, and with the New York School of poetry, there is nevertheless no way to argue that in any way they share a common creed.

Codrescu's lineage went back into Charles Olson and the Beats on one side, and into European surrealism on the other.

Olson was not a Christian, although his father was Swedish, and the son may have picked up the Lutheran ethos from that culture. In Tom Clark's biography of Olson, he made it clear that Olson's mother was a devout Catholic, but that Olson did not wish to adhere to the faith. However, Olson was a good citizen, and wrote intensely about his chosen city of Gloucester with a remarkable insistence on saving its better qualities, and he often defended the Portuguese and their Catholic faith in his great sequence *The Maximus Poems*. Olson opens his 600-page poem with an invocation to a Christian muse who stands on top of a Catholic cathedral in Gloucester.

George Butterick, in his *Guide to the Maximus Poems of Charles Olson*, writes in reference to these lines, "On top of the Church of Our Lady of Good Voyage on Prospect Street in the Portuguese community of Gloucester, overlooking the harbor, is an eighteen-foot statue of Our Lady holding a schooner as described.... She is the invoked muse of the poem, and, as Olson has said (conversation with the author, June 1968), 'the poem is a voyage, and I want a good voyage.'" (11).

Indeed, Olson was willing to allow his own son to register in a Catholic school, and as he studied cosmic gods through his Jungian phase, he came more and more to accept the Catholic God of his upbringing (Clark 319). Olson's mother's faith was Catholic, although he had a "clear preference for [his] father" (Clark 5).

What would constitute a school, if not a common creed, or a manifesto?

Charles Olson wrote that the time-space dichotomy was a major axis on which American literature moved. Olson indicated that time was occluded in American literature and that this made for a new and better literature than the European. "I take SPACE to be the central fact to man born in America, from Folsom cave to now" (11). Charles Olson wrote, "It is space, and its feeding on man, that is the essence of his vision, bred in him here in America, and it is time which is at the heart of Christianity" (100).

Although influenced by the Beatnik ethos of exploration of American realities, none of Codrescu's immediate circle have surrendered their brain to a guru or a given Christian denomination, nor do they seek to stun the reader with overwhelming emotion so as to close down the capacity for rational examination of the curious phenomena of contemporary urban life, nor do they seek to drive themselves like a phalanx into American culture. Their work does not aim to proselytize, but this is often a handicap in that it may seem that unlike Allen Ginsberg they have nothing urgent to say. Even Gregory Corso, the most comical of the original Beat generation, is often aiming for larger emotional and intellectual impact than the Investigative Poets. The younger generation's is a poetic of the understated moment, the little moment at the edge that might otherwise be overlooked. The awareness of subliminal visions, in which ordinary life is enough, is beautiful all by itself, is their practice. Their work reads like sketches in notebooks, rather than finished poetry. In Codrescu's "Juniata Diary," in *Comrade Past & Mister Present*, he publishes a diary of various trips he made to teach at a school in southern Pennsylvania, and makes entries such as this: "In the student-union men's room: 'Beware of gay limbo dancers'" (81).

These notes belittle the idea of an author creating great works that are meant to stand outside of time. Instead, these works exist in time, but they disorient the metanarrative of time and show odd things going on that challenge the general consensus. These are witty collectors of moments, which are not united into a seamless narrative that is intended to put the reader into a state of certainty.

An important passage in Tom Clark's book on Charles Olson might indicate how these writers formed into a school without consciously attempting to do so. Olson's war on time in favor of space became a leitmotiv for the next generation. And yet time sneaks back into their work. Clark writes, "Olson invited his fellow survivors to 'put war away with time, come into space,' and emphasized his defiance of the temporal" (113). Clark continues in this vein, "An 1823 comment of the Hungarian mathematician Bolyai Farkas to his son — 'many things have an epoch in which they are found at the same time in several places, just as the violets appear on every side in the spring' struck Olson as directly applicable not only to projective geometry but to the postmodern pursuit of knowledge in general; the quote became for him a touchstone statement on the process by which a plurality of minds may arrive unbeknownst to one another at parallel advances, and thus an image of a common intellectual 'company' which he would always find particularly gratifying" (114).

Of this school only Codrescu has read deeply in recent continental philosophy, and only he can make himself understood within the stuffiest academic corridors, or within a fishing boat in Alaska, as well as among his peers. He has the widest range, the widest discourse community, and therefore his voice has the greatest power and greatest influence, although he is utterly dependent on the other poets of this group for reference points and for support. Although he is certainly aware of Marxist thinking in both the East Bloc and within the west, his thinking is deliberately and somewhat ferociously along Nietzschean lines. As Nietzsche writes, "'On ne peut penser et écrire qu'assis' (G. Flaubert). [One cannot think and write, except sitting.] There I have caught you, nihilist! The sedentary life is the very sin against the Holy Spirit. Only thoughts reached by walking have value" (*Nietzsche* 471). Codrescu's work is nomadic. It is unstable and doesn't set up fences, and perhaps his only clear preference is for deterritorialization.

This emphasis on movement between intensities is found throughout the writings of this new school of democratic humorists. It is also found in the work of Gilles Deleuze, to whom Codrescu sometimes links his thinking. Of the French postmodern school, it is Deleuze's concepts that Codrescu most frequently cites within a positive framework. He, like the other members of his school, rejects the polite closure of reality under contemporary Marxism, and this, more perhaps than any other factor, accounts for their critical nonrecognition. Nietzsche writes, "When stepped on, a worm doubles up. That is clever. In that way he lessens the probability of being stepped on again. In the language of morality: *humility*" (471). This is a lesson this group of poets seemingly won't be taught. Nietzsche writes, "I mistrust all systematizers and I avoid them. The will to a system is a lack of integrity" (471).

Like Nietzsche, these poets see philosophy as the beginning of a degradation into systematized thinking, of which Hollo's anti-philosophical poems above show an ample illustration. The move is towards experience and away from an understanding based on other people's blueprints. They are characterized by fresh vision, wit, paradox. Codrescu takes this lumpy school of writers and frames them in his writings into an outlook, a poetics, which has taken several decades to cohere. I asked Codrescu to write about his affiliation with this group of poets:

> In terms of our personal connections, Ted Berrigan was my father teacher of American horizontality [i.e., things as things are interesting; easy before you transcend]; Anselm Hollo is my erudite older brother and Whitmanic-ironic soulmate; Ed Sanders is my fellow satirist, activist & newspaper publisher à la Ben Franklin and Mark Twain. They each embody different American spirits: Ted: courage & long-distance [range, as in his cowboy satire, "Clear the Range,"]; Anselm the American idiom & learning & bardic all-night soulfulness; Ed, socialism, anarchism, and public activism. If you want American kin, you might mention, in addition to Whitman, WC Williams, Mina Loy, Robert Creeley, Paul Blackburn, Joel Oppenheimer, Frank O'Hara, Kenneth Koch, and John Giorno. Also, my contemporaries: Tom Veitch, with whom I collaborated on poems and a novel; he became God and is now a printer in Vermont; Dick Gallup, who has all but abandoned poetry and now drives a taxi in San Francisco; Eileen Myles, lesbian presidential candidate and lyric-narrative poet; Elaine Equi, Chicago surrealist, one of my contemporary epigones; the late Jim Gustafson, Detroit hardass surrealist, a one-man kickass band; Jeffrey Miller, who died young in 1977 but left behind continually amazing spiderwebs of grace that get better with time; Bill Knott, who teaches in Boston and is very odd; Lorenzo Thomas, sound sophisticate black poet, teacher in Houston; Victor Hernandez Cruz, who was my challenger in the World Heavyweight Poetry Championships in Taos, New Mexico, 1990, and whose W.C. Williams tinged work drinks in salsa surrealism. You can put all these — and some I forgot to mention — under my Love Umbrella. The only thing that radiates a big enough field and takes in past and present simultaneously is Love. You can make THAT retroactive, anything else will smack of hubris [e-mail of November 20, 1999].

Their poems are brief. They have something in common with the New York School, but they are not merely a second generation, or third.

John Ashbery and Frank O'Hara and Kenneth Koch are admired, but no one of these newer poets based their own practice entirely on such forebears. They are all domestic, married, and teaching in university positions, at least occasionally, even though they are mostly all sympathetic towards ecology, they are not in favor of depopulating the cities, or in living out in the woods with an outhouse for a toilet. The most useful term is Investigative, because this is what all of these poets are doing, and they say so repeatedly in their poems, as well as in their nonfiction work. The term belongs to Sanders, although it has echoes in Codrescu's term "outside." *Investigative* Poetry is useful for describing a mentality that is alert to the Outside, more so than the New York School of poets, which many of these younger poets see as their most basic point of relation. Against nature poets aligned with Wendell Berry and Gary Snyder, these poets have kept a sense of their love for what is living and somewhat wild within picturesque cities. Opposed to the usual love of art and museums which characterize poets who live in cities, they are continually opening up systems by showing that which is outside which doesn't belong to any known system.

This new generation of poets, for instance, has turned against art, and distrusts it, while O'Hara and Ashbery made a good part of their living as art critics. O'Hara worked at the Museum of Modern Art, and many of his poems are dedicated to painters such as Larry Rivers and reference the works of Jackson Pollock and others. This newer generation of poets is disgusted by museums, or at least suspicious of them, and turns instead toward daily reality of people outside the closed system of art. In Hollo's poem, "In the Land of Art," he writes, "the artists/ work on the art farm" and everything they do in life has to do with the closed, claustrophic world of art. They go to art dances and art movies and wash their clothes at the art laundromat. "When they get sick, they go to the art hospital./ & when they die, they're buried/ in the art cemetery./ & that's the life of the artists/ in the land of art" (*Outlying Districts* 21).

Codrescu explains the mind-set behind the disgruntled feeling this group feels towards art. In his short piece, "Why Art?," for NPR, Codrescu asks why there are art vandals afoot. What he objects to is that art is worth more than life. "When a painting by Van Gogh goes for some $54,000,000, one can't help wondering at the great gap between the living and the dead. A middle-class man in an industrially developed country is worth about $600,000 in insurance. The difference between him and 'Irises' is $53,400,000, which is either the price of publicity or the price of a nameless something we don't quite understand.... Can this large sum reflect the absolute power of advertising over the acts of basic life? ...So here comes this man, tormented by these and other questions, carrying a shotgun. A hammer may have been sufficient when the price was in the thousands. Millions call for firepower" (*Raised by Puppets* 108).

In the preface to Nietzsche's *Twilight of the Idols*, he sounds off against the stuffy professors who prefer art to life. "Nothing succeeds if prankishness has no part in it.... For once to pose questions here with a hammer, and, perhaps, to hear as a reply that famous hollow sound which speaks of bloated entrails" (*Portable Nietzsche* 465). Against the idols having replaced life, Codrescu and his friends practice philosophy with a hammer. As Codrescu wrote on the backside of Rodin's Thinker in 1967 in Detroit, "What's this pig thinking about? The time for revolution is now!"

Codrescu's strongest rival for major theoretical significance in what I have called the Investigative School is the poet Ed Sanders, as it is he himself who supplied the name. His novel *Fame and Love in New York* (Turtle Island, 1980) satirized the charlatanry of the art world. His ingenious masterpiece *1968* (Black Sparrow 1997) is a highly readable lyrical epic of perhaps the most tumultuous year in American history. Sanders himself played a bit part in 1968 — he knew top members of the Yippie party personally, as well as key poets, and his band The Fugs played alongside major rock groups. An eyewitness, Sanders combined his personal observations with a lifetime's archival collecting on the period and organized it with an inspiration based on Greek general and historian Thucydides. His poetry is sharp, witty and intensely readable, almost always trying to notate the monadic "worlds" of various groups, such as the Veterans of Foreign Wars Crawling Contest to the Yiddish Speaking Socialists of the Lower East Side (see his *Collected Poems*).

Against thinking as an end in itself, these Investigative Poets propose travel, notes from the real world, noted down with witty paradoxes and sharp fresh observation. When I left the dreary school of art I had first attended, and ended up going to Naropa Institute in the late 1970s, one of the first assignments Ed Sanders handed me was to go and sit outdoors in the same place for twenty minutes every day and write down what I saw. Over the years I have practiced this exercise I have seen midget nuns and fire trucks and doughnuts heaped with ants on the sidewalk. As Codrescu puts it, "Giving up the ideal for the real is our only job" (*Disappearance* 190).

With roots in William Carlos Williams, Whitman, the New York School, Investigative Poetry is anti-art to a new extreme, and interested in notes of an alternative world written down in a vernacular that is sharp, direct, and against the will towards systems, and closure. Codrescu's formulation of a manifesto of this school in *Disappearance of the Outside* marks him as one of the school's two theoretical leaders, and his abundant poetry and nonfiction work marks him as one of its leading and most successful and energetic practitioners.

Frank O'Hara, while surely an exciting poet in the realm of experience, is not remembered for his critical acumen, in spite of his invention of "Personism," which shows considerably more critical intelligence than its somewhat playful presentation would suggest. When we think of O'Hara, we don't think, we are caught in a fresh world of charming fun. Fun was his central criterion, and although O'Hara is not thought of as a canon-building critic, it is he who canonized the notion of fun, and this criterion might be added to Benjamin's as one way to judge the various poems of the Investigative School. Looking back through American poetry to the poems of Walt Whitman, for instance, there is manliness and catalogues of pleasure, but the whole oeuvre seems slightly dated precisely because of this lack of a sense of fun, and also because of a certain predictability in terms of what things from the Outside Whitman will allow into his poetry: It must be powerful, it must be life-affirming, it must have a mythical tone. In Poe and in Melville, too, the central criterion of letting the weirdly banal marvels of the outside come in has not yet emerged. This begins perhaps with William Carlos Williams and the Objectivists. It has taken Anselm Hollo and Andrei Codrescu, two recent immigrants, to insist on this central American quality, most strongly instantiated in O'Hara's work, and since then a canonical quality within the New York School of the last 40 years. Part of the fun of America is mindless movement, as Codrescu celebrates it in his book *Road Scholar*— getting in a car and going places. Speed is a subcriterion of fun, as Codrescu writes:

> &
> I hate everything that moves faster than my body because
> everything that moves faster than my body
> does so by a cheap trick
> [*Selected Poems 1970–1980* 65]

To Codrescu, the body is a toy. Life is a toy to share with friends. He is open, democratic, and more inclusive than many of the other members of the school. Codrescu has opened his world up to strangers, with his ceaseless appetite for new experiences. "I crave strangers," he writes *In America's Shoes*, "They are like foreign cities at night to me" (157). He even speaks to strangers on the bus. Chance meetings with Polish secretaries working undercover on novels, or with members of weird religious denominations in upstate New York do not occur in the writings of many of his colleagues. Codrescu, with his appetite for strangers, is generous, open. In this sense, Codrescu seems to embody Walt Whitman's definition of the American poet in the Preface to "Leaves of Grass": "The American bards shall be marked for generosity and affection and for encouraging competitors.... They shall be kosmos ... without monopoly or secrecy ... glad to pass any thing to any one ... hungry for equals night and day" (*Whitman* 15).

Codrescu's journal of more than a decade, *The Exquisite Corpse*, was an application of these interests. Many contributors were first-timers who did not know the editor personally and who sent in their work blind, were published, and then never published again, vanishing into the night, or sometimes sticking around and publishing in the journal for a decade or more, although not publishing much of anywhere else. His journal was a microcosm of his interests: a journal of reportage, based on cities, and funny happenings in those cities, which was in turn meant to inspire new happenings and show how many possibilities were still available. His journal is implicitly against big egos and describes a poetic that would include not just nature and people but also cities, even, and especially overlooked cities, rather than leave them out. One could read letters written in weird English from Estonia, or from Korea. It is especially urban life with all its gritty hilarity that was chronicled, in contrast with the green movement poets such as Gary Snyder, who argues that communities should be divided up according to river systems. The poetry of certain ecoregionalists, such as Gary Snyder or Wendell Berry, who see urban life as an atrocity committed against other life forms, is clearly from a different ideology. Snyder and Berry have a strict set of criteria for what can be let in from the outside, and it is certain to be positive and life-affirming. One doesn't find cannibal ants or dolphins raping one another in their nature poetry, although this is part of nature. Instead, we find nature acting as if it was saintly, as if nature had attained the grace of a

Zen master, or the most enlightened elements of humanity. Ironically there is no *outside* in the writings of Snyder or Berry. Ordinary humanity is included among the monadic poetry of Codrescu and Hollo and Sanders and Clark, and mental systems have just as powerful an interest as natural systems, but there are a lot of strange marvels in their poetry that simply don't fit into any system. Codrescu and contributors in his journal saw urban life as a fascinating aspect of contemporary life, and were hardly going to urge everybody back to nature, to work in agrarian communes. Codrescu likes the fun of big cities, and he is constantly cataloguing and discriminating over all the joys and paradoxes of urban existence.

The invention of a name and a set of criteria has been partially achieved by borrowing an idea from Codrescu's book *Disappearance of the Outside* and linking it to the moniker invented by Sanders. Investigative Poetry is an important new tendency in contemporary poetry, which, although it has clear precedents in the poetry of Williams, the Beats, and the New York School, and in postmodernism, has a very strong code of its own. The code is against closure into meaning. Because there is a major difference between Codrescu, Sanders, Clark and Hollo's work and that of the Beats and New York School in general, they need to be considered separately. Codrescu is thought of as a second-generation New York School poet. It wouldn't be fair to call Codrescu or Hollo members of the New York School, however, because most of their work wasn't written in New York. The long hilarious lines that characterize Frank O'Hara or the abstraction of John Ashbery's work can't be found in the minimalist, reality-centered work of Tom Clark. In that sense, and in others, they are not second-generation members of the New York School.

I wrote to Codrescu to delineate how he differed from the New York School, in particular, and whether he considered himself part of the same discourse community with second-generation New York School poets such as Larry Fagin and Ron Padgett.

He wrote:

> We worked under the same umbrella but there were others who were part of the same discourse-community of that same moment [New York–Bolinas 1966–1973]; Michael Brownstein, Lewis Warsh, Bernadette Mayer, Elinor Nauen, Alice Notley, Jim Brodey, Gerard Malanga, Jim Carroll, etc.—anyone involved in the St. Marks Poetry scene during those years. But for a full range

of my friends and literary cross-pollinators you have to also include a number of poets from other scenes. Bill Knott & the Chicago surrealists; the Detroit hardcore experimentalists like Jim Gustafson, Mick Vranich, Bradley Jones, Faye Kicknosway; the San Francisco Beats and Surrealists Michael McClure, Diane diPrima, David Meltzer, Jack Hirschman, Nanos Valaoritis, Harold Norse, etc. [I'm not talking about literary values here but intense human contacts held together by poetry]; and you can count in humanly and poetically all the people I've read and associated with because of my poetry anthologies, *American Poets Since 1970: Up Late* [4 Walls/8 Windows] and *American Poets Say Goodbye to the 20th Century* [4 Walls]; *The Stiffest of the Corpse, 1983–88* [City Lights], and *Thus Spake the Corpse: An EC Reader Volume I, 1989–1998* [Black Sparrow, 1999], volume 2 will be published in 2000, and of course, EC itself, in its paper run from 1983–1998, put me in the company of hundreds of enlightened souls — human temperature though not lacking in [mostly lost] meta-illumination. So your job is to figure out where to place me! [e-mail of November 21, 1998].

Indeed, how to identify this urban nomad, such an intense insider in so many outsider groups? Codrescu's world is large. Seemingly the entire outer world is cathected, and nearly everybody within that outer world. Even the things of the outer world, not only cities obscure and famous, but ordinary things, every variety of fork and pencil, make their way into his poetry and nonfiction pieces. So many friends who pop up in his work. As Andy Warhol put it in another context, "In the future everyone will be famous for 15 minutes." However, in Codrescu's work it is not only his own insider group he is talking about, and not only people and animals outside the art world, but things, which get their day. "No ideas but in things," William Carlos Williams wrote, and in this poetry, things get their 15 minutes, too.

In the poem "Love Things," which appeared in *Selected Poems*, Codrescu inventories a love for things, and things that love him:

> I want to bring myself/ to love all things/ to find, inside all things,/ their claim to me, the place where/ their sexuality is hidden./ For all things have/ a claim to my love … all creation/ is objectively valid [121–122].

"Love Things," is a typical poem of Codrescu's early period, although perhaps more homogenous than many others. In it, there are only a few of the interruptions that disturb the dreams of the others. In the middle of the poem, just where he has been talking about the great sex he has been having, there suddenly appear in capital letters the words: "CUT OFF THAT HEAD!" The lines appear without explanation, and can thus be read in a number of ways. One is the Lacanian idea of castration. Just when one is in the middle of a pleasurable episode, the inner police step in, and interrupt the pleasure, demanding tribute to other men, who hold the power. Another reference might be to the Queen in the "Alice in Wonderland" stories, who suddenly steps in and gives an order for a decapitation. Codrescu's life has been mixed up with such unpleasant realities. Real policemen, rather than inner policemen, the infamous Securitate, who arrested many of his friends, and their intrusions have come to seem expected, and could be yet another way to read the poem. The poem is an attempt to love all things, to love the whole universe, a drunken disregard for the pain of things. I wrote to Codrescu to ask for more information on the poem and he said,

> What you are hearing here is the voice of Christ. He cannot afford to refuse love to anything because that's his job. You may call this "psychological," or about the "torments of love," but, like in most of my poems, a parallel discourse could be heard, investigating ontological matters. Love was the credo of our generation.... I tried to reconcile unconditional love with reason and all I could come up with, at that time, was poems [e-mail of November 24, 1998].

I asked him if there was beauty in his poems, and how we were supposed to read them, since many of them are so obscure.

> Beauty's there in love checked by irony, a constant battle between sentiment and intelligence. That's how language sparks. You may want to look up here Paul Celan, Benjamin Fondane, Tristan Tzara and Ilarie Voronca, for a matrix for this work. People are afraid of misunderstanding poems, which is why most would rather not, at all. Ruralism, TS Eliotism, Poundianism, williamsism, confessionalism, iowa cornponism, translatese surrealism, languageism,—all these guilt-provoking little analytic machines [some no more complex than a crowbar] have made it nearly impossible to read a poem unanxiously. The basic system is a confrontation with all intelligible systems. My poems are meant to engage your fears [e-mail of November 24, 1998].

Codrescu's poems push one into an experience of undecidability. They are a thicket of signs, many of which mean the reverse of what they say. The poem "Against Meaning," for instance, turns out to be an exercise in carefully controlled meaning.

Like the other members of the Investigative school, Codrescu finds the outer world to be his source of inspiration and loves all things in it. But there are other aesthetic practices and thoughts that lie under this objectivist aesthetic. Codrescu has deep sources in Romanian poetry, and especially in the poet Lucian Blaga, the one poet Codrescu has extensively translated from Romanian. Blaga wanted to preserve the primal mystery of things, and so does Codrescu, leaving in his poems a non-closure, a sense that everything has not been said, and what has been said is sometimes deliberately obscure. In the poem "Against Meaning" he writes, "Everything I do is against meaning./ This is partly deliberate, mostly spontaneous/…This is partly to confuse the police…/But through a little hole in the boring report/ God watches us faking it" (126). Note the extreme clarity of the language, which is however found in an ambiguous context in which clarity itself is something to be afraid of. This need to conceal, this fear of the police, is not something that can be found in Frank O'Hara's poetry. O'Hara lived in a more wholesome world. There is always a sense of the police, and dungeons, lingering in Codrescu's unconscious. Many of his early friends disappeared in underground retention rooms, and this image continually resurfaces in his poetry, a poetry of the unconscious turned inside out, moral values made concrete, the mansions of the mind turned into actually pleasant places to live, and horrid places to die. In the poem "Irony as Nursery" appear quite suddenly the lines: "And then to think,/ miserably, over a cup of coffee, how the map/ is all dots of jailed men hanging/ from bare electric bulbs in underground prisons/ swaying between light as we see it/ and the wall of light in the dark" (134–135).

Codrescu is not a member of the New York School in that he lives in New Orleans, and travels, and has an underground world of the Romanian Jew, and exile, a dark basement, as inner map, a room which most Americans can only understand through various rumors which seem as distant as the torture rooms beneath medieval castles. For Codrescu, this is not only a psychological reality, but one that has been turned inside out and keeps him awake at night. He doesn't live or think as if he was an exile from New York City. His work is simply not about New York

City (although he does love the city), nor is he one of the insiders in that scene. In addition, he does not have the same concerns that the New York School had, except that he shares with them a certain interest in fun. Codrescu's vortex, moreover, is unlike that of Hollo, or Larry Fagin, or Tom Clark's. They share a few central values, but not to the exclusion of all other values. Fagin is funny and observant, but it is impossible to imagine him risking his neck to help bring down a corrupt regime. Fagin's work doesn't have that sense of political urgency. Hollo is charming, but he doesn't have the same risk-taking agenda that gives Codrescu's nonfiction writing on Romania its profound sense that we are living on the edge of an abyss. Hollo's Finland was one that stood its test against communism, outnumbered 50 to 1, and the Finns held Stalin's Marxist tank divisions to a draw, to general Western jubilation. It cost the Finns plenty, including a fourth of their country as compensation and half of the adult male population was wounded or killed in the effort, but the Finnish experience of the latter twentieth century was not as unfortunate as the Romanian experience. Finland remained a democracy, with democratic traditions, and has enjoyed the prosperity and high level of education of the western Scandinavian democracies as a result. The Finns had adequate food, housing, and excellent educations, while the Romanians had none of these things, as everything that could be skimmed was sent to the Soviet Union.

Deleuze and Guattari chart the impact of history on literature in *Anti-Oedipus*. It is not only the family that has an effect on the psyche, but larger issues of war and peace. We exist in a social and historical field.

> The father, the mother, and the self are at grips with, and directly coupled to, the elements of the political and historical situation — the soldier, the cop, the occupier, the collaborator, the radical, the resistor, the boss, the boss' wife — who constantly break all triangulations, and who prevent the entire situation from falling back on the familial complex and becoming internalized in it.... There is always an uncle from America; a brother who went bad; an aunt who took off with a military man; a cousin out of work, bankrupt, or a victim of the Crash; an anarchist grandfather; a grandmother in the hospital, crazy or senile. The family does not engender its own ruptures. Families are filled with gaps and transected by breaks that are not familial: the Commune, the Dreyfus

Affair, religion and atheism, the Spanish Civil War, the rise of fascism, Stalinism, the Vietnam War, May '68 — all these things form complexes of the unconscious, more effective than everlasting Oedipus. And the unconscious is indeed at issue here. In the shadow of the fantastic phallus distributing the lacunae, the passages, and the articulations. Structures exist in the immediate impossible real. As Witold Gombrowicz says, the structuralists search for their structures in culture. As for myself, I look for them in the immediate reality. My way of seeing things was in direct relationship to the events of the times: Hitlerism, Stalinism, fascism [97–98].

To read the different poets in Codrescu's circle, and to read Codrescu himself, is not so much to regard them as individual figures, alone with their families. We must see them in history, as being divided and transected by vectors which force them in new directions. Anselm Hollo's Swedish-speaking father, his German-speaking mother. A long history of the libido in just those two descriptions. Hollo's family is rather illustrious, with one brother on the Finnish Supreme Court, his father an important translator in the capital city of Helsinki. Codrescu's family forced to share a toilet with a neighbor family in a provincial city. In Romania, short on food, especially meat, the angry fights over a slice of beef, a head of cabbage. Poetry is transected by history, which is transected by ideas.

Many writers have not had to confront the dangers Codrescu has faced, and yet not everyone has been a religious minority in communities that despised them, or an anarchist enemy of a communist state. And fortunately not everyone has had to run the risks of speaking up in such situations. But this is part of what makes Codrescu's writing so interesting: all the cracks in history that run through his unconscious. Codrescu's writing constantly references the skulls of his ancestors, cracked and buried beneath the marketplace in his hometown. Jews have had a tragic millennium, and Eastern European Jews among the most tragic, and those who are left have had a burden of bearing witness to the Holocaust, while maintaining enough sanity and optimism so that life could be lived, and not only as an onerous political agenda. Codrescu's writing has a larger relevance because it is not only fun, it is also smart, musical, and fresh, mostly wishing to leave behind the horrors of World War II and the Old World and look forward to the building of a more playful, tolerant society. He takes huge risks and has come a longer distance than any other of these poets, risking his life, and becoming the stated enemy of the deadly Ceausescu government in the process, his name forbidden to be mentioned in crossword puzzles. At a time when some of his Romanian friends were being hunted by former members of Securitate, and shot and killed for their work (I'm thinking of the religious scholar Ioan Couliano, who was assassinated in a toilet during a classroom break at the University of Chicago for having made broadcasts against the post–Ceausescu regime, which he claimed was merely a continuation of Ceausescu-ism by other members of the same gang), Codrescu remained publicly visible and continued his denunciations in spite of death threats warning him to desist.

How can he go on under such circumstances, hunted by the secret police of a state based on terrorism. He wrote:

> The business of living under authentic political threat does cause occasional stress — especially when I suspect that my apt. is bugged, or my phone and computer, or both. The best thing to do is to live as if They, like my readers, are only another Audience. Which they are.... I have an unshakeable faith in the greater purpose of creation and see my job in it as helping along by immobilizing the purveyors of ideologies. There are counter-revolutionary forces at work that can only be defeated by the use of laughter, humor, paradox, tai-chi like turning back of force, imaginative leaps that leave them in the dust, and unwavering support for the meek of the earth. The solution is the relentless cultivation of paradox for purposes of pleasure. I believe also in miscegenation [of people and ideas] and in the ultimate creolization of the specie. I believe also in cross-specie fertilization, and support all genetic advances in the hope of getting wings and a tail in my lifetime [e-mail of November 21, 1999].

Whitman wrote: "The attitude of great poets is to cheer up slaves and horrify despots" (17). "The coward shall surely pass away. The expectation of the vital and great can only be satisfied by the demeanor of the vital and great.... Only toward as good as itself and toward the like of itself will it advance half-way. An individual is as superb as a nation when he has the qualities which make a superb nation. The soul of the largest and wealthiest and proudest nation may well go halfway to meet that of its poets. The signs are effectual. There is no fear of mistake. If the one is true then the other is true. The proof of a poet is that his country absorbs him as affectionately as he has absorbed it" (27).

Since Codrescu is often citing Whitman, I asked him if he could describe a little anthology of those poems of Whitman's that he considered central. He wrote:

"Whitman matters in block. He only wrote one poem and it's all tangled up with his beard" (e-mail of November 19, 1999).

That poem is a song of America, its possibilities, its dreams. America is the great Outside, unassimilable into any strict metanarrative, it has so many cultures and countercultures that they can never be turned into one story, dictated by a tyrant. The poetry of the Investigative school uses as a litmus test the undigestibility of the poem. If it cannot be reterritorialized into a totalitarian platform, and if it challenges those who are trying to do this, it is a good poem. This is a poetry that exists as a counterbalance to the great systems of capitalism and communism. It is neither the one nor the other. The song of America is a story of the American outside, which Codrescu picks up, and uses as dystopian contrast to the Romanian inside, the American dream as compared to the Romanian nightmare.

11

Edward Sanders/Charles Manson:
The Family

While the Investigative Poets do not generally articulate limits, in several of their books they are forced to do just that. Ed Sanders' *The Family* and Codrescu's book *The Hole in the Flag* are such attempts. *The Family* deserves an examination of its own as it provides a parallel to Codrescu's look at Romania, which follows.

Manson, we are informed, was "gang-raped in reform school" (*Family* 386), and he was a convict, a small-time hoodlum, and a possible hit man (161) and yet infiltrated the flower-power movement. Manson often repeated the words from Revelations 9 as he prepared his followers to kill. "Neither repented they of their murders, nor of their sorceries, nor of their fornication, nor of their thefts" (124–125). Sanders, to counteract this vicious gang of hoodlums and their psychotic creed, read the Bible, too. "I was reading the Book of Jeremiah. I was searching for a tone to take in setting to text the accumulated gnarls of data that were swirling in my travel cases and filing cabinets" (393).

In an age of multiculturalism in which tolerance asks us to tolerate almost anything, it is a useful exercise to think about the Manson family. Manson was a racist who was looking forward to a destruction of the black race. He hated women and wanted to control them completely. He turned everyone around him into a killing machine. After the infamous murders of Sharon Tate and her friends, Manson's cohort Tex was proud of what he had done. "Tex laughed and told Snake, according to Snake, that he killed Sharon Tate: 'I killed her. Charlie asked me to. It was fun'" (312).

Once in the Family, it was hard to escape. "Clem had been assigned bed-check duty and discovered the girls missing. He yelled immediately for everybody to roust out and capture the runaways. Manson had issued proclamations that if they found anybody escaping, they were to beat them up, or worse" (341).

Discipline inside the family was delivered with insane ferocity, but his ferocity would have embroiled the entire country.

Manson wanted to create a racial holocaust. To do so, he considered various plans. "Manson used to talk about pouring LSD into the L.A. water supply. They believed mass acid use would cause citywide violence" (133). The idea of the violence was to set off a "big race war" (132) and in the effort of that, "Charlie put up a picture of a white elite ultimately ruling over a black population" (132).

Manson was ordered to death row in San Quentin for his crimes (432).

Sanders' book is a moral examination of the problems caused by free love and drug abuse when they are extended to the criminally insane.

An anonymous participant in the Manson family festivities told Ed Sanders that Manson was fascinated by films depicting animal and human sacrifice. The Family screened such films during the long summer nights. "There were three types of films that he seems to have witnessed: 1) family dancing and loving; 2) animal sacrifices; 3) human sacrifices" (190).

"They cut up a dog. Then they brought in a girl in there — two girls. They took their clothes off and poured the blood of the dog on top of the girls. They just held the dog. And they took the girls and they put the blood — and the bodies — all over both of them. And everybody balled the two girls ... it was a couple, two couples — they were being, uh, but I'm not, you know, this was a while ago..." (Sanders 191).

Sanders' informant goes on to talk in nauseating detail about the kinds of home-made films the Family enjoyed. The madness and suffering they invoke seem to have a parallel in the feeling of suffering invoked by the Dionysian tragedies of ancient Greece. The plays were part of the festivals for Dionysus. Seemingly, the ritual outcast of a scapegoat is what the festivals were based on. René Girard writes, "The unanimity attained through the intervention of the surrogate victim must not be lost. The community stands united before the onslaught of 'evil spirits' and remains faithful to its vow to reject mutual hostility" (*Violence* 124). It is this ritual violence that expels the actual violence felt within the community. "A collective murder that brings about the restoration of order imposes a kind of ritualistic framework on the savage fury of the group, all of whose members are out for one another's blood. Murder becomes sacrifice" (*Violence* 124).

How is it that Charles Manson and his group came to embody the destructive characteristics of the 1960s? While many others were apparently involved in the same kind of activities, the Manson family went further, and they attacked famous citizens and spread such terror that it was imperative that they be caught. Did flower power partially use the myth of Manson in order to exonerate itself? After the rock festival of Altamont, in which the Hell's Angels beat a black man to death, it became increasingly hard to believe in the innocence of the countercultural community. They could not police themselves. Throughout the '60s there was an atmosphere of violent confrontation with the police, with families, accompanied by a turn towards gurus in the form of Charles Manson and Jim Jones, among many others. Sanders' book traces this defection from democratic principles, and does so with a tone that increasingly turns away from the comic celebration of the '60s and recaptures a tone of moral urgency and indignation. Sander's *Family* is an adult book, and marks the rite of passage of the '60s, and perhaps a return from the infantile opposition to authority to an increasing sense of the need for cooperation with competent authorities. Towards the end of the narrative, Sanders befriends policemen, attorneys, and others involved in the agonizing separation of the good and evil in the operation of society.

The problem of meaningfulness became more important as the Investigative Poets, through no fault of their own, were forced to move inside as they sought a moral line against the likes of Manson. Sanders helped himself to recover the moral line by reading the Book of Jeremiah (383). While Sanders was not the only one to write a significantly moral book, it is significant that Codrescu's book on Romania, and Clark's various books on criminal mischief within the American poetic community, show that this group of poets is united by a need to continue to articulate ethics, as well as playfulness.

Girard asks, "Is it a mere coincidence or should we suspect that far from being as hopelessly irrelevant to contemporary problems as the intel-

ligentsia believes, the biblical text is much more relevant than the Oedipus of Freud or the Dionysus of Nietzsche?" (*To Double-Business Bound*
227).

As Codrescu returns to Romania to witness the aftermath of the
winter revolution of 1989, he emphasizes the humorlessness of the Ceausescu regime, but what apparently brings the regime down is the eviction
of a Christian bishop.

12

Good/Evil: Ceausescu

In Andrei Codrescu's book *The Hole in the Flag*, he describes his return to Romania during the heady weeks following the uprising in Timisoara in December 1989. To preface the journey back, he writes of the unstable conditions in which the militia, the police, and the infamous secret police (also known as *Securitate*), and the army all had different roles and often didn't know what side they were on. Were they inside or outside? Could any of them be trusted? "The police, which had its roots in *polis* (community) would, it was hoped, function only to keep the peace" (23). Codrescu doesn't articulate a good and evil, or criteria of judgment. To set Codrescu next to a serious Romanian Christian will illustrate the difference.

Ceausescu's regime collapsed on Christmas Eve in 1989. For over 20 years Ceausescu had come to be the single acceptable viewpoint in Romania, with all others being mercilessly crushed. Poets and artists were particularly susceptible to being crushed, because they dared to recognize their own authority. Richard Wurmbrand, a Romanian pastor, has written that Christians in Ceausescu's Romania were also susceptible to being crushed, but that it was they who brought down Ceausescu's regime.

> The prisoners ... had to abjure all their convictions, political or religious, for which they had been sentenced. They had to promise full allegiance to Communism. Any method that would produce results was permitted: severe beating on the soles of the feet

and on the genitals; breaking teeth with gravel; forcing prisoners to ingest feces and urine; sleep deprivation; forbidding them to go to the toilet; and any other degrading measures. Men had to be reduced to heaps of fear, nothing else [30].

As Ceausescu and his men sought to impose their single philosophy on 20 million people, there nevertheless remained something that couldn't be beaten out, or killed. In a chapter titled "How the Revolution Began," Pastor Wurmbrand describes the capacity of Romanian Christans to witness to their faith while being murdered by the top dog and his henchmen:

> A Romanian bishop, one of the many who became stooges for the Communists, fired the Reformed Pastor Tokes of Timisoara for preaching faithfully. When he was to be evicted from his home and church, a crowd of Christians of all denominations and several nationalities surrounded his house and obstructed the police. The number of demonstrators grew. When they proceeded to march towards the center of town, the army was called out to stop them. The soldiers began shooting, and many were killed or wounded. Little children gathered on the steps of the cathedral and sang religious hymns. Again the troops fired, and some children died. The rest sought shelter in the cathedral, but heartless priests had locked the sanctuary.
>
> Then an amazing thing happened. The entire crowd, instead of fighting the army, knelt and prayed. This was too much for the soldiers. They refused to shoot any more. Meanwhile, the whole town had gathered. Pastor Dugulescu seized the opportunity to address everyone from the balcony of the Opera House. A poem by Constantin Ioanid, "God Exists," was recited. The crowd shouted, "God exists!" Leaflets with the text had been distributed. Some who knew the music began to sing the song that had been composed for the words. Soon thousands joined in singing it again and again. It became the song of the revolution [22].

Singing and jokes interrupt the rational. They bring in another perspective. So does the transcendent aspect of Christianity. As Slavoj Zizek writes,

> With regard to the notion of the act as real, this means that an authentic *act* is in between Time and Eternity. On the one hand, an act is, as Kant and Schelling have put it, the point at which

"eternity intervenes in time," at which the enchainment of temporal causal succession is interrupted, at which "something emerges — intervenes out of nothing," at which something takes place which cannot be explained as the outcome/result of the preceding chain [to put it in Kant's terms, the act designates the direct intervention of the noumenal dimension into phenomenality; to put it in Schelling's terms, the act designates the moment at which the abyssal/atemporal principle of identity — "I did it because I did it, for no particular reason" — momentarily suspends the reign of the principle of sufficient reason] [93].

The perspective of heaven explodes the temporal plans of humanity and brings into the temporary a notion of justice that can suddenly give men, women and children the courage to stand up to Ceausescu and his armies. Pastor Wurmbrand writes, "In Sibiu, two Orthodox priests who were lifted onto tanks asked everyone to kneel for prayer. The demonstrators, numbering thousands, as well as soldiers and officers, did so. An 'Our Father' was said together by those who still remembered prayers. Soldiers and citizens embraced. It was no longer possible to repress the uprising" (24).

It is difficult to find the precise fillip that sent the chain of dominoes tumbling. Another form of opposition was play. This is where Codrescu's aesthetics can be usefully contrasted with Wurmbrand's. Play is a powerful aspect of the Romanian avant-garde, from its earliest practitioners, such as Urmuz and Tzara, to its most important critical defenders, such as Mihai Spariosu and Marcel Cornis-Pope and Andrei Codrescu himself. Spariosu, a contemporary literary critic and Romanian exile for many years, writes in a summary of his career "Exile, Play, and Intellectual Autobiography," that exile was a positive phenomenon for him. "Then exile could also be understood as *atopia,* that is, as an experience of the void or emptiness. Far from being negative and threatening, this experience may be seen as an experience of the unknown, both within and without, characteristic of all truly playful activity" (214).

Codrescu's poem "À Francis Ponge" is a direct slap against the rational ideals enunciated by Ceausescu and instituted by East Bloc partisans of totalitarian politics, and a lyric poem to the ability to reinvent oneself at every step.

> We don't want to be examples. We just want
> to happen. Where would the police be without examples?
> Where the professor? Where the state? Where the censor?
> [*Selected Poems* 115].

Against the idea of a static identity, Codrescu positions motion, style, and the concept of the Event. Deleuze and Guattari write in a similar vein: "We have seen this in the case of the painter Turner, and his most accomplished paintings that are sometimes termed 'incomplete': from the moment there is genius, there is something that belongs to no school, no period, something that achieves a breakthrough — art as a *process* without goal" (*Anti-Oedipus* 369–370). Against the Oedipalizing psychiatrists who attempt to make examples of us, and attempt to show that we always correspond to their mental maps, Deleuze and Guattari write that

> on the other, the schizorevolutionary, pole, the value of art is no longer measured except in terms of the ... gushings of mercy and pity knowing nothing of meanings and aims [the Artaud experiment, the Burroughs experiment] ... art as experimentation [370–371].

But what can create the "gushings of mercy and pity" that Deleuze describes? Is it postmodern irony, or the ancient practice of prayer, spoken quietly into the heart of an enemy? Pastor Richard Wurmbrand writes,

> Then there was the Malmezon prison in Bucharest, where I had been in both Fascist and Communist times (it was much worse under the latter). During the war, six brothers and sisters were there. It was a loose arrangement, with male and female prisoners together during the day. On one occasion the commander, a colonel, entered the room and shouted, "I heard that you sing your hymns here, which is forbidden. What kind of hymns are these? Let me hear one."
> We sang, "O sacred head, now wounded, with grief and shame bowed down." He turned around and left without saying a word. Many years later I heard from Filip Shmuilovici, an outstanding Hebrew Christian who had been my fellow prisoner on this occasion and now lives in Israel, that the colonel had become a brother in Christ. Our singing might have helped others to salvation as well [43–44].

Against the ideological torture administered by the communists, the evangelical Christians of Romania proposed a counterevangelism composed of nothing but songs of redemption and grace, sung even toward their most brutal tormentors. Believers sang and danced in prison, befuddling their captors who believed only in brute strength and only in material reality. The prisoners prayed for Ceausescu and his men and converted many of them, until the mass conversion of December 1989, when an entire army betrayed its master. Fortunately, there is something in the human being that cannot be pounded out, there is something which always remains free. Compared to Wurmbrand, Codrescu's own denunciation of communism is quite fierce, but he doesn't replace it with anything. Codrescu's humor and playfulness never becomes a dogma. It never forms into a prescription of any kind, but it does tend to preference friendliness.

Codrescu writes, on meeting an American professor on the plane to Bucharest,

> I had spent three cramped hours from Paris listening to an obnoxious professor from Brooklyn College who was writing a book on the Romanian Communist Lucian Goldmann. He was going to Bucharest to talk to Goldmann's old Communist pals, some of whom had only recently been put to pasture by the revolution. Others were former honchos of Ana Pauker and Gheorghe Gheorghiu-Dej's regimes. "Doesn't it strike you as ironic," I asked him, "that the only Marxists left now are American academics?" [*Hole* 211].

In *Ay, Cuba! A Socio-Erotic Journey*, Codrescu discusses humor as one of the ways in which the folk art of the proletariat subversively tried to give another perspective to the heavy-handedness of Ceausescu. Discussing the similarity of jokes in communist Romania and in Castro's Cuba, he writes:

> The jokes were familiar to me. They came from the culture of the Joke, which was the common culture of all socialist countries. One can dispense with serious histories and study solely jokes for a complete picture of the birth, decay, and collapse of those regimes.... Toward the end, the jokes were the only thing still holding the people together.... I told them that in Romania now the binding cement of political humor had all but crumbled,

leaving in its wake the bitter taste of a hundred specialized idioms
[132–133].

As Codrescu reentered Romania in 1989 he had been gone for nearly
a quarter of a century, and he was barely able to speak the language. He
didn't remember the rules and was silent. Finally, in Bucharest, he was
offered oranges by young revolutionaries. Oranges had been unavailable
during the Ceausescu years, and were, in fact, a forbidden fruit. He joked
in Romanian.

> "I will not eat a ... political prisoner," I said, and amazingly they
> laughed, understanding the metaphor precisely. I said this in
> Romanian, and until now, even after Adrian introduced us, I had
> not spoken to anyone in Romanian, holding back for the right
> moment. This was the right moment.
> You do not belong in a place until you have made a joke in the
> native tongue. That's the true passport of acceptance. Now they
> converged on me" [*Hole* 106].

Joking indicates a constant ability to evolve, to dance, to make a
new step up, and to change the rules. First, all the inside rules have to
be learned by heart. Only at that point can there be creative friendship.
The ability to joke together is the basis of friendship. It is impossible to
imagine a friendship in which joking doesn't play at least some part.
Common amusements, as Aristotle points out, and common sacrifices,
create family connections. "They are created by friendship, for friendship is the motive of society" (*Aristotle on Man in the Universe* 302).
Without the ability to creatively make jokes, friendship is impossible.
Friendship is only possible with the background of common rules and
yet a certain innovative attitude towards them. Joking is only possible
where there is a certain amount of freedom, as it is implicitly a democratic format in which many different perspectives vie for the mind of the
reader. Ludwig Wittgenstein asks, "What is it like for people not to have
the same sense of humor? They do not react properly to each other. It's
as though there were a custom amongst certain people for one person to
throw another a ball which he is supposed to catch and throw back; but
some people, instead of throwing it back, put it in their pocket" (83e).
Codrescu writes in *The Hole in the Flag* that there were some leaders of the National Salvation Front who came into power after Ceausescu's death who were more popular than others with foreign reporters

simply on the basis of the quality of their humor. "Aurel Dragos-Munteanu was a personable man with a relatively gentle sense of humor, unlike [Silviu] Brucan, whose demonic humor struck most reporters as downright sinister" (86).

Communities form in joking relationships. The ability to laugh together signifies a mutual appreciation of certain values. A demonic sense of humor, as Silviu Brucan was felt to have, is only appreciated among demonic people. One can imagine the demonic sense of humor among torturers in the underground prisons of Romania, as they laughed among themselves of the things Christians and avant-garde poets said when their spines were being broken with sledge hammers, and their feet burned with hot irons. Kantian aesthetic philosopher Ted Cohen writes in his book *Jokes: Philosophical Thoughts on Joking Matters* that joking and laughing together creates a sense of communion, which is why it is so disastrous when one tells a joke and the other does not respond. One is alone. Sometimes one cannot join. But suppose your joke is a success? "Thus they join you. And then they join you again, if the joke works, in their response, and the two of you find yourselves a community, a community of amusement. That is what I call the *intimacy* of joking" (40).

Codrescu writes that he was two different people in Romanian and in English, and the cultural shock caused by going back and forth between the two systems created a gargantuan gap in his own sense of his self as he went back to Romania with a rough American media who were unwittingly breaking every unwritten rule of Romanian politesse. This made Codrescu feel his Romanian-ness.

> The polite, even delicate Romanian elicited information obliquely, through reminiscence, wit, and inference. The American was direct, rude, quick to get to the heart of it. In addition to the historical circumstances that made everyone confess, there was a basic psychocultural difference between Romanians and Americans. The reason — incomprehensible to a Romanian — why it was possible for an American to be so direct was that an American wasn't offended if he was told that it was none of his business. Telling an impertinent questioner off was the right, democratic thing to do. But for a Romanian it was rude not to answer a direct question, so he preferred to lie rather than honestly tell his tormenter to "fuck off." Also, Americans did not

judge the information they obtained in the same way that Romanians did. They were rarely shocked by it, and they never considered it a confidence unless expressly told that it was. The
American press, of course, has no concept of confidence [104].

Codrescu's media colleagues were trampling all over delicate Romanian sensibilities, asking forthright questions that Codrescu considered
impossible to ask. A true insider in both systems, Codrescu was able to
joke in both languages. Codrescu's story of his return is in fact chiefly
notable for its tone of persiflage, which only infrequently becomes a
lament, or a tone-poem to the Romanian landscape:

> We began to see the first pointy haystacks that are characteristic
> of rural Romania. I have never seen haystacks like these anywhere
> in the world, and I watch for them. ...With snow on them they
> looked like the peasants' lambskin hats.... I had always loved the
> touchingly tender way the Romanian haystacks dot the fields, a
> kind of writing legible only to crows [146].

In an essay on the American left of the early 1970s, collected in *The
Dog with a Chip in His Neck*, Codrescu writes:

> The politicos, as I remember them, seemed to me notoriously
> incapable of grasping paradox, possibly because they lacked a
> sense of humor. They were taken seriously only by the FBI,
> which, likewise, lacked the elementary organ of humor. These
> twin bummers, politicos and their fuzz brothers, acted or rather
> reenacted the shadow ideological quarrels of the 1930s, unaware
> of the fact that the languages of the ideologies they invested with
> such magic powers had in fact been emptied of meaning. I was
> possibly more aware of the bankruptcy of ideological discourses
> than many of my contemporaries because I grew up under a Red
> totalitarianism that used all the buzzwords of community and lib-
> erty but meant exactly the opposite by them [50].

In Nicolae Ceausescu's speeches, for instance, the only thing missing is a sense of humor. If it weren't for that, we might think this was a
freedom-loving democrat.

> We declare most firmly against the imperial policy of force and
> dictate. Life requires that this old policy should be done away
> with entirely. History demonstrates, day by day, hour by hour, we

might say, that whatever has been built on strength, dictate and pressure of any kind has, in the end, collapsed under the blows of the struggles of the peoples, of the wide masses. All the big empires that were looking forward to an eternal life are known to have crashed, one by one, and free, independent nations rose on the ruins of those empires which had subjugated the peoples [*Romania's International Policy of Peace* 28].

Codrescu's writing follows the general poststructuralist trend towards a strong critique of top-down institutions, which are not conducive to friendship. Where there is such an institution, there is felt to be an injustice, because they are not playful, but authoritarian. And yet, without museums, universities, hospitals, dictionaries, train tracks, and other support structures that will outlast our own physical selves and be there for children, and grandchildren, how is it that we are going to live and pass on our way of life? Someone has to set a timetable. Coming from Stalinist Romania, it is possible to see where Codrescu would have a problem with strong government and any kind of organizational factor that would last too long. This doesn't mean that Codrescu would like to dismantle anything permanent. He has raised a family, gotten tenure within a state university, has many deep and lasting friendships. His poems are not the work of an utterly chaotic crazy man, but the work of a flexible, inventive, and devoted citizen. It is important to see the work of the Investigative Poets — many of whom have raised families, all of whom have maintained friendships for decades — as the work of citizens. Although they probably have collective FBI files that would take up several warehouses, as they are frequently oppositional advocates and thus citizens in what is maintained as an open society, none of them are devoted to destroying law and order, but rather, in fact, towards maintaining it, while also creating a lively and loving democratic culture in which no one faction gets the upper hand. It is a community based, finally, on aesthetics. Their politics is neither conservative nor Marxist, but is rather based on playfulness and friendship without bosses.

The founder of postmodernism, Jean-Francois Lyotard, was one of the first radical French philosophers to turn away from extreme radicalism and a closed interpretation, as he was one of the first to see the problems it caused. Lyotard's realism, and his explicit faith in representative democracy, is announced several times in his later volume *Postmodern*

Fables. "The notion of a conversational minimum is surely indispensable to liberal, democratic politics.... I don't see what can be opposed to it if we agree that there is no political alternative to liberal democracy, as seems to me from now on to be the case. That's why I don't think it's fair for Rorty or others to authorize themselves to hear resonances of leftism, revolution, or even terrorism, in my defense of the differend" (133). We have come to a critical juncture in history where top-down organizations all over the globe have been destroyed by the resentment that they create. Christianity has also caused resentment where it has dictated moral rules such as whether dancing or card playing are permissible. Whenever people seek to rule one another it brings out the most unpleasant aspects of humanity. While Codrescu's ludic surrealism does not seek to legislate, it also avoids authority. Communism and Christianity are competing authoritarian systems. Codrescu frequently compares them, but for him, communism has no redeeming features. Communism and Christianity are the two great competing metanarratives of the West. Christianity is itself composed of many denominations with various attitudes toward authority and community.

Political scientist Anne Sa'adah investigates the origins of the French, British and American revolutions in her seminal volume, *The Shaping of Liberal Politics in Revolutionary France: A Comparative Perspective.* In it, she writes, "Revolutionary politics are, by definition, exclusionary, and were so in England and America, as in France" (13). What then constituted the difference between the American Revolution, in which the leaders held a trust in one another, and never scapegoated one another, and the French Revolution, that ended in an orgy of blood? The big difference is perhaps the Protestant character of the American population, Sa'adah argues. Whereas the French revolutionaries were enlightenment atheists such as Voltaire and Robespierre, and were appealing to a group that had long seen the Catholic Church in collusion with the crown, the American and British revolutionaries saw their God as covenantal rather than hierarchical, as the best friend they had rather than an implacable foe. Sa'adah writes:

> While Protestantism in no manner represents a sufficient condition for the type of revolution and revolutionary outcome that obtained in England and America, it does constitute a necessary condition. From God we receive a property in ourselves; by God we are held responsible for and constrained in the way we use

ourselves and one another. Not by accident did Locke, who elsewhere struggled inconclusively with theological questions, feel
compelled to assign Providence an explicit role when he came to
write the second *Political Treatise* [72].

The American Revolution had been prepared for by more than a century of covenantal discussion that included tremendous dissent and an
emphasis on freedom of opinion in which every citizen could speak. The
link between Puritanism and liberalism is not direct or completely understood, Sa'adah writes, but it is there:

> Protestantism in all its forms confronted the believer with the
> Bible, so that each man and woman might read and accept the
> Word. With no resource left to them but the power of verbal per-
> suasion exercised from the pulpit, the Puritan minority was natu-
> rally led to insist upon the right of men of diverse views to
> express themselves freely, the right of listeners — themselves read-
> ers and often expounders of Scripture — to arrive at their own
> conclusions, and the right of like-minded men and women to
> join voluntarily in "gathered" churches where they might appoint
> a minister of their own choosing. Dissent proliferated [73–74].

When Locke wrote his treatises he did not do so in a vacuum but
within the groundswell of the Reformation, in which the notion of gath-
ered churches, dissent, liberty, the direct relation of man and God, were
well-known intellectual currency. Sa'adah writes, "Thus there was a language of liberty — and of politics — common to England and America in
the seventeenth and eighteenth centuries: a language couched in allusions
to property, Scripture, and the established constitution.... French liberalism spoke to a different historical experience, drew on a different reser-
voir of cultural and religious references, and developed within different
restraints" (76).

As we look at different societies and their political experience over
the last 300 years we must not see them as divorced from religious questions. French surrealism inherits the Jacobin distrust of religion and
covenantal politics. French surrealism and poststructuralism inherits the
same tendency toward scapegoating and suspicion that has not been a
part of American politics. While the American and English revolutions
were built on a century or more of Protestant political rhetoric, the French
revolution, Sa'adah writes, as the Stalinist and the Nazi revolutions, had

different historic and rhetorical conditions as background. The French liberals lost out to the radical Jacobins because "their fears and aspirations never coalesced around a coherently motivated and systematically pursued plan of action" (79). While the Puritans had God to rally around, and to hold as common ground, the French radicals did not. Nearly a century before the French Revolution, Louis XIV forbade theological dissent. "Even pamphlet warfare, so prevalent in Stuart England and so important to the evolution of seventeenth-century English politics, was severely restricted in Louis XIV's France" (96). Without God, there was only political power. Sa'adah writes, "The eighteenth century paid the price of Louis XIV's and Bossuet's momentary victory, as militancy fell to the skeptics and atheists who, thanks to Louis's policies, identified religion with divine right kingship and intolerance" (96). The French then did not have a language in which they could discuss their differences. While America turned to what Sa'adah called a politics of *transaction*, the French turned toward a politics of *exclusion*.

> For all the conflict legitimated by the triumphant ideology's individualistic emphasis, the result was what is sometimes called consensual politics. Conflict did not end, but it assumed certain characteristics. The stakes of politics and the advantages of power became subject to both explicit and implicit limits.... The stability of the rules, rather than substantive uniformity, became a primary index of the health of the community. Stable rules guaranteed the manageability of conflicts [5].
>
> Finally, from one end of the political spectrum to the other, the politics of exclusion sponsored an enduring nostalgia for moral unanimity and a deep-seated aversion to politics. In this account, in a well-constituted society, politics would represent a very minor activity. Politics would be a one-shot deal: After all the enemies had at last been turned out of the city, the friends would gather in a grand meeting of like-minded individuals, not to organize competition but to celebrate community.... Roughly summarized, this is the pattern of politics which I call the politics of exclusion [19].

In French surrealism we can see that this was the politics that came to be practiced by André Breton, who excommunicated rather than submit his organization to the necessary twists and pulls of democratic transactional politics. Bitter debates within the French revolution lacerated the opposition and insisted on absolute purity and virtue from within the Jacobin ranks, and abolished any opposition.

> Thus Saint-Just charged Danton after the latter's indictment: "You accused Roland, but more as an acrimonious imbecile than as a traitor...," Saint-Just cited this lapse as proof that Danton too was a traitor. The logic that prompted the transfer of the politics of exclusion from appropriate objects [the king] to inappropriate objects [the plausibly loyal opposition] discouraged the consolidation of liberal institutions, since the effect was perpetually to reopen revolutionary questions, forcing the opposition into ideological self-consciousness and intransigence, while fragmenting, isolating, and diminishing the supports of the new regime. The effects cut all the more deeply because as a conception of political life, the politics of exclusion now permeated all sectors of French public opinion; as a model of political behavior, it affected the opposition[s] as much as it did the men and groups in power [161].

Such a model of exclusionary politics became a template for French revolutionary thought. It continued, perhaps, to operate throughout the twentieth-century left, and can be seen in the perpetual crises within the surrealist ranks, in which one surrealist after another was tried and excommunicated. Leafing through the *Archives du Surrealisme*, edited by Marguerite Bonnet, one can read the copious notes on the Philippe Soupault trial, as well as many others, as authors were tried for everything from smoking English cigarettes to publishing journalism to failing to adhere to the French communist party. In the politics of exclusion, no dissent is tolerated, and dissenters are excommunicated.

Codrescu does seem to implicitly critique Christianity as well as communism, and especially is critical of those who attack outsiders. He is implicitly inclusionist, and doesn't practice exclusion. I know of no one with whom he has broken. For Codrescu the alternative to Christianity or Marxism appears to be a Lyotardian-Deleuzian postmodernism in which friendship and listening takes the place of powerful orders from above. Within the group of Investigative Poets one could almost argue that there is an implicit covenant of support and good will that is virtually unshakeable. But where are they headed? If the two great metanarratives of the West are Christianity and Marxism, then must an alliance be made with one system or the other in order to make any headway into the general culture? Early surrealism under Breton chose Marxism and then backed off, and seemingly had no myth whatsoever. Could surrealism try the other option? For Codrescu, Christianity has many positive references throughout his work and is a redeemable option, while Marxism is not. Indeed, Codrescu hesitantly credits Christianity for its role in the events of December 1989. Discussing Lutheran minister Lazlo Tökes, he writes, "Listening to Tökes, I had the feeling that great events are sometimes possible because of the moral force of a single human. That is, of course, a Christian belief, and Christianity may, in spite of Georgescu and in spite of the church's own dark past, be a force for the good in Romania. There is an unavoidable religious dimension to the Central-Eastern European revolutions of 1989. From the Roman Catholic church in Poland to Bishop Tökes's small ministry, Christianity played a major role…. It will not do to ignore this problem as does *The New York Times*, for instance, which printed Václav Havel's speech before the United State Congress, but left out all references to God and miracles" (*Hole in the Flag*, 208–209).

Nevertheless, Codrescu is very critical of Christianity's lack of playfulness and sometimes sees it as a system as rotten as Marxism. Directly after the positive quote above, Codrescu downplays the role of Christianity in Bishop Tökes's character. "He [Tökes] seemed to be simply *decent*. His sermons … were *only* [my emphasis] the considered thoughts of a man who decided to speak out" (209). Codrescu is darkly critical of the Greek Orthodox church in Romania and its role in propping up Ceau-sescu's legitimacy and his tip of the hat toward Tökes's being "decent," does not imply that Codrescu is now without a distrust of Christianity in general. Indeed, his approval of Tökes and his provisional approval of the work of Christians in the revolutions of 1989 runs somewhat counter to his prevailing opinion.

13

Surrealism/Protestantism: The Blood Countess

Codrescu is not on the side of the Protestant Reformation that Anne Sa'adah claims forms the watershed of inclusivist and transactional politics. In *The Blood Countess*, Codrescu's novel about a Hungarian countess who cannibalizes and rapes her own servants, Codrescu describes a Lutheran pastor whom he dubs Comrade Hebler. This text appears to slip into an abyss awaiting from within his own Old World-surrealist-exclusionist vocabulary. Codrescu straddles massive worlds. While he is often inclusivist, he has slips into exclusionism especially where it includes Marxists or Christians. Comrade Hebler is a murderer, like the Stalinists to whom Codrescu explicitly compares him. Moreover, Lutheran Hebler hates the Jews, as is discovered by Countess Bathory's childhood friend and biographer, the hunchback Andrei:

> Andrei had been told by Hebler that Doctor Luther hated Jews because the Jew had been punished by God, and that it was up to good Christians to erase them from the face of the earth. When Andrei asked how this might be accomplished, Hebler, his eyes blazing with fury, said that "we must burn their synagogues and kill them in the flesh, especially the converted ones who hide under the Christian cloak, erasing all the debts that they have bewitched us into contracting" [86].

This character reappears in the story, several hundred years later, in the 20th century, and runs the history class in Stalinist Hungary.

> Comrade Hebler had asked the class to speculate on what it was that might have motivated the Hungarian tribes to be nomadic. Was it lack of resources, the search for food?
>
> I appear to have answered, "The joy of plunder and rape."
>
> The class burst out laughing, not because they found the answer wrong, but because it so obviously ignored the prevailing ideology, which found only the forces of production and class struggle relevant to any given situation, no matter how distant.
>
> Hebler brought his ruler down on the desk with such force that it broke in two. "Feelings do not create history!" He shouted. "History is 99.9 percent sorrow! The only joy there is, is felt by people when they triumph over the rich!"
>
> Comrade Hebler then reported me to the school authorities for my remark about the joy of plunder and rape. The Party committee charged with ideological vigilance at the gymnasium was well aware of my unhealthy social origins. My remark was viewed as a direct challenge to the new interpretation of history that they were at such pains to provide [303].

Codrescu links Lutheranism with Marxism, not only due to his upbringing, but because of his postmodern surrealistic philosophy. He sees them both as closed systems.

Lutheranism is in fact violently opposed to Marxism, and was partially responsible for bringing down the East German state and it was also one of the few institutions that stood up to Nazism. Robert Goeckel, a professor of political science, has written in his book *The Lutheran Church and the East German State: Political Conflict Under Ulbricht and Honecker*, that "the Soviets found that in the early postwar period the churches were often the only intact organizations that were relatively untainted by collaboration with the Nazis.... The Soviets' recognition of the churches' not inconsiderable opposition to Hitler's rule and the personal experience of German Communists jailed with members of the Confessing Church — along with the force of circumstance — led them to grant the church a honeymoon" (41).

The Lutheran church remained intact throughout the Soviet occupation of East Germany and helped organize resistance to the Russian imperialists in the latter 1980s. Although Vladimir Lenin had opted for a politics of militant atheism, and this antagonism intensified during the Stalinist period, the Soviet system never succeeded in eradicating Christianity, and in periods of relatively mild repression, it was Christian criticism that stepped directly into the breach. It was the Christian Alexander Solzhenitsyn whose *One Day in the Life of Ivan Denisovitch* caused such an enormous furor in the mother country in the early 1960s. It was the patriarchal Polish pope whose "armies" dismantled the Soviet juggernaut and its allies in Poland. Alexander Dubcek, a Lutheran, was the leader of the Prague Spring in 1968. Estonia's large Lutheran minority (approximately 35 percent) had led revolts throughout the 1980s. In East Germany, 59.2 percent of the population were Lutherans in 1970 (Goeckel 41). During the Soviet occupation, the East German Lutherans were able to maintain autonomous newspapers, as well as religious studies and peace programs, and to provide a mild but insistent voice of criticism against the government's militarization and repression. In the circumstances, even mild criticism should have been seen as heroic, but in Codrescu's narratives, almost all Christians, but especially mainstream Protestants, are invariably suspect, because of their apparent closure to the spirit of play.

In 1970, shortly after Codrescu left Romania, only 1.1 percent of Romanians were Lutheran (Goeckel 10), while Eastern Orthodox made up 80 percent. Jewish people (who made up 0.5 percent of the Romanian population), like Protestants, were a suspect and mistrusted minority, and perhaps had little opportunity to interact with one another, and had in many cases lapsed from their faith. When I asked Codrescu what he was doing with the Lutheran Hebler in *Blood Countess*, he wrote, "About Lutherans and such, I can't answer your questions. I love God, I hate churches. I enjoy talking to Jesuits and rabbis" (e-mail of February 14, 2000).

Because of Codrescu's background of growing up in Stalinist Romania, (he caught only the opening years of Ceausescu's Romania), he has been somewhat jaundiced towards the idea of long-lasting institutions, especially if they argue for absolute values of justice or truth without being able to embody them. Most Christian denominations are absolutist, as are most Marxist institutions. Codrescu's work is always to crack open absolutism and introduce a hilarious postmodern negative capability. His journal *Exquisite Corpse* is one of the most important conductors of negative capability in the American literary world of the latter part of the twentieth century, and it has endured into the twenty-first. It is devoted to iconoclasm and to a joyous pillaging of any and every sacred institution in favor of the pleasures of the body and the concept of now, however ironically inscribed.

Jean-François Lyotard and Gilles Deleuze, also seeing the depraved character of the Maoist Cultural Revolution that beset Paris throughout the 1970s with so much self-righteous twaddle, also came to distrust and resent pious institutions, and permanence, and to privilege one-sided eroticism, and private experience, and to spend the majority of their work defending such sensations from the public sphere. Institutions, at least for Deleuze, are swept aside, and his work barely considers them (Lyotard's considerations of the future of education in *The Postmodern Condition* could be considered as an example of the provisional acceptance of institutions, but there is no similar endorsement of schools in the work of Gilles Deleuze).

The surrealists have a long genealogy in utopian anarchism, and in that domain institutions are generally decried. Max Stirner, for instance, writes, "The Revolution aimed at new *arrangements*; insurrection leads us no longer to *let* ourselves be arranged, but to arrange ourselves, and set no glittering hopes on 'institutions'" (316). Stirner put nothing above the body, including ideas. "My intercourse with the world consists in my enjoying it, and so consuming it for my self-enjoyment. *Intercourse* is the *enjoyment of the world*, and belongs to my self-enjoyment" (Stirner 319). Here we have a statement that would seem to concur with the ideology of the *Blood Countess*. As Stirner writes, "The critic ... will never comprehend that above the *bodily man* there does not exist something higher" (356).

Hannah Arendt, however, warns that since the body cannot be shared, it cannot be considered the foundation of a public life. "Hedonism, the doctrine that only bodily sensations are real, is but the most radical form of a non-political, totally private way of life" (*Human Condition* 112–113).

The surrealists believed in eros and the marvelous as their ultimate concerns. This social vision is based on inventive poetry, and the writings of these authors are filled with the kind of fun and verve that their social vision of society requires. But seemingly the fleeting sensation of pleasure is all that holds Fourier's and the surrealists' communities together. There is no covenant beyond immediate pleasure. It is often claimed that the surrealists did accept difference, but their numerous excommunication trials reveal this not to be the case. They had a strong sense of rejecting those who did believe in time, in money, and tried to take care of their families within it. Along with many of the modernists, they tried to suppress art itself, or to make life into perpetual beauty.

Although Codrescu condemns Marxism, he has no ethical system with which to replace it because the avant-garde (especially that segment that has turned primarily to French surrealist thought for its vocabulary) for well over a century has sought to rid itself of moral maxims or commandments. This is the dead end of much surrealism. Slavoj Zizek writes, "What if the suffocating character of the pagan universe lay precisely in the fact that *it lacked the dimension of radical Evil?*" (122).

The Christian universe posits an absolutely good Father and a profoundly evil figure in Satan. The Christian universe clarifies, and it is not relative. It is absolute. Moreover, in the pagan universe there is no end to time, and the beginnings are obscure. In the Christian universe there is an alpha and an omega and a moral meaning to time.

The key to Codrescu's work is time. What does it mean? Codrescu appreciates cities, especially those vestiges of older cities. He is not a treehugging nature lover but loves instead things that last and give pleasure over the course of generations. His question is, How do some cities prosper, and why do some things go bad? This is also Gilles Deleuze's query. To find out why the Russian Revolution or psychotherapy went bad means we must turn toward moral understanding and toward an articulation of limits.

In Codrescu's imagination the ideal individual is a permanent marginal in a permanent diaspora from the societies based on time. Codrescu's world is an ideal that works on a much different plan than American Protestantism. Out of a Calvinist world in which success was considered a sign of grace, Codrescu asks us to find not the opposite, but rather to suspend the thought of time and to live in the moment. But in order to do this, the marginal must ironically live within a prosperous and longlasting community, the kind of community that surrealists themselves have never been able to build. Codrescu praises the ephemeral.

The Blood Countess wanted to live forever by bathing in the blood of virgins. Codrescu says in the Collins interview, "Rivers of morality flow out of immortality, which makes it, from my POV (that of Eternal Immorality) immoral. Immorality, the noun, is a god, while *The Blood*

Countess was both about the immortality of immorality and the immorality of immortality" (18).

This same destruction of the moral and metaphysical aspect of time found its equivalent among the Imagists, and within William Carlos Williams' famous phrase, "No ideas but in things," by which he begins his disjointed epic *Paterson* (6), an epic that has neither time sequences, a study of character, nor anything but a massive jumble of descriptions without discernible discretion regarding the moral or aesthetic value of those things. Williams' positivism finds its nadir in certain of Tom Clark's poems, in which a critique of the pointlessness of American existence without a sense of any higher value than temporary pleasure is pointed out:

Things to Do in California (1980)

Play beach volleyball
Make surfboards & live at Dana Pt.
Pick up chicks galore
Shine it on & get a good suntan
Catch cancer from the chemicals in the water
Die a grotesque death
Have a movie made about your life
Make sure you look thin in every scene
[*Paradise Resisted* 102]

In his latest works Codrescu has turned increasingly toward the religion of cities, investigating them and comparing them, and appreciating their sense of morality and their beauty. This is a theme he opened in *Blood Countess* with its implicit investigation of evil. In his novel *Messiah*, he compares Jerusalem and New Orleans and arrives at a new and inventive vision of his own that seeks to combine the religious and the hedonistic in order to posit the good. We will see the consequences of this in the following chapter, but also an emerging spirit of questioning toward the stability of those values.

14

Messiah/Messiah: The Return of Paganism

Codrescu has recently returned to the novel form. *Messiah*, which appeared in 1999, is a critique of time and its use in the West. Ostensibly following the careers of two young women, the novel is also a critique of places that are based on time. One of the young women, Andrea, is first associated with the city of Jerusalem, which Codrescu describes as a city of blood and anguish, filled with quarrels instead of humor (297). The other young woman, Felicity, is associated with New Orleans, which is a place lost to time. Andrea represents the spirit, and Felicity represents the body. It is only when the two get together that they can experience an orgasm, and together, they become the new Messiah, spreading happiness and erotic energy everywhere they go, and signaling an end to the Christian era at Mardi Gras 2000.

Codrescu's critique of Christian Hegelian Marxist time and its constantly putting everything into the future is foregrounded throughout the novel. I asked him via e-mail if it was his hippie background that made him believe in the Second Coming. "I don't remember any hippies believing in the Second Coming," he wrote back. "We believed in third, fourth, and fifth comings, all in one night if possible" (e-mail of February 20, 1999). While Codrescu's fellow Romanian E.M. Cioran had a Gnostic conception of time, in which *The Fall into Time* (the title of one of his books) was the misfortune of having been born at all, and was thought to be a nasty trick of a charlatan God, Codrescu sees this world as eminently liveable and when he does veer between cynicism and idealism, he prefers idealism. In *Messiah* the forces of disorder and physicality are arranged against the Christian forces that represent hypocrisy, lurking perversity and a painful attempt to reinscribe their spiraling pattern of time on the populations of the globe. In other words, the Christian notion of a spiral in time, that all of life has a meaning as seen from its end point, disgusts him. This clockwork meaning is being played out progressively in time, leaving nothing but meaning in its wake. Against this notion that the world is composed primarily of meaning, Codrescu posits a world of meaningless sensation, in which pleasure and play are the primary units of value. Codrescu is not building a system at all, which is why it is difficult to systematize his work. His work is a bomb that explodes systems, preconceptions, in order to let in the paradoxes and aporias of the present, but the result is a rather vague theodicy, or understanding of evil. As Codrescu's heroes race to ward off Armageddon in *Messiah*, they are described as a weapon forged against certainty: "Together, they were an arrow drawn against certainties, verities, eternal truths, gospels, edicts, writs, primers, laws, stone tablets" (346).

The traditional avant-garde saw themselves as getting us someplace, as leading the pack. Time was an arrow, and they were the sharpest point. These progressivist time machines point to a future that will never be reached. Whether Hegel, or Marx, or the traditional avant-garde, there was a future orientation. In Codrescu's work, there is no future orientation. The orientation is towards a present, and futurists are considered as fascists. In this, as in so many other ways, Codrescu resembles Walter Benjamin, who argued against the ability to see into the future, and against the modernist turn towards the occult, which Codrescu satirized in his spin through Taos, New Mexico. Although generally in favor of surrealism, Benjamin writes, "I am not pleased to hear it cautiously tapping on the windowpanes to inquire about its future" (*Reflections* 180).

Unlike surrealists, whose sense of time was convulsive, Marxists in the East Bloc worked within time frames generally of five years. In Endre Bojtar's study, *East European Avant-Garde Literature*, he writes, "Thus, in East Europe, constructivism-surrealism placed the (entire) *totality* of art into the future, its worldview being a future-centered totality.... The future-centered totality, of course, had the inherent danger that — as pointed out by the contemporary Marxist critic, Kurt Konrad — the work might reflect an incorrect or false totality, either by losing contact with the present or by directly deducing the future from the present" (91).

To this extent, Codrescu is not a member of the traditional avant-garde in that he is not an arrow racing to a blueprinted future, nor is he a Marxist. He doesn't believe that there is a better future unrolling meaningfully according to some blueprint in time. Throughout *Messiah* this is repeated. Two thousand years after the birth of Christ, Codrescu's novel deconstructs the notions of millennial activity. Although set at Mardi Gras in the year 2000, Codrescu has said that it could be "2020, if you like," (e-mail of February 19, 1999). While time is destroyed, or tampered, or played with, throughout the novel, it is place that matters. Codrescu wants to reorient humanity away from its obsession with time, and the future, and foreground the present. It is only in the present that erotic invention can be found. This is a critique of Hegelian-Marxism and its emphasis on a future, as well as a critique of capitalism, for which time is money and you are what you own, as well as a critique of Christianity. Instead of these, Codrescu wants to posit the body as the central source of value, in place. The body is not time, for the body is living, and time is not money, that is, it is not time which is most valuable. It is the body. Codrescu's notion of history is limited to orgasms. The second coming is not more important, he says, than the fourth or fifth. To spend one's time wisely, Codrescu would posit, is not to accumulate capital in the form of dollars and cents, but to spend it in the form of physical pleasures. These pleasures are not individual, however, but all the more powerful when they are shared. To this extent we can see a critique of *The Blood Countess* in that her pleasures are rarely shared and are usually had at the expense of another. Shared pleasure is the beginning of a positive politics. Against the future-oriented arrows, against those with a spiraling notion of time that will come to a peak during an Armageddon, Codrescu's idea of time is Proustian.

One could easily put Codrescu's work in the Proust-Benjamin lineage, in that his work is not only about his own past, but about utopian splinters of the past which he hopes to reopen and insert into the present. In Gilles Deleuze's book *Difference and Repetition*, he writes:

> Combray reappears, not as it was or it could be, but in a splendor which was never lived, like a pure past which finally reveals its double irreducibility to the two presents which it telescopes

together: the present that it was, but also the present which it could be.... It is always Eros, the noumenon, who allows us to penetrate this pure past in itself, this virginal repetition which is Mnemosyne.... Where does he get this power? Why is the exploration of the pure past erotic? Why is it that Eros holds both the secret of questions and answers, and the secret of an insistence in all our existence? [85].

Codrescu's *Messiah* is primarily erotic, as is all of his work. The erotic cannot be placed in the future, or in the past, but in both of these folded into the present, through the eternal return. Time's great pattern is brought into a tight ball, and then exploded. To come five times in one night is Codrescu's only goal, to fold love into the form of voluptuous emotion, not in order to get somewhere, but in order to arrive in the eternal present. This is the aim of Codrescu's protagonists, who are only interested in history to the extent that it will make them come. They cybersurf on the Internet only in order to make love with figures from history. History has no other reason for being.

Because Codrescu rids himself of time, however, he also rids himself of morality and completely sacrifices the very possibility of orthodox moral language. Since Aristotle, character was linked to plot, which is a sequence of events arranged in time. Aristotle writes, "Character is that which reveals moral purpose, showing what kinds of things a man chooses or avoids" (13). Without this movement through time, morality is impossible. Deleuze himself admits to this in his book on Kant. He opens by writing, "The first is Hamlet's great formula, 'The time is out of joint.' Time is out of joint, time is unhinged" (vii). However, Hamlet discovers after the death of Ophelia that he was himself in love with her, and in finding this, he rediscovers the possibility of love for beauty, and in doing so, rediscovers the possibility of morality as well. He exclaims at the beginning of Act V, "There's a divinity that shapes our ends," which is glossed by Harold Jenkins in the Arden Shakespeare: "The present passage shows Hamlet recognizing a design in the universe he had previously failed to find" (557). The belief in a design is a belief in the possibility of meaningful action through correct judgment. The surrealist left would have us undo judgment, and indeed one of Deleuze's later essays is titled "Pour en Finir Avec le Judgment" (In Order to Finish With Judgment), based on a play by the surrealist Antonin Artaud. To remove the possibility of judgment removes the possibility of morality and that in turn destroys the possibility of action. What's left is theatre of the absurd. Shakespeare, however, was not an absurdist, but had seen a meaning in time. Shakespeare's Christianity is shown at the end of *Hamlet*. Until Hamlet can find a meaning in time, he cannot act. Humans can only act in a moral sense within time. After being struck by Laertes' poisoned rapier, Hamlet falls, but forgives Laertes, for both have been tricked by the treacherous king. Hamlet says to Laertes in regards to his being guilty of Hamlet's death, "Heaven make thee free of it" (Act V, Scene 2, line 337).

Time is strange within Christianity as it appears to be something that functions within the earthly realm and yet does not function in the afterlife, creating a sense of two separate kingdoms. Theologian Mark Wilms writes in his essay, "The Rebirth of Luther's Two Kingdoms in Kant's Commonwealths," that Kant held a Lutheran disdain for the Enlightenment. "Just as Luther believed that the secular realm, while serving an important function, cannot take the place of the kingdom of the gospel, so Kant's ethical commonwealth cannot be forced into existence by the political authorities" (3). It is Kant that Lyotard prefers to Hegel when he writes against such a junction of the earthly and the heavenly, "As Kant understood, ethics and aesthetics are analogous but they were separated by a chasm, and that only the transcendental illusion (that of Hegel) can hope to totalize them into a real unity. Kant ... knew that the price to pay for such an illusion is terror. The nineteenth and twentieth centuries have given us as much terror as we can take" (*Postmodern Condition* 81). This key disjunction of the two kingdoms provides an opening, a sense of that which lies outside the material realm and only occasionally penetrates it in bursts of revelation.

In a short piece titled "History" in the collection *The Dog with the Chip in His Neck*, Codrescu writes, "History is no place for the faint of heart. It's full of hidden intentions, unforeseen results, and above all, bodies" (71). Because he gives such short shrift to time, Codrescu doesn't pay attention to continuity through time but tends to concentrate on little moments that incarnate wonder in which time within our realm appears to be heavenly.

Eros and play are what Codrescu poses against the worker state of his origins. If Marx, Hitler ("Arbeit Macht Frei"), Ceausescu and company would have liked to pose man's identity as "homo faber," Codrescu would like to see man (and equally women) as "homo ludens" or "homo eroticus." In *Messiah* he describes the clitoris as a "monk," (151), and after a nun falls out of her habit and into the arms of a lesbian, Codrescu writes, "She would combust spontaneously before the beauty of this shameless orphan. A new millennium would begin tomorrow, but the promise of redemption no longer applied to her. She would belong wholly to her time. Sister Rodica surrendered to the flame and took Andrea in her arms" (200). The end of Christian history is played out in a lesbian orgasm in a strip joint (293). Karl Marx rematerializes in the novel as a black ditch-digger in New Orleans. Codrescu writes, "He had not given sufficient thought to the problem of time in *Das Kapital*" (245). "Was there truly a progression toward a better future, or had he, as his enemies implied, been misled by the stubborn utopian messianism of his Jewish genes?" (245). In wiping out time, Codrescu wipes out morality.

Against redemption, in which the soul is returned to heaven without having been soiled by its contact with the earth, Codrescu's vision is one in which the soul only comes to life with the flowering of the body's ecstasy. This in turn seems to be a turn away from the Jewish tradition, in which the angel enters from without. In Codrescu's work, the angel is desire and comes from within. Desire opens heaven. Memory is born in the damaged lesbians as they make love for the first time together. "The air filled with gold specks like a rain of sequins, and quite a few of them heard a sound like the beating of wings. On the wake of this encounter came another gift: Felicity remembered who she was and what she had been doing. So sudden was the return of her memory that it seemed to be part of the sexual quake, rather than an aftershock. She moved away from Andrea and looked around as if seeing the place for the first time" (293). Felicity's orgasm is repeated in Andrea, who can also remember for the first time, and the contagion of spontaneous memory gain spreads throughout New Orleans: "All the people on all the streets of New Orleans were experiencing convulsive waves of remembrance. People sat on their stoops or stopped on street corners or leaned against walls, crying" (294). These memories are chiefly erotic, as every kiss is remembered by every human being for a brief hour in New Orleans. This was the Second Coming, as understood by Andrei Codrescu, and this is why these two young women are both separate halves of the new Messiah, whole only when they are together and making love.

In the Lutheran-Marxist time-spiral the value of the worker is as a being redeemed either by its work for God or for the state. Codrescu's investigative project is to return dignity and value to the human herself, not at some future time, but now, in the present. To change the meaning of man from soul, or worker, to player, to gourmet, to experiencer of voluptuous sensation and promoter of a humorous Aphrodisian carnival is Codrescu's rather extensive goal. Although it makes fun of all other utopian projects, it is a project as earnest as the man's who stood before the line of tanks in Tianamen Square and forced history to stand still for a moment.

The heart of Codrescu's work is in his poetry, and this is his center, the only law to which his work corresponds, because it is here that his art can best capture those orgiastic moments outside of time. All of Codrescu's life has been predicated on such moments, such moments as are heard on the radio, when time seems to miraculously stop, and a Transylvanian voice appears, and all work ceases, and the sense of a different scale of values based on love, humor, and play appears and for a brief moment we enter Codrescu's psychic state: where time is not money, but we are money, valuable, golden, in and of ourselves, and we become aware of ourselves in space, and what we are doing, and a rustling beauty can be heard like the fluttering of wings.

15

Codrescu/Codrescu: Conclusion

The surrealists struggled to bring the nonsense of Dada into a progressive narrative but failed. They tried to link surrealism to Marxism but had to admit it was a disaster. In the brief tract *Prolegomena to a Third Manifesto of Surrealism*, written in 1942, Breton admitted that surrealism lacked a progressive myth. Surrealism was officially dissolved in the late 1960s shortly after Breton's death.

For Codrescu the lack of a progressive surrealist myth has meant the invention of new pleasures without a larger picture having to do with ultimate meaning. Perhaps the question of ultimate meaning was waved away in a Dadaistic gesture arising from within cultural and historical conditions in early twentieth century Romania that led to a nihilism best expressed in the small oeuvre of the Romanian genius Urmuz.

The literary output of Romanian writer Demetru Demetrescu-Buzau (1887–1923), aka Urmuz, consists of eight prose poems that he wrote to entertain his nieces and a nonsense essay and a short poem. The longest of Urmuz's works is the Fuchsiada, a translation of which by Julian Semilian, appeared in Andrei Codrescu's journal *Exquisite Corpse* (Summer 2002, Cyber Issue 11). This piece is about four pages in length. This small body of work is so rich in nonsense that working out its implications took the rest of the twentieth century not only in Romania, but through Dada/surrealism, and theatre of the absurd, in the avant-gardes of Western culture generally. Throughout the work of Urmuz is a struggle to understand the separation of nature and spirit, or the difference between animal and human life. Many of the heroes are married to animals. In Urmuz's one essay, "A Little Metaphysics and Astronomy," he undertakes to understand the origins of the universe.

> So what would be the point of doggedly insisting on discovering some cause, and a single cause at that, and the first one as well, when all cause is unfortunately, an effect in turn begetting other effects, devilishly tangled and complex.
>
> So what good would it do to look for a single cause, an initial force which we would like to be [and had better be] a generative force also, when the force would stubbornly insist on generating only multiplicity out of itself; calling for countless millions of men, flies, sponges, beasts, stars, even at the price of their suffering; calling for the sawfish and the trunkfish, for pointless and unnecessary distances and speeds [Urmuz 95].

As Codrescu has recently turned from poetry and miniature essays to the novel he has had to deal with the need to tell a meaningful longer story with a beginning a middle and an end, and some sense. A novel with a protagonist, an antagonist, and a moral meaning through time is the basic structure of the novel, but Codrescu finds such conventions laughable. In his novel *Casanova in Bohemia*, Codrescu's hero wants only the pleasures of sex and gourmet food and to be left alone by moralists. Codrescu writes:

> He [Casanova] said that buttery golden macaroni captured the sun. At the other end of the spectrum ... cuttlefish cooked in its own black ink in the Veneto captured the night. In between, there were stellar dishes such as ziti sprinkled with Parmesan, noontime zuppe de verdura, Tuscan cheeses filled with afternoon, fruits for every hour of the day that constituted a sort of paradisical clock, and sweets that corresponded to every emotion, from the sighs of a young girl in love as embodied in lemon ice cream, to the rich pleasure of a courtesan in the last glow of her youth, fully present in amaretto chocolate and peach liqueur [*Casanova* 126].

And yet at the end of the novel, considering his increasingly weak pulse and failing body, he contemplates ending his life. Codrescu's Casanova says, "Suicide is a reasonable option [to old age] ... but I am also a Christian and it is a sin" (147).

Codrescu emigrated from Romania in the 1960s with Urmuz in his suitcase. Codrescu revels in the ambiguous liminal twilight between night and day. In mystery, in humor, in the nonsensical and the irrational, he finds his poetry. Can there be anything progressive in such a narrative? Unlike Urmuz, Codrescu does not commit suicide, and appears to use Christianity as a handrail at key moments, as in the case cited where his central character Casanova calls suicide a "sin." While the surrealists did write testimonials, they are ultimately pessimistic because no real meaning could be found in the stories they relate. Urmuz himself could not find a beginning or an end to the universe. It is "devilishly complex" (95). As first Dada and then surrealism sought the magical outside of timelessness, short poetry has come to be its favored medium. Can Codrescu create a surrealism that can be repotted into a different soil in which a progressive narrative can grow?

The surrealist poet Octavio Paz offered the Reformation as an answer to the lack of a central myth for the avant-garde. In speaking of the conditions of Russia and Mexico, and how they remained in bad shape compared to western Europe, Paz writes,

> There is a similarity — as yet little explored — between the Spanish and the Russian traditions: neither they nor we, the Latin Americans, have a critical tradition because neither they nor we had in fact anything which can be compared with the Enlightenment and the intellectual movement of the eighteenth century in Europe. Nor did we have anything to compare with the Protestant Reformation, that great seedbed of liberties and democracy in the modern world [119].

And yet, Paz could not bring himself to go back into the church. He writes, "I do not believe in eternity" (131).

Romania, too, could be considered along with Spain and Russia as lying outside of Protestant influence, and the avatars of the avant-garde there have been almost uniformly atheist, and the churchgoers have been largely within the non–Protestant tradition of Eastern Orthodoxy.

Among Codrescu's innermost circle in America, Robert Creeley was raised as a Baptist, Ed Sanders' mother was intensely Christian and taught Sunday school, Tom Clark was raised as a Catholic, and Anselm Hollo was raised as a Lutheran in Helsinki, Finland. Codrescu was raised within the Jewish faith. No one of this group are churchgoers, however, and all are more or less opposed to the church or see it as irrelevant. The endless night of the Urmuzian universe is partially countered by a muted Christianity in Codrescu's later work, and we have seen in Ed Sanders' work that a reliance on Christianity as a source of values came to the fore for him while studying the Manson family. Casanova has principles, as does Codrescu, but they are not firmly grounded, or rather they are not categorical but contextual, and even provisional. Whether surrealism could flower in a soil other than ludic nihilism remains unlikely, but surrealists were interested in political reforms and often denounced unjust governments. Yet they never created a firm set of standards, or elaborated a creed, or invented a myth with a beginning middle and end. Their litmus tests were the marvelous and ejaculatory love — ephemeral events as opposed to enduring institutions such as the family or a faith in God.

Codrescu continues to tell marvelous love stories. In September 1986, while walking near Seattle's Space Needle, Codrescu told me that he wanted to live in a city of lesbians where he was the sole man. The city would be called Atlantis and would be in the shape of a giant ear. Marcel Detienne, in his book *Dionysos at Large,* writes that Dionysus was the god who represented the "Stranger within, the god who could turn anyone he pleased into fire and blood" (Detienne 53). The god of the Greek drama, Dionysus represents the marvelous, the sudden shifts of reason into poetry and exalted phrase. He is "god of an urban territory" (24), but he is himself from somewhere else, "both strange and foreign" (9). Meeting Codrescu is like being in the presence of Dionysus. He is obsessed with sexual pleasure and sees its likelihood in almost everybody. Detienne writes, "Who can blame the people of Athens for being dubious about a strange god who appeared before them in the troubling form of a large, erect penis?" (32).

Dionysus is surrealistic, and surrealism is Dionysian. As mythologist Johann Bachofen writes, "The sun ... exalts men's eyes to contemplate the greater glory of the male power. The diurnal luminary ushers in the triumph of the patriarchate.... This is the Dionysian stage of father right, the stage of the god who is celebrated both as the fully developed solar power and the founder of paternity. ...Like the sun in its fullest virility, Dionysian paternity is the phallic fecundator; like Sol, the Dionysian father forever seeks receptive matter in order to arouse it to life" (114). André Breton writes in *Nadja,* "As for her, I know that in every

sense of the word, she takes me for a god, she thinks of me as the sun"
(111). Surrealism is under the sign of the unstable god Dionysus.

Breton concludes his most famous novel, "Beauty will be convulsive, or will not be at all" (*Nadja* 160).

In *Messiah*, Codrescu seeks to reunite the city of flesh and the city
of angels, or the heavenly city, and he seeks to do so on this earth, but
realizes this can only be done in flashes of time when the two kingdoms
and the two genders momentarily intertwine, when the eternal is suddenly present within the temporal. For surrealism the eternal is present
in the temporal in the form of the symbol of an ejaculating penis.

Codrescu is appreciative of embodied beauty, but it is a beauty without limits, and to which his poetry makes explosive reference:

> The Lower East Side of New York
> moved eternally by a rhythm
> "beating outside ordinary time".....................
> I was in love but with no one in particular [*Alien Candor* 215–216]

That Codrescu is at his best in poetry and in the short radio message indicates the limits of surrealism, but also its strengths. It is not
guided by a longer story, a story with meaning attached that offers a guide
to moral action. It is rather guided by short explosive Dionysian revelations, when the temporal is invaded by a divine presence. Codrescu's
importance is to continue the surrealist tradition of the dérive into many
American cities and towns and keep the form alive within his journal
Exquisite Corpse. Codrescu's narratives operate without an allegorical
dimension, without an Armageddon or an end to history, with his sole
source of meaning the experience of convulsive ecstasy. Without having
a larger meaning, the idea is to retain playfulness against severity and
whimsicality against an angry structure.

An important aspect of Codrescu's future work is the attempt to
build a surrealist novel — a form banned by Breton. As Codrescu continues to work in these longer frameworks he must also move from the
short explosive nonsense of Urmuz into the re-creation of meaning that
transcends the personal and formulates the communal. Will Codrescu
succeed in this quixotic quest? What's exciting about his work is the
crossing of borders, where he seems to be able to permeate different
domains. Americans have always leaped across seemingly unbridgeable
chasms and made friends. Codrescu contains multitudes. He is a Roman-

ian who has learned to befriend himself as an American, although he keeps an amused eye on this American as well as on his Romanian self that he is always in the process of introducing.

In the novels, Codrescu wavers when his characters return to the Old World, a metaphor it seems for a return as well to the vicious nationalism and bitter resentments practiced there. His relish for the doings of Countess Bathory or his hatred for what the Romanians had done to the Jews slips in and his aesthetic appreciation returns to the horrific history of the Old World. The promise of the New World was that all these resentments carefully nursed and handed down over centuries would be relinquished and peoples would focus on the development of their communities. The buildings and urban aesthetics of the New World, widely decried for their lack of meaning and historicity, have at least the benefit of being young and not weighed down by the past. In them, it is possible to invent a new poetics. Codrescu's greatest contribution is to extend the lineages of Dada — a group similarly disgusted with the nationalisms of left and right after the First World War and with all the progressive myths that were only killing people — or legitimating the killing of people — and to provide a forum a style and a comic vision that would provide young writers from around the globe with a chance to develop an alternative to the politics of resentment. That alternative is humor and poetic invention — not after some five-year plan or another but to let life be life right now in the moment — this is the gift Codrescu has brought with him to these shores, where time and money are thought to be identical. Codrescu comes from outside of America and arrives in a democratic country and within a circle of poets that has been distrustful both of Marxism and Christianity, the two great metanarratives of the contemporary West. Of the two, Codrescu appears to prefer Christianity. In a long poem in the collection *Alien Candor*, Codrescu places the dictator Nicolae Ceausescu into a Christian hell for his many crimes that include defacing a historic cathedral:

> In our mutual country several thousand miles to the east
> That mad dictator Ceausescu, a triple-chinned gargoyle,
> Whose place in hell is being kept by toothless political
> Prisoners fanning the flames with tracts
> [he had once succeeded the man who'd overthrown
> the queen the dead man loved]
> was ordering the demolition of the ancient capital

to make room for statues of himself.
A 16th-century church gave way to a badly executed bronze head.
[270–271]

In this passage, Codrescu clearly prefers the remnants of the Christian order to the demonic and hellish mentality of dictatorial communism. Without a larger myth, the extraordinary is missing in surrealism, and this has marked a downturn in adherents to surrealism, with Codrescu being one of the last great ludic surrealists. Codrescu has drawn upon the legends of Dracula and Urmuzian Dada and Casanova in order to re-create surrealism in its heroic moments. And while the European branch of the movement appears to have died with the throes of Marxism, it appears that the American branch looks longingly toward an alliance with liberalism. This can be seen in certain passages of the postmodernist Jean-Francois Lyotard, and now can be seen again in some inklings in Codrescu. If this alliance is to take place, perhaps surrealism could flower and survive in the new soil of American liberalism with its centuries of Protestantism lying underneath in the notion of the covenant. Like the eastern half of the Roman empire that continued to thrive long after the death of the western half, so American surrealism could rise again with Codrescu as its avatar long after the French version has become a dead letter.

Appendix A. Andrei Codrescu from a Romanian Viewpoint, by Roxana Maria Crisan

[Shortly after completing the manuscript for this book, I received a senior essay from a young Romanian scholar, Roxana Maria Crisan. With her permission, I have included some portions of this very comprehensive and yet pungent senior essay as an addendum with the hope that all or parts of it will eventually be published in a volume of its own. Crisan offers a viewpoint that I cannot, which is that of a Romanian insider living in the town of Sibiu where Codrescu was born and raised. She also provides nearly a hundred pages on the Romanian revolution. While I quote only very cursorily from this masterful essay, it is meant to give a larger context to Codrescu's own valuable insights and to give a larger indication of the country and city from which he has immigrated.— Kirby Olson]

SIBIU

Andrei Codrescu's birth town, Sibiu, was founded by Saxon Germans soon after the year 1000. Originally inhabited by a German population, the town later developed into a multiethnic center that also included Hungarians, Jews, Romanians and Gypsies. Sibiu is the Romanian name of the town; Germans call it Hermannstadt and Hungarians refer to it as Nagyszeben. When looked at from the top of the hills surrounding it, the burgh resembles an intricate concentric pattern; streets and defensive walls curl around the church in the main square. A huge spider web, the fortification system made up of bulwarks, bastions as well as escape tunnels, spreads throughout the city, recalling the time of the Turkish assaults. Life and people are molded to fit this medieval structure: "Like all medieval cities, Sibiu was connected by a rich, albeit empty, underground system. In his deepest heart he knew that he too was built in the same way and that inside him there were the abandoned networks of extinct cultures" (*An Involuntary Genius in America's Shoes* 51).

1.1 THE PIED PIPER OF HAMELIN

According to a famous legend, the Pied Piper of Hamelin cleared the town of mice and rats by playing his magic flute in the year 1284. Because the citizens of Hamelin refused to pay him the money they had promised, he laid the locals' children under a spell and took them away. Allegedly, the children were piped off to the city of Sibiu, where they grew into craftsmen and tradesmen. Andrei Codrescu feels for their new status as rich burghers; prosperous and influential, inhabitants of Sibiu aroused the envy of their neighbors, who attacked them. Consequently, they kept building bigger walls while expelling or executing all the people who were different from them. The intolerance and foolish pride which once characterized their parents in Hamelin continued to create victims: "In the seven hundred years that have passed since they first got to my hometown, the good citizens expelled Jews, if any of them were foolish enough to settle here, banished or tortured anyone who worshipped in a style different from their own Catholic religion, and burned witches in the town square" (*The Devil Never Sleeps* 168).

1.2

Andrei Codrescu spent most of his childhood and teenage years wondering at the magic force of his native town. There was a mystic melancholy about the squares, plazas, churches, passageways, cobblestone streets, gas lamps which always inspired him to dream of forgotten epochs. Although he was brought up in communist Romania, the future writer felt that the baroque architecture and the medieval atmosphere of Sibiu safely ensconced him in a fantastic time dimension: "I realized that Sibiu, my hometown, was the exact opposite of the Communist party" (*The Hole in the Flag* 160).

In the 1950s, children played "Russians" and "Germans" instead of "cowboys" and "Indians," but everybody refused to be Russians. Andrei Codrescu had different playfellows: Peter, his next-door neighbor, was Saxon German; Alex Schlesinger, his best friend in elementary school, was a Hungarian and Yiddish-speaking Jew; Ion Vidrighin, his *bodyguard*, was the son of a rich Romanian peasant. When they got into a fight on the street, the boys insulted one another in the usual way, mocking the opponent's intelligence or looks, and afterwards, they proceeded to the "national" level: "'stinking kraut' would be followed by a 'dirty kike' by a 'dirty hun' and a 'lice-riddled Gypsy.' The richness of our vocabulary of ethnic insults was wide and deep. It reflected, all too easily, the more elaborate prejudices of our parents, which, in their rabid form, had already resulted in countless tribal bloodbaths" (*The Hole in the Flag* 260–261). At home, Codrescu spoke German with his mother, Hungarian with his grandmother and Ilona, the baby-sitter; Romanian was the official teaching language; all three idioms were used simultaneously on the street.

Sibiu is also the place where the modern writer learned to pray. Years on after having left Romania he could still pray in his country's tongues. A sacred formula locked inside his heart, the Romanian multilinguistic core survived the confrontation with the omnipresent, international, rich English:

> Now this whole portion of myself is a remote and inviolate island in the middle of what is a totally inimical personality. This is crystal clear when I look at the languages in which I pray, whose words, with the exception of my sacramental formula, I have totally forgotten. While millions of people speak these languages in their everyday lives, I have retained only their essence.... My daily language is now American and the tremendous distance between the linguistic kernel of sacrality and the huge territory of my human relations in Anglo-American is also the distance between God and my soul. They stand opposed to each other, these two tongues — of my soul and of my life... When they meet

(recognize) each other, the resulting tension cracks the world. Everything parts like a curtain and the traveling words leave. The soul rises [*An Involuntary Genius in America's Shoes* 260–261].

Christmas in Sibiu resembled an orange. Before going to school, Andrei sat in line for bread and milk eager to find out if anyone knew when the oranges would arrive from Israel: "They were huge, thick-skinned, individually wrapped Haifa oranges, imported from Israel" (*The Dog with a Chip in His Neck* 244). Covered in snow, the medieval houses decorated with wreaths and twinkling lights were ready to welcome the exotic carolers. An inviting smell of strudels, walnut pies and roasts guided oranges to the doors of fruitless Romanians:

> Every day, from the first of December onwards, my mother discussed with our neighbors the burning question of oranges.... When my mother and I finally sat down with our oranges on Christmas day, we peeled them slowly, kissed the plump slices before we actually bit them, closed our eyes and, as the heavenly juice sprayed our palate, we fancied that we were cured of every-thing that ailed us. (The curative powers of oranges were whispered about in awe in my home town: a single orange was said to bring a dead man to life.) [*The Dog with a Chip in His Neck* 244].

Andrei Codrescu published his first poems in the local newspaper. A rebel teenager, member of the UTC (Union of Communist Youth), he managed to offend the Party Secretariat in Sibiu by writing, "The Eagle," a piece of literature dedicated to the very UTC. Urged to repent for his irresponsible actions in front of Comrade Rana, Secretary General, the young poet reinforced the ingenuousness of his verses by defiantly raising the collar of his uniform: "Eminescu, the greatest Romanian poet, had syphilis. Caragiale, the greatest playwright, was a dropout. All the other greats had run away with the Gypsies, killed themselves, fallen into the river, had been put in jail.... Does the Union of Communist Youth have a medicine for me? If so, is it bitter or sweet?" (*An Involuntary Genius* 78).

1.4

The Jewish community of Sibiu had lost most of its members by the time Andrei Codrescu visited the synagogue for the first time. World War II and communism dramatically changed the lives of Jews and consigned to oblivion their cultural heritage. Accompanied by Berl, his school colleague who had long curly sideburns and whose father was a fervent believer, Andrei Codrescu contemplated the old Spanish-style edifice. As he walked up the brick alley covered with moss looking at the fading Jewish letters on the frontispiece, mixed feelings overwhelmed him. The atmosphere was strange and pleasant at the same time, but nothing seemed familiar. Besides having lots of fun while bathing in the synagogue's decrepit swimming pool together with Berl's cousins, the holy place did not make any impression on him. Andrei heard about his grandparents and his father's commitment to the Jewish community: during the war, when the Nazis patrolled the city, his grandmother hid together with the frightened believers every day behind the old synagogue, praying to the Lord to save their lives; his father fought on the partisans' side; nevertheless, his grandfather's bazaar, where cheap trinkets were sold, served as a screen for resistance meetings and Jewish services. However, the boy did not feel like truly belonging to his ancestors' world. What fascinated young Codrescu was an old Jewish cobbler who repaired endless rows of shoes while uttering mysterious words from the Talmud. He was living on a little street behind Andrei's high school; very often, the secret admirer would crawl on his stomach to a rear window and watch the fabulous personage at work. During these days of keen observation, Andrei Codrescu came to understand the essence of his origin:

> I saw an old Jewish cobbler in there, sitting on a low stool in the middle of a room containing only an open Talmud on a rickety stand, and a long shelf full of shoes waiting to be repaired. He always had a few nails between his teeth, and he liked to hum as he worked. One time he was fixing a high-heeled red shoe. He had a magnifying glass screwed into one eye and he was tapping tiny nails into the heel with a wooden tool. At night, he studied [*An Involuntary Genius in America's Shoes* 340-341].

Intending to open a "Museum of the Jews" (*The Dog with a Chip in His Neck* 248) after the Jewish population had disappeared, the Nazis despoiled Eastern European synagogues. American GIs in Europe found a warehouse full of Jewish religious objects at the end of the war. Among the stolen objects was the Torah from Sibiu. The sacred book was taken to the United States, where the Shalom Synagogue of Dallas, Texas, adopted it. "'We give this Torah to children to hold,' the rabbi said. 'That way each one of them becomes responsible for the soul of one Jew from Sibiu'" (*The Dog* 249). Rabbi Kenneth Roseman of the Shalom temple invited Andrei Codrescu on February 9, 1996, to participate in the ceremony of rededicating the Torah of Sibiu: "The Torah, the sacred scroll on which the Bible is written, is said to contain all the souls of the people living in the community. If so, surely, the souls of my grandfather and grandmother and those of their mothers and fathers and many before them, were contained within" (248).

1.8 THE SIBIU COMMODITY EXCHANGE

On July 12, 1997, the Sibiu Commodity Exchange was inaugurated. The modern building next to the railway station, where twenty-five brokers operated financial transactions on first-rate computers, hit the headlines: "'The First Futures Trading in Romania Organized on the Occasion of the Exchange's Official Opening!' trumpeted *Tribuna*" (*The Devil Never Sleeps* 115). There were four hundred companies on the exchange list. Titu Ancua, Codrescu's high school colleague, invites the writer into his sumptuous office "overlooking the ancient spires of Sibiu" (115). As the conversation carried on, Ancua told his former colleague the incredible story of his going into the exchange business after having been trained as a veterinarian and having managed a pig farm before the events of 1989. He placed an advertisement in a New York émigré newspaper asking for financial counsel in banking. Luckily, the person who answered the advertisement was Thomas Curtean, a brokerage genius born in Sibiu, who had previously contributed to the development of many American financial institutions. Mr. Curtean wanted to return home and buy the house where his parents used to live. As a result, he and Titu Ancua made a deal according to which the newcomer moved into Ancua's house for several months, until the exchange had been created. During this period of time, Thomas Curtean trained the future brokers for free and monitored the construction of the enterprise. Nevertheless, laws regarding the functioning of exchanges did not exist, which meant that anyone could hit the jackpot if he held the initiative and pulled the right strings:

> "What are the laws regarding exchanges?" I asked. "That's the beauty of it!" shouted Titu. "There aren't any!" Titu was writing the laws. He was rightly proud of his initiative and full of

enthusiasm for what his attitude portended. It meant that anyone with the nerve to seize the initiative (and with the necessary connections, naturally) could make a bundle in Romania. In this respect, Romania is where Poland, Hungary, or the Czech Republic were seven years ago [115-116].

1.10

Speaking to Cornel Lungu, the director of the Brukenthal Museum, in 1997, during his fourth visit to Sibiu after the revolution, Andrei Codrescu found out with great disappointment that no action was taken either to preserve or to renovate the old city. In addition to this problem, there was also a lack of political support in the field of tourism, which could have improved the state of the local economy. When Codrescu brought the matter to Ancua's attention, he came up against a wall of indifference. The new entrepreneur blamed the local government for the deplorable state of Sibiu's architecture; he also stated that only after the historical buildings had been sold to private investors and laws regarding preservation had been adopted would renovation programs be put into practice: "It was amazing to hear such resolute market ideas: Had so much time passed since 1989 when he'd been the director of a collectivist enterprise?" (116). In the meantime, buildings of great historical and artistic value were falling down.

1.11 HOME

Andrei Codrescu returned and continues to return to Sibiu in search of his childhood. He would walk under the Liars' Bridge where he used to sunbathe in the summertime, go around ancient plazas, put his cheek against the big door of his house, built in 1456, look up to the sloping roofs and smell paprika, strudel, or cabbage while going past the locals' windows.

4.1 TIMISOARA

A western Romanian city of one million people shatters the world. "The cradle of the revolution" (*Hole in the Flag* 52), Timisoara witnesses the beginning of the eight epoch-making Romanian days. On December 15, in front of Reverend Lazlo Tökes' house, three hundred people gather: Hungarians, Romanians, Serbs and other minorities join hands while shouting, "We are not leaving!" (*Hole* 69).

What is going on? Demonstrators build a human chain while opposing the eviction of Reverend Lazlo Tökes. Minister of the Reformed Lutheran Church in Timisoara, he receives the order to move to a small country seat, far away from the city. Through his person, repressive action is taken against the Hungarian democratic movement. In the light of ultranationalist party decisions, Hungarians set up a democratic forum whose representative is Lazlo Tökes. But the reverend's democratic speech also touches the heartstrings of Romanians, Germans, Serbs, Gypsies, etc. Everyone, ethnic identity notwithstanding, feels persecuted and demoralized.

News about overthrows taking place in the countries nearby reaches the people of Timisoara via Yugoslavian and Hungarian media — Timisoara lies close to the border with Yugoslavia and Hungary — Radio Free Europe, and Voice of America. It follows that Reverend Tökes's eviction, inevitably followed by arrest according to Securitate procedures, gives frenzied people the opportunity to do something. When militia units gets to Lazlo Tökes's house, a young man bursts out, "Down with Ceausescu!" (*Hole* 28). A few seconds of heavy silence pass. Only now do demonstrators realize how tremendously heavy, not to mention sickening, the burden they have been bearing inside is. Other slogans are shouted all through the night of December 15, repeated again and again by the ever-growing crowd. Hundreds of thousands of people chant into Maria Square the poetry of the revolution. "Down with the dictator!, Goodbye to fear!, Ceausescu will fall!, Freedom!, Dignity!" (28).

Sunday, December 17, protestors move to the central squares. Spring is in the air; it is 22 degrees Celsius, an extraordinary temperature given the time of year and the place. A helicopter hovers around the scene at 5 P.M. People point clenched fists to the sky. "Nobody leaves until the dictator gives!" (28). Tanks and soldiers behind white shields occupy strategic locations that give access to the main square. Luckily, they do not yet suppress demonstrations. Soldiers are asked to join in: "You are our brothers!" (28). Parents hold children. Celebrating, people share food and sing.

As night falls, things change dramatically: an armored carrier is set on fire; a newsstand explodes; shop windows are broken; small fires burn on the side streets. Disoriented, demonstrators voice pacifist principles: "We are nonviolent! Peace!" (28). Addressing soldiers, they implore, "Come join us, brothers! You, too, are Romanians!" (28-29). Snapshots, taken at the scene, show soldiers in distress. Soon, they are ordered to shoot. Some disobey, throwing their guns away. Political officers pull traitors out of formation and shoot them on the spot. Unfortunately, most soldiers stick to rules and duty. Civilians cry: "Blanks!" (29) in a desperate attempt to calm those around. Children are held up for soldiers to see them: "Brothers, don't shoot our children!" (29). An orchestrated killing presents itself: machine guns on armored carriers fire at nests on balconies of buildings ringing the square. Hell on earth: panic-stricken, demonstrators stumble over one another; others refuse to budge singing *Arise Romanians!*, *Dance of Unity!*, national songs forbidden under Ceausescu's regime; shot, some go on singing. "Murderers! Down with Ceausescu! Liberty!" (29). Victims shout as they run. Bullets are the only response. There is blood on the ground. Wounded and dead, both protestors and mutineers are put inside anonymous vehicles, one of which looks like an ambulance. Later, the wounded transported within the so-called ambulance are found shot; the shooting must have taken place inside the *ambulance*. Just as unusually as it started, the springlike day ends with a cloudburst: heavy raindrops, lightning and thunder.

A clear blue sky calls people back on Monday. This time they meet in front of the cathedral. On the highest step, a woman waves the tricolor while people sing: "Arise, Romanians! Arise!" (30). Children light candles for the victims. Tanks return in the afternoon. Only this time many soldiers fraternize with *the enemy*. Others shoot into the air. Volleys of shots can be heard from the nests, yet people are out of range. In spite of dangers lying in wait, all those present share the same feeling: there is no going back. They will be here the next day, the day after tomorrow and so on, until both dictator and communism shall fall.

The first journalists to report news from Timisoara are Yugoslav, Hungarian and Soviet. During a Hungarian radio broadcast one can hear machine-guns firing and glass breaking. The Tanjung correspondent on the square estimates 5,000 to 10,000 dead. According to a Hungarian reporter filing from the cathedral, the death toll is 7,500. Most of the news seems to be part of a horror movie scenario: corpses in carts are taken to mass graves where they are hastily buried. On Wednesday,

December 20, a Pole gets to Budapest and confirms having seen "them tossing the dead into the river" (30). Hospitals lack free beds and medicine; there are patients with open wounds lying in the halls.

4.2 The University Square

> Moments before the end of the decade I stood in the cold, ice-covered center of the University Square in Bucharest, Romania, and said a brief prayer of thanks. The only light came from the small sea of candles burning in the snow at the martyrs' shrine before me. Bits of paper taped to a Christmas tree at the center of the shrine fluttered in the bitter wind. Penciled awkwardly on them: "Thank you, children, for dying so that we could be free!" "Your young lives ended here for us!" "You brought us Christmas!" "Good-bye, my child, you died for the country!" There was still blood under the layers of ice and snow under my feet. They had also died so that I could stand here for the first time, twenty-five years after leaving my homeland [*Hole in the Flag* 15].

Andrei Codrescu celebrates New Year's Eve in the heart of Bucharest. He opens a bottle of Hungarian champagne bought on the way home and drinks to the revolution with a group of NPR journalists. The night is quiet, but it's the calm before the storm, hopefully. Enterprise, vivacity, and wakefulness in the attempt of reaffirming one's identity as a free man: this is the storm Codrescu envisions for his country and its citizens. The square with its metro entrance assumes the role of a crossroads. Long journeys across two continents and an ocean mysteriously bring the writer to the starting point.

4.5 The Palace of the Republic. The "Sistematizare."

Andrei Codrescu gets the first glimpse of Bucharest from the window of his train compartment. A mammoth edifice, that only a mega-Mussolini mind could have created, overtops cupolas of churches and apartment blocks. This is the Palace of the Republic, symbol of Ceausescu's policy of "sistematizare" (124). Europe's most complex building site of the time, the construction has no common foundations but three layers of secret tunnels communicating with all strategic places in Bucharest. Tunnels that support a circular commune with the presidential palace in the middle, such is the imminent architecture of the whole country. Romania is due to step into the new millennium from the position of a 90-percent industrialized country. However, the industrialization plan can only be fulfilled through systematization: destruction of Romanian villages and historic buildings. Memories of icons, twin Byzantine towers, shady porticoes and long galleries belonging to the Vicreti Monastery overwhelm Codrescu; now they are only dust in the wind. Prisoners of matchbox sized flats, the people of the capital have witnessed a fierce combat between construction and destruction, both unlimited. Does December 1989 set a limit on further construction? The palace is only two-thirds finished because of the Ceausescu's ever-changing orders with regard to new rooms and decorations. Villages still exist and historic monuments stand. When Noah Adams, NPR's journalist, asks the chief architect the above-mentioned question, the answer is affirmative: "We will have to finish what we started.... There are objective conditions in the development of a city" (125). A Marxist phrase, *objective conditions* have pulverized both habitations and inhabitants. As for the tunnels, they perform a narrative role during the revolution; built to stand the test of nuclear war, provided with the latest technology, missiles, delicacies, they are considered to be the terrorists' base of operations. Such terrorists, some of whom are said to be Palestinian and Libyan, show up out of metro entrances or fake gravestones and shoot civilians. Frightening stories based on a common scenario — tunnels and terrorists — are told and retold. The young Front representative, in charge of the ministry where the chief architect has just committed to continuing *sistematizare*, strongly disagrees: "Ceausescu's sistematizare policy was criminal. The destruction of Romanian villages and historic buildings were acts of cultural genocide. All new building must be immediately stopped" (124). Somehow his words fail to reassure Andrei Codrescu, who anticipates that many high-ranked public figures still share the architect's opinion.

Appendix B. Five Interviews with Codrescu by Kirby Olson, Mid–1980s through July 2004

JUNE 1986

This interview was conducted by telephone. Codrescu was in New Orleans, and the interviewer was in Seattle. A terrific thunderstorm was in progress in New Orleans.

KIRBY OLSON: How did you get up this morning? Do you get up slowly or what? Do you have an alarm clock? I thought I'd begin with the personal part of the interview.

ANDREI CODRESCU: I think I got up with an erection. That's the only alarm clock I go by.

KO: One of the recurring images in your books is the urge to own a gun. You have even titled a book of poems *License to Carry a Gun*. I met a Chinese guy yesterday who said that he had recently immigrated from China. The big reason for him to move here was that he heard you could own a gun. I asked him whether he owns a gun now and he said no, but the ability to own one was great. Do you own a gun?

AC: No, I don't, but essentially he was right. The ability to be a major criminal, the idea of having the choice of violence is intoxicating. *License to Carry a Gun* ended up on gun store shelves in Ohio along with *Gun Digests* and bibles. A similar thing happened to Brautigan with *Trout Fishing in America,* which ended up on the shelves of tackle shops. Just recently someone who had been a convict in 1970 at Folsom Prison told me at a reading that he had had the picture from the front cover of that book on his cell wall and when he sees it now it always reminds him of prison life. He gave me a copy of a pretty rare tape by Charles Manson. Us extreme surrealistic poets have to stick together, you know.

KO: You wrote in the book *Life and Times of an Involuntary Genius* that you had a choice between leaving Romania or going into the army. You chose to leave. Have you ever wished you had made the other choice?

AC: No, I never have. Being in Romania is the same thing as being in the army. The government regulates everything. I was fortunate enough to get out at a certain time when there was a temporary lull in the horror.

KO: Do you ever wish to go back to Romania, even as a tourist?

AC: Of course I would like to return, but there are problems. I was talking with a Romanian cultural commissar several years ago. Next to him was a young blond SS type monitoring our conversation. We spoke of high literary matters until the SS guy got up to go to the bathroom. The commissar leaned over to me and whispered, "You *are* being widely read in Romania. Don't come back for several years, though. It is much too dangerous." When the SS guy returned I said, to cover this up, "So, would it be all right if I came to Romania?" "Of course," he said. "You can stay in my house!"

KO: Do any of your early Romanian literary pals continue to publish?

AC: Oh yes, they write but they don't say anything, which is prudent. They are good bureaucrats. Today the cultural commissars are very sophisticated — even a mild protest can land someone in big trouble. There are two people I would like to find out about, but my inquiries are always met with silence.

KO: It seems that you come out of a tradition of crazy comic Romanian intellectuals. I'm thinking of Urmuz, Tristan Tzara, Eugene Ionesco, and E.M. Cioran, among others. Is there something that makes Romania a breeding ground for intellectual anarchism?

AC: Yes, in the Balkans we have a tradition of absurdist writing. It is a tactic for survival, like an underground shelter on wheels. The Balkan metaphysical methods are becoming high currency now because human beings everywhere are powerless. The whole world is becoming Balkanized.

KO: Your ex-wife Kyra, whom you had to leave behind in Romania, what has become of her?

AC: She has just emigrated to Canada with her second husband. She married the only other Jew in my hometown — my colleague in kindergarten — he became a chemical engineer. They are trying to figure out how you start to live again.

The interview ended here because Codrescu's kitchen started to flood.

An Interview with Andrei Codrescu on His Novel *Messiah*

This and the other interviews were conducted via Internet from Finland in late November and December 1998.

KIRBY OLSON: A repeated refrain throughout this novel is that "Time means nothing." I find this dubious in that, by the very nature of mathematical progression, and the word Messiah, this is a second coming. As you know, Marx said history repeats itself, the second time as farce. Is this a farcical reenactment of the first theophany? Are you implicitly mocking the first coming?

ANDREI CODRESCU: All second comings are farcical. They take a lot more exertion, they are a lot less spontaneous, and they are overly self-conscious. I am, however, not mocking any coming because I find them all wondrous, miraculous, a disruption of unrelenting "reality." Coming suspends historical time, therefore a state of "no time" is the desired effect. The intervention of the divine, miracles, are humanity's constant and oldest wish. My two protagonists, Andrea and Felicity, come into history at a time of great expectations and are greeted accordingly by a humanity enslaved by machines.

KO: The notion of arrival is stated and restated throughout the book. People are going, and some of them are coming, or trying to come. This movement of intensities, gatherings and separations, is somehow crucial to the narrative dynamics of the novel. Had you designed these comings and goings in advance? Is there an end to coming and going? To the labor of arrival?

AC: Astute observation, informed by real pathos. Obviously, there is no end to pedestrian strife, as the Ecclesiastes put it. The only pedestrian exits we know are birth and death. The existence of nonpedestrian exits is what *Messiah* is concerned with and, as you well framed it, these exits can occur only in the contexts of a gathering of intensities, of comings and goings.

KO: In your travel book, *Ay, Cuba: A Socio-Erotic Journey*, which was apparently written at the same time you wrote *Messiah*, there is a similarity in that you turn towards the future as a space of hope, although this hope is based on very little progression from the past. Is the future, in your mind, linked to the past, or can the future be a leap out of old preconceptions, old paradigms? You seem to indicate throughout your work that you think people can leave their pasts like snakes shed skins. In your epistle to new immigrants at the end of *Road Scholar*, for instance, you write that new immigrants must leave behind their old hatreds when they come to the New World. Is it possible for this leap to occur, or are you only hoping that it is? What kind of emotional event must take place for such a break to happen?

AC: To start with the last question, the emotional event that must occur is a symbolic death. The human must "die" in order to become a shaman. The rupture involves a complete abandonment of one's former life which then becomes, as it did for Lama Cohen, a "fine silver ash at the bottom of her self." Without this death there can be no new life. Several such symbolic deaths might be necessary in order to maintain a fragile hope in the future. The Marxists of Cuba harvested great energies from the promises of their utopia, but they misdirected and misused them because the blueprint was faulty. The flaw of the Marxian blueprint was making the means of redemption the private property of the Party, and basing the production of redemption on reason. In *Messiah*, the means of hope-production are truly in the hands of the people, who are a priori unreasonable, and open to miracles. (At least to scriptural, literary miracles.) To answer another of your questions, the future is only linked to the past to the extent that it can recast the past to suit its needs. The past is an anthology of narratives, none of which are to be trusted. After all, people never "lived in the past." They lived in the present and that present was arranged to suit their immediate needs. The "past" becomes past only through worn literary devices: storytelling, nostalgia, kitsch, false memories.

KO: In the Hegelian and orthodox Christian conception of time, spirit enters matter in order to see itself in space, to come to know itself. According to Hegel, the second coming was already Napoleon, who entered Jena to the tune of cannon shots, and brought the freedom of speech to the people, which meant the end of history. Of course, a few years later, Napoleon crowned himself Emperor, and created the vicious Napoleonic code, which still animates the laws of "New" Orleans, and which have nothing to do with the central libertarian principles appended to the constitution, principally the first amendment, our central liberty, and one which is not a given in the French context, which has laws against hateful speech, for instance.

AC: Ho, there! The Napoleonic Code in Louisiana has to do mainly with property settlements. The U.S. Constitution functions as well here as it does anywhere else. As for the idea that "spirit enters space to know itself," I can only hope so. From this perspective, we welcome its attempt at self-knowledge and humbly wish that the spirit finds us educational.

KO: Time, in the Hegelian sense is linear, or at least a spiral, which culminates, and, Hegel was historically wrong, in that his pick of the man who instantiated the Second Coming turned out to be a small-minded prick with dreams of personal glory which superceded his interest in a happy society. This speaking in the name of freedom, in the name of the Second Coming, always turns out to be a farce in which the dictator (Napoleon, Ceausescu, Castro) turns out to be ever so human in terms of personal vanity.

AC: Just because Hegel sucked up to temporal Power, as do most so-called "philosophers," once anybody notices them, does not invalidate the spiral model, which has no "end of history," or "second coming" attached to it. The spiral is infinite, it just evolves. There is a great temptation to declare an "end" at the points where the spiral leaves the circle, but it's just a human failing. The model will not be exhausted until it is — and then we'll ALL know it, not just Hegel or Mao. Jews are wise to keep waiting for the Messiah — it's the waiting, the process, the hope, that is productive, not the product.

KO: Do you continue to believe, as per your hippy origins, that there will be a genuine Second Coming?

AC: I don't remember any hippies believing in the Second Coming. We believed in third, fourth, and fifth comings, all in one night if possible.

KO: Such a moment will be a leap out of all the viciousness and terrors of the past, the constant bloodletting and criminality of humans as an animal species linked to the Tyrannosaurus Rex more reliably than to the notion of generosity and attention which animated the Christian project at its conception, and that men and women, collectively, can leap into a state of permanent mutual aid?

AC: You posit sides where there aren't any. If anything, hippies believed in the "Christian project at its conception," as you well put it.

KO: It would seem to me that a concommitant interest of yours, played out as well in this novel but in a minor key, is that *The Fall into Time* (as your fellow Romanian E.M. Cioran titled one of his books) can also be seen within a Gnostic conception, in which the descent into time is a nasty trick played by a charlatan God, and that the only way out is up, and that peace will never reign on this earth.

AC: That's correct.

KO: Cioran went so far as to rage against the misfortune of being born. It seems that your entire literary effort is predicated against this principle that this earth is unacceptable for utopian habitation, and that you are constantly arguing that it is, if people would only completely inhabit their bodies for the time permitted, and also accept the reality of the situation, including death. About Felicity, you say: "She had denied death life; and death, displeased, had taken her orgasm." Again we are back to the notion of time as the central problem throughout these narratives. Space, you've dealt with, and even law, you've dealt with. In this novel, the forces of disorder and physicality, are arranged against the Christian forces which represent hypocrisy and lurking perversion. You've reversed the perspective. The novel opens with a comparison of Jerusalem and New Orleans, and reverses them such that New Orleans is the city of saints, and Jerusalem is a city of blood and anguish. Is this a central axis, that to live in one's body in time, as they do in New Orleans, supposedly, is this the closest we will get to Paradise?

AC: I can't add much to this. Your analysis is astute.

KO: In a similar way, you've reversed the traditional perspective that Christ is male, and now you make Her into a Lesbian duet. Is this not a mockery of the notion of Time instantiated in Hegel, and yet still not an acceptance of Cioran's notion of a "Fall into Time," but rather some kind of Christian hedonism along the lines of perhaps the German philosopher Hamann?

AC: Is Hegel's Time "male"?

KO: Hegel mentions at one point, in a footnote around page 200 of *The Phenomenology of the Spirit* (I forget the page exactly) that it is interesting that the universal spirit (which may, to some extent, be coequal with time, in that it organizes time into periods) chooses to "procreate and urinate from the same aperture" which would indeed make it male. Hegelian time is a clockwork rapist, forcing space to do its bidding, and leaving no room for anything but *its* meaning. But Hegel saw all of this as beautiful, for some reason. The early Gnostics, on the other hand, did have a group of libertines, principally in the city of Alexandria, who felt that they should break the ten commandments, specifically those regarding sexuality, in order to gross out the false God by drinking cups of sperm and menstrual fluid in the church. They saw the fall into time as hysterically ugly, and wanted to double its horror, in order to end it. They were run from the cities by the orthodox Christians, and destroyed. In your world view, there is a similar view that those things which have been repressed, or called filthy, ought to be allowed: lesbianism, for instance, and cybersex, and sex between mismatched classes (based on age, or race, or other categories which would go against the purity codes) but that this wouldn't be against a Gnostic god, but rather for pleasure, which you insistently link to the spirit. In this sense, it seems that you do not believe that time has any meaning, in that there will not be an ultimate time, an end to history, but that there will be good moments in time, perfect moments, which are punctuated by sexual pleasures, by charm, spin, uniqueness, moments outside of time, and yet within time, and principally within bodies who have yearned and sought for them. Is time a line, a spiral, a set of circles, or merely dots?

AC: Again, this is correct. And let me add to my admiration for the spiral, my now committed admiration for dots, circle sets, and all whirling atomic and subatomic chaos play.

This interview appeared in the online journal George *in December 1998. The original interview took place on November 21, 1998. Codrescu was in New Orleans, and the interviewer was in Tampere, Finland.*

INTERVIEW ON POETRY,
NOVEMBER AND DECEMBER 1998

KIRBY OLSON: I'd love to get really personal, and go past your bank account, into the deep mysteries of your body: do you have regular blood pressure, do you go to the bathroom normally and without pain — how much do you deposit, is it regular? However, I can't find a way to link this to your aesthetic practice. My problem is stress: dealing on the one side with the remnants of the classical liberal tradition and their emphasis on greatness as in coherence and complexity, with their belief that the world is eminently logical and can be studied, and on the other hand with the neo–Marxists, who think the world will get better by demographic representation — and that we have to balance the canon by skin color and gender and then the problems in the street will cool. I just think that everything is a paradox, and every solution is a new kind of murderous problem.

ANDREI CODRESCU: Thanks for leaving out the bowel questions — although I am one of the founders of The Bowel Movement (which had its public display and termination at Intersection Center for the Arts in San Francisco, ca. 1975); it was an offshoot of Actualism, the Midwest-based movement which Darrel Gray wrote the "Actualist Manifesto" (published in the *Exquisite Corpse*) for.

It's sad that you allow the history of Western civ to wreak such havoc on your body. We had that problem licked around 1967, but it has returned with a vengeance, to torment serious young people like yourself. Of course, you also see the solution, which is the relentless cultivation of paradox for purposes of pleasure. My intellectual pleasure consists almost entirely of watching both sides of the aisle squirm with frustration. On the other hand,

I have an unshakeable faith in the greater purpose of creation and see my job in it as helping along by immobilizing the purveyors of ideologies.

KO: I guess everybody feels marginalized — and I suppose that's why Kafka hits home universally (I got this idea from a critic named Charles Altieri who said something like this in a conference once). You're a Jew in an unfortunate century, a poet in a country where nobody reads poetry, and a genuine political target for the collapsed regime in Romania. What is your source of strength, if it's not religion, and not nationalism, and not politics of any conventional variety? I asked that of the artist Christo years ago, and he said it was his mother that gave him his strength.

AC: That's a Medusa-knot of questions. The answer is that I do what I do. After all, I chose the quasi-public life. Chaos takes care of the rest. There is no point in either worrying or carrying a pistol because, as Robert Gal puts it, "the unexpected comes unexpectedly." As to the other business, the job is to teach courage. That's what Ted Berrigan was: my courage teacher. In turn, I try to be of use. Everybody's desperate, you won't find a soul not in torment. Giving them a kick in the ass — by confirming all the reasons for their despair & then still moving as Galileo said — that's Good Work. There is a spark there in people but you have to blow hard to keep it flickering. Christo's right: my mother was pretty loving, though completely insane (and given the demographic data, what else is new?).

KO: You regard the poetic adventure as something of a heroic act, and something of an act against nature.

AC: The most heroic act, the most unnatural, and the best way to explore with language — as opposed to the plodding essay or, as I call it, the sentence of the unfinished sentence. The penalty of explaining yourself.

KO: Most poets end their poems saying nobody loves me, I can't get a proper date, or I want to blow my brains out. Your poems frequently end with an assertion that you are loved. What is this act of blessing yourself, and why is it that no other poets do this?

AC: When you say "no other poets do this," that's precisely the point. Each poem should — ideally — be a complete critique of every poem that came before it. Every poet wants to be unlike every other poet. You should listen to those endings in their double meaning, which is serious and ironic at the same time. Of course, poets are loved and not loved.

KO: Your poems don't "flow." They shift direction, abruptly, even rudely, considering the idea of a poem, in general, is to put someone into a dream and drift them along quite nicely. Your poems are jagged and lively. A central value seems to be mental alertness.

AC: Here I think that we are running into a bit of prejudice brought about by the norm in middle-of-the-road Am Po, which is a flowing, as you say, "quite nicely," in either a narrative or a confessional way, or both. Irony, humor, rerouting, disconcerting, jabbing, keeping your reader awake, making up beings, are not part of the tool-kit of the expression and language-poor poesy of so many of my contemporaries.

KO: There is no beauty in your poems in the sense of a lush being-in-love kind of feeling which Pound and others offer—the experience is rather one of brilliant conversation.

AC: Here you are, in my opinion, wrong. You are perhaps too influenced by reading my essays. The fact is that beauty abounds (but not in description). It's in there in love checked by irony, a constant battle between sentiment and intelligence. That's how language sparks. You may want to look up here Paul Celan, Benjamin Fondane, Tristan Tzara, and Ilarie Voronca, for a matrix for this work. Beauty, certainly not in the Pound sense you mention or in some other haiku-ish manner, is in a kind of resisted astonishment at what can be "abducted" (Charles Russell's word) from the world. See the ending of one of my works: "The beauty is in what shocks me least." A person under shock-attack, or media-attack, meditating in an "emergency," sees beauty as rest. The act of poetry, or any act, under current conditions, is an act of war. Beauty is suing for peace, which is to say, banality, order, triviality, property.

KO: In your poem "Love Things," you seem to think that all things have a claim on your love. A claim? Are you kidding?

AC: Ah, Kirby! Kirby! Yes, of course you are right that I'm both not kidding and kidding. But here I'm mostly not kidding when I say, "All things have a claim to my love," because what you are hearing here is the voice of Christ. He cannot afford to refuse love to anything because that's his job. You may call this psychological, or about "the torments of love," but, like in most of my poems, a parallel discourse can be heard, discussing ontological matters.

KO: I'm intimidated when I read your poems because they are like walking through a mine field of possible mistakes of reading, which is why I think no critics dare to do it.

AC: You may be right about this. I've had people (and translators) read my poems *exactly* in the opposite way from how I meant them, most notably Robert Bly. I had to insult him grievously for the faux honor he did me of misunderstanding my poems on the stage of the SF Art Institute. The problem it seems to me is in the reader who usually brings baggage to the works. This is, of course, inevitable, but in the case of most American readers the baggage is the heavily ideologised nonsense about poetry which has dripped steadily into everybody for decades. Ruralism, ts eliotism, poundianism, williamsism, confessionalism, iowa cornponism, translatese surrealism, languageism — all these guilt-provoking little analytic machines (some no more complex than a crowbar) have made it nearly impossible to read a poem unanxiously. Which is why most people would rather not, at all. It isn't that people don't love poets. It's that people are afraid of (misunderstanding) poems. Well, in my case, I require *All Your Baggage*, because my poems blow it up as they go along. They are meant to be acts of cultural subversion, to engage your fears.

KO: "Love Things" is incredibly heterogeneous. In what way is it unified? You reference voodoo, the Iron Curtain, fruit (several times in several different ways) as well as purple Hula Hoops.

AC: Get over "unified." Everything contained in a book or any measurable object is "unified." There is no way out of it.

KO: Your reference to Bill Knott clues me in somewhat, as he is about as inclusive and weird.

AC: I'll buy this.

KO: Is love a thing?

AC: I'll quote Creeley here: "The body is the plan." But one assumes, in Gnostic fashion, that either love or dread, or both, are constantly at work throughout and before history.

KO: Is that then the reason for the title of the poem "Love Things"?

AC: The title is ambiguous. It's either "The Things of Love," or an ironic injunction, "Love Things!" Or else.

KO: You are a depraved hedonist?

AC: Hedonism is hard work — and only a means to investigate the mind of God.

KO: Can you differentiate between Hula Hoops and people? Do you love them both equally?

AC: Love was the credo of our generation. We were sacrificial lambs. I tried to reconcile, as I've said, unconditional love with reason, and all I could come up with at the time was poems. But please read the later work in *Alien Candor*. You'll have a sense of the evolution.

KO: In your poem "A Francis Ponge," you contrast events favorably with examples, and style favorably with virtue.

Virtue and examples are static, perhaps easily linkable to Platonic forms, and Aristotelean logic. Style and events are about movement (Bergson, Deleuze), against static fixity, and rigidity. This poem would fit into a solid Deleuzian reading.

AC: Yes, sir.

KO: In the poem "Against Meaning," the poem admits to faking.

AC: "Against Meaning" is an exercise in meaningful, clean phrasing.

KO: Walt Whitman, in the poem "A Still," reclines in the future and is readying the house for the party.

AC: Correct — it was my most utopian phase. I would never write anything like that now. I was horny. Horniness views the future in a utopian light: when I get laid, it will be heaven.

KO: In "Fascinations," which ends with you being loved again, there is a great line:

> One day there is a party for the whole galaxy
> But some, it seems, aren't ready to party.

AC: Right again. It's Eros against Thanatos — all the way, come who may. Those were the days, my friend. Not that last night was half shabby.

KO: I have the feeling that your generation didn't separate high and low, art and life, and as a result a lot of people died.

AC: Death is a tollbooth on the road of excess that leads to wisdom. Why do you think so many of us — Berrigan, Jeffrey Miller, Jim Gustafson & many more — ARE dead? You can get Nietzschean here, or listen to the Doors.

KO: I'll return to poetry for one last question. Poetry is a hard battle and you need a team of good guessers to work at it along the lines of a cross-word puzzle. Alone here in Finland, I could use hints.

AC: I'll try to help, but not in figuring out a system (which to me is fairly obvious — a confrontation with all intelligible *systems*—), but I do remember the exact provenance of most lines and, in re-reading, I can certainly point out to you blindingly obvious things that most people seem to miss. But don't be afraid to *read*. I remember working hard at "The Skaters," John Ashbery's poem, to unravel the elegy it is.

INTERVIEW ON POLITICS, NOVEMBER 1998

KIRBY OLSON: You seem to constantly compare those communities that serve the clock: the Christian church, or the communist party, for example, with those communities that don't live for the future, but live for now. Do you see love as needing to extend over time, or can it only happen in the moment? You seem to have a great faith in sexuality which is not borne out by most people's experience. Can you explain this value system, and why it is better than the faith that many people feel in the Catholic Church, or in the communist party?

ANDREI CODRESCU: I think what you are asking is why do you prefer hedonists over ascetics? I grant you asceticism and Northern rejection of instant gratification lead to the buildup of wealth and insure the continuity of well-built communities, while hedonism and Southern squandering lead to poverty. That is the world geography: the prosperous North stays that way through sexual repression while the profligate South stays poor. See: North and South America, Northern and Southern U.S., Northern and Southern Europe. The fable of the Ant and the Grasshopper is as active as it always was. Having granted you this, I invite you to listen to Jesus: "Sooner will a camel pass through the eye of a needle than a rich man into the kingdom of Heaven." Was Jesus for the grasshopper? Yes, because wealth creates injustice and "injustice," as the Bruderhoff elder in *Road Scholar* puts it, "leads to war." Wealth, unless it flows by establishing an exchange in libidinal currency, leads to stasis. The libido is the only commodity desirable enough to the North to melt its stores of frozen wealth. But love is not just a commodity, it is the very medium of exchange, movement itself. Wealth remains merely symbolic (a record of denial) unless it is traded for what the people of the South freely give away. Hence, according to Jesus, there is no need of wealth at all. Accumulation is only a tic but, paradoxically, it is one that insures the well-being of the next self-denying progeny. My point is, bankers are born not made, ditto for lovers. But lovers work without an intermediary, there is no matter between them and spirit. And yet, as long as they are embodied, they need their Northern patrons. That is how the paradox functions.

KO: In Cuba, you meet seemingly hundreds of teenagers who will sleep with tourists for next to nothing. The only moral comment you make on this is in the context of a preacher *not* taking sexual advantage of one of these kids, but trying to convert her instead. I think most American readers of the book will find this disturbing, although a smaller group will find it appealing. I'm not sure what I'm asking. What is the age of consent in Cuba? In Europe, as you know, it is different in each country. For instance in Holland it is 11. In France, it is 15 and three months. In Finland, it is 18. In America, it varies from state to state, but Monica Lewinsky, for instance, was thought to be too young by many at age 21. Is age a necessary yardstick of maturity? What did you think of these kids on the street, if I could ask you to think about it from an ethical perspective?

AC: This question is full of repressed anger. Isn't life, joy, and squalor (after all the prettiest flowers spring from murk) worth attention? Are you making a case against poetry, against joy, against the sun? All the delicate trembling that takes place along the vast surfaces of the tactile world, isn't that what a poet attempts to render momentarily visible? And if not, why not? Savonarola stalks the streets of Florence still, as does Kenneth Starr. Whom do they work for? Satan, the dark angel, the antilove, the rationalist, the dry seedpod. There has been entirely too much grandstanding on "ethical" issues in the US lately to let it go without exposing the sheer hypocrisy. (Which is pretty evident by now.) The "ethics"-spouting hypocrites are nasty perverts, see Freud. Happily, sometimes, when a new Inquisition or Puritanism rears its ugly head, American common-sense corrects it.

KO: You seem to always be looking for the special qualities of a place, the gold, or poetry, of a place. What would you say is the gold of Cuba?

AC: Its people.

KO: The entire Caribbean is impoverished. The island of Haiti, just across the water from Cuba, is perhaps even poorer. The average caloric intake per day of a Haitian is about 1,200 calories, which isn't enough to live. Meanwhile, the top 3 percent of Haitian landowners live in luxury, drive Cadillacs, can fly to vacations in Paris, and support sparkling swimming pools. Isn't this disparity of wealth enough to make the poor want to slaughter the wealthy capitalists and become communists? Do you see an alternative to capitalism or communism?

AC: Yes. Good social policy implemented with equitable taxes.

KO: There are two emotional peaks in your book on Cuba. One is when your father is freed as a chicken is destroyed against your back by a Cuban practitioner of Santeria. The other is when you make love with a sexy revolutionary doctor. These two incidents step out of the ordinary into another world. It seems that this is where you want to take the reader — into a world outside of normal time, into a world of dense emotional experience, when time is suspended, or made so dense that it becomes golden. Given that these are the most valuable experiences, and that those who have them are richer than those who do not: Is the ratio of such experiences higher in Cuba than in America?

AC: Yes, because there aren't so many status symbols and simulations of emotional realities in the way.

KO: What other countries might you like to visit?

AC: I don't "visit" countries. I infiltrate them.

INTERVIEW ON THE NOVEL *WAKEFIELD*, DONE ON JULY 12, 2004.

KIRBY OLSON: The character Wakefield doesn't really change from beginning to end although the scenery does. He goes through different cities and the arms of different women. Could this novel be called a picaresque?

ANDREI CODRESCU: He changes enormously, Kirby. His last act is so uncharacteristic of the Wakefield who sets out on his journey, it would seem ex-machina, if the ex-machina (the Devil) wasn't himself a character in the book. The editor was very much against that ending, just like Tolstoy's editors were against the ending in *Anna Karenina*. Tolstoy wrote several different endings until he returned to his original (and right) one. Part of the point of Wakefield journeying in 90s America is that the entire culture is against the possibility of change. The fact that in the end he does is a testimony to the power of an individual (even a typically passive fin-de-siecle American) to go against the grain. Wakefield's journey is only apparently picaresque: he does go with the flow, but the flow is programmed by a society that requires appointments (his speeches go on on time), demands "openness," sets standards for "taste," and costs a lot of money. The end of the '90s in the U.S. is a historically closed "gilded age" a la Mark Twain, or F. Scott Fitzgerald. There were three such exacting (and unconscious) dream epochs in the 20th century. Wakefield's is the last. The "true life" he's looking for is impossible in such a time (maybe in any time) and he finds that no matter how much conscious attention he pays to what befalls him, he will not be allowed to make his experience coherent or "authentic." This is ironic and redeemed only by the uncharacteristic decision he makes in the end. The farther irony is that he commits his Camusian act in the belief that he's pleasing the Devil, but the Devil doesn't give a damn — he has his own problems.

KO: One of the final segments of E.M. Cioran's *Tears and Saints* has him admit, "I am altogether too much of a Christian. I can tell from the way I am attracted to beggars and deserts, and from the insane fits of pity to which I am often a prey. All of these amount to various forms of renunciation. We carry in our blood the poisonous dregs of the absolute: it prevents us from breathing yet we cannot live without it" (118). If two of our most avant-garde figures — yourself and Cioran — can't shake the biblical metaphysics — do you think that perhaps the rest of us should just return to it?

AC: I'm not sure about return, but it makes sense for people to want to lead a decent life. If returning to Christianity gets the trick done, fine. The danger of returning to the comfort of a belief-system known more for its abuses than for following the original program is that the returnee may become intolerant of others. The fervor of converts is dangerous like all fervor and it can be employed to destroy even as it soothes. My Devil is not at all the fundamentalist devil of the pre-Enlightenment, he's a central European kind of cultured devil familiar from literature, opera, and popular entertainment. He's the devil of Marlowe and Bulgakov, not the devil of Revs. Falwell and Robertson. He's actually an ally of (the sleeping) God, who threatens to wake up God if the bureaucracy of Hell keeps going against the individuality of humans. My devil is deeply interested in the torments and contradictions of individuals, he feeds on that turbulent matter. The new Hell cares more for large, apocalyptic, bureaucratic solutions — it doesn't give a whit for humans.

KO: There is an irony through the book that Wakefield is diverting himself on his quest for his true life. He has sex, he has drunken escapades, but by the end of the book what he really wants is silence, or a moment's peace. Finally, in the last sentences, "He heads home, to read. What else could a silence-loving man do in a hammer-wielding world?" What book did he intend to read?

AC: Indeed, Wakefield is looking for peace, but it's the peace of a bourgeois reader in a civilized city, not the deliberate stilling of the mind of Buddhists, or the hubris-filled peace of seekers after transcendence. He wants to re-read, more than he wants to read. His apartment is filled with books he wants to return to. If Wakefield were a writer he might want to re-read Gogol. As it is, he'd probably plunge into the multivolume of Casanova's "Histoire de Ma Vie." He doesn't want to renounce the world, he just wants to renounce the distractions of his culture.

KO: How does your Wakefield relate to Hawthorne's short story? Hawthorne relates the incident of a man who leaves his wife for twenty years, and is assumed dead, although he is living a couple of blocks away. Your Wakefield spends some time with his alienated daughter, but they go to the movies. So their time is mediated and isn't really together. Could you say anything about "family values"? Is family life a kind of Christian renunciation that the Nietzschean will to power finds naturally despicable?

AC: Hawthorne's Wakefield made an escape in the mid-19th century, a time when escape was already impossible for a modern man. My book begins with this, from Hawthorne's Wakefield: "Imagination, in the proper meaning of the term, made no part of Wakefield's gifts." Hawthorne isn't dissing Wakefield here, he merely states that imagination was already in big trouble in a world where a man was entirely trapped by his obligations of work and family. No matter how much imagination Wakefield might have had it would have been insufficient to change the circumstances of his life. He's a married London clerk living by a clock set by urban capitalism. If it was so hard for 19th century Wakefield to escape, think how much harder it is for a late 20th century Wakefield who must make a superhuman effort just to get away from television. Both of these men, these working drudges (albeit my Wakefield's job seems to be more interesting) want only to claim a piece of unprogrammed time for themselves. Family "values," whatever those are, have nothing to do with it. Hawthorne's Wakefield is more sinister than mine because his escape involves some weird stalking of his wife, who he sees as part of the system of bondage. My Wakefield is a reasonably attentive husband (even though he's, conventionally, divorced, and his ex-wife is pursuing her own madness), and he does pay a "mediated," as you say, attention to his daughter Margot, an alien in her own right. In a perfectly Christian world — preferably in a peasant setting — Wakefield might pass for a model (undivorced and unhappy) father and a model for his (strange) children, but it would be a formal arrangement based on a conscious decision to surrender his independence and his imagination. He would be resigned and dutiful, like most of the unhappy folk who keep things running. The paradox (and the irony) is that late 20th-century America seems to be full of "escapes": cruises, television, canned sex, yoga retreats, etc., but none of them are born of individual initiative; they are all "approved" means of letting off steam. The only force that remembers the mandate of the original "liberty" that humans were granted in Paradise is the Devil, the first rebel. He was hurled out of Eden because he wouldn't abide by God's one rule against knowledge. The Devil's quest since has been to foment rebellion against rules, divine or human, and to remind people of their original endowment. He's more pathetic even than Wakefield, because he keeps being a libertarian in a world where nobody knows how to be free.

KO: You write well about food. "Avgolemono is a lovely soup, light, pale as the crest of a wave, filled with sun, the rice like grains of sand on the beach at Kios" (236).

AC: A book without food is like a kiss without honey.

KO: You write, "When Wakefield was young and poor his friends, who like himself were poor, despised luxury. He should feel sad about the loss of idealism, but he doesn't. These days he enjoys good food and other expensive pleasures" (217). In your hippy days you were part of a revolutionary generation, and now have become rich (at least by comparison) and in this text you appear to find the youths of the Seattle World Trade riot to be somewhat

misguided. You ask whether America is truly the cause of global misery —
"Is American prosperity from coffee to cheese really the source of all global
misery?" (223), and also you make fun of the notion of "culturalimperial-
ism" (225). What am I asking?

AC: First of all, you are making the mistake (common to some readers) that
Wakefield is me. I went to great lengths to make Wakefield NOT me. I lent
him some of my experiences, but in each instance he acts exactly the opposite of the way that I did act in those circumstances. You can look at the
book as a kind of autobiography "a rebours" (Huysmans' words), a mirror-
image autobiography, or an "if" autobiography; if I had reacted differently
how different might things have turned out? Wakefield lives my life with a
different character: he's passive, I'm not. That said, his reflections about the
changes he's lived through in America are ironically contradicted by reality.
In one sense, the book is an argument with some of my former or current
idealism: I still think social justice is essential and I'm outraged by the cal-
lousness and excesses of the rich. Wakefield often goes against my most cher-
ished beliefs, and I often hated him for it. He brings the cultural relativism
of the late '90s (which is, easily, in the air) to matters that shouldn't be
approached in that light, justice and love chief among them.

KO: In a world in which God no longer exists, which is the world of many
today, something must fill the space of meaning that this former system represented. Some now find the meaning in pleasure, or in love, or in restoring
ancient architecture. Would Wakefield be a story about post-Christian life, in
which movement and what Deleuze called "becoming" is privileged over "being"?

AC: Here is another irony: Wakefield is completely a creature of "becoming," but he's unhappy by this constant "becoming" because he feels that it
robs him of something essential, a something he naively thinks is "peace to
read." The transcendental urge still flickers in him but it's toward a domes-
ticated sort of ideal. He assumes that God is asleep, unlike the Devil who
knows that God is asleep. When his very modest ideal becomes impossible
because of the Restorer next door, he resorts to a violent and absurd act that
could be as strong as a conversion, but turns out to be just sad and funny.
I'm not sure what you mean by a "post-Christian life," I don't think there
was ever a "Christian life," unless you mean that thing monks do.

KO: Your Wakefield is a pessimist, and argues that pessimism is the secret
to his vocation as a witty cynic. E.M. Cioran writes, "The more I read the
pessimists, the more I love life" (101). You and Cioran are both from the
city of Sibiu in the Carpathians. Do you share a sensibility with the other
inhabitants of that city, or how would you characterize your parallel relationship with this philosopher, and the Dadaist tradition that also came

from Romania? French surrealism through Breton and others spoke of love — the courtly tradition of Provence and poetry. Romanian Dada through Tzara, Cioran, Ionesco and others rarely speaks of love. Is pessimism central to the Romanian contribution to global culture?

AC: Cioran and I are both from Sibiu, a medieval city that was both a model of bourgeois life and the site of Dracula's massacres. Witches were burnt in the town square. The Carpathians surround the city and offer the possibility of escape. When city life became unbearable because of either religious intolerance or conquest, the oppressed could always dream of melting into the pristine valleys and peaks around them. The town is honeycombed by escape tunnels into the mountains. Cioran and I both escaped to the West, as have many of the artists you mention, and we brought with us the following certainties: sooner or later an invader will shatter your peace (and kill you), but it's possible to escape into the mountainous peaks and valleys of the imagination. We held nature as the sacred refuge from persecution and monotony. Nature is also where the Devil (old Pan) lives. We brought Pan (the Carpathian devil) to the cities of the West and made works that hold the resplendent promise of escape and freedom. Romantic love was for Western poets the ultimate refuge from bourgeois life, but for us Thracians (whence Orpheus hails) Romantic love is only part of the greater world of Pan and Orpheus, the god-singers of Nature.

KO: The optimism of the hippy movement. How do you see it now?

AC: Well-meaning, still valid for small communities. The movement was ruthlessly destroyed by the Reagan "revolution," but the ideal is flawless. See, I'm not Wakefield.

KO: You remain a poet although it has nothing to do with luxury or with creating a marketable product. Even in Wakefield there are great passages that equal your best pages of poetry. You also cite great poets such as Ted Berrigan and Frank O'Hara. The surrealist movement under Breton, as you know, banned the novel form in order to focus on poetry. Do you see a future for the poetic, surrealist novel?

AC: Yes, because of its capaciousness, which can contain poetry, recipes, stories, overheard conversations, and philosophizing. One needn't call it "novel," because this kind of genre-ing (or gendering) is confusing. The novel has changed formally almost since the beginning: the great first novels of Rabelais, Laurence Sterne, and Cervantes did not follow any rules for the "novel." Before that, the epic cycles were narrative poems. Let's just call the things "books" and be done with it. Books have a future, though a shaky one in this age of electric and ephemeral writing.

KO: I have a question as to why you are so drawn to other historical periods — along with Umberto Eco, Garcia Marquez, Raymond Queneau, Susan Howe, J.L. Borges, J.M. Coetzee among a hundred others — you are a postmodern writer with a penchant for re-creating other periods in history. What exactly is this about? Is there a theoretical reason for your doing this?

AC: There is no "theoretical" backing, but an affective-theoretically-evolving way of thinking based on rabbi-questioning and the Romanian exaltation of the imagination plus the native humor. And a bit of fantasy-fiction. The epochs I'm drawn to form a secret ambition to dig into certain ideas of the 17th century (*Blood Countess*— the beginnings of European nationalism), the 18th century (*Casanova*— the Enlightenment), the second-half of the 20th century (*Messiah, Wakefield*— the ultimate fight between the religious view and desacralized return to paradise). That leaves me with the 19th century, where I project a book about Tesla and Twain, and another on the first half of the 20th century that will be on Tristan Tzara and Dada.

Appendix C.
Works by Codrescu

Websites: codrescu.com; corpse.org
Vita: Born in Sibiu, Romania, 1946. U.S citizen, 1981.
Poet, Novelist, Essayist, Screenwriter, Translator
MacCurdy Distinguished Professor of English at Louisiana State University
Editor of *Exquisite Corpse*, online literary journal at www.corpse.org
National Public Radio commentator
Archive at Hill Memorial Library, Louisiana State University

BOOKS

2004 *Wakefield: a novel* (Algonquin Books).

2003 *It Was Today: New Poems* (Coffee House Press).

2002 *Casanova in Bohemia, a novel* (The Free Press).

2001 *An Involuntary Genius in America's Shoes (and What Happened Afterwards)* (Black Sparrow Press, reissue of "The Life & Times of an Involuntary Genius," 1976, and "In America's Shoes," 1983, with new forward and coda-essay). Memoirs.

2000 *The Devil Never Sleeps & Other Essays* (St. Martin's Press). Essays.

2000 *Poezii Alese/Selected Poetry*, bilingual edition, English and Romanian (Bucharest: Editura Paralela 45, 2000). Poetry.

1999 *A Bar in Brooklyn: Novellas & Stories, 1970–1978* (Black Sparrow Press).

1999 *Messiah, a novel* (Simon & Schuster).

1999 *Hail Babylon! Looking for the American City at the End of the Millenium* (St. Martin's Press 1999, Picador, 1999). Essays.

1999 *Ay, Cuba! A Socio-Erotic Journey.* With photographs by David Graham (St. Martin's Press, 1999; Picador, 2001). Travel/Essay.

1997 *The Dog with the Chip in His Neck: Essays from NPR & Elsewhere* (St. Martin's Press, 1996; Picador, 1997).

1996 *Alien Candor: Selected Poems, 1970–1995* (Black Sparrow Press).

1995 *The Muse Is Always Half-Dressed in New Orleans* (St. Martin's Press, 1995; Picador, 1996). Essays.

1995 *The Blood Countess, a novel* (Simon & Schuster, 1995; Dell 1996).

1995 *Zombification: Essays from NPR* (St. Martin's Press, 1995; Picador, 1996).

1994 *The Repentance of Lorraine, a novel* (Rhinoceros Books, 1994, reprint with new introduction of 1976 edition by "Ames Claire").

1993 *Belligerence, poems* (Coffee House Press).

1993 *Road Scholar: Coast to Coast Late in the Century*, with photographs by David Graham. A journal of the making of the movie "Road Scholar" (Hyperion).

1991 *The Hole in the Flag: a Romanian Exile's Story of Return and Revolution* (Morrow, 1991; Avon 1992).

1991 *Comrade Past and Mister Present, poetry* (Coffee House Press).

1990 *The Disappearance of the Outside: a Manifesto for Escape* (Addison-Wesley Co. 1990; reissued by Ruminator Press, 2001, with new essay).

1989 *At the Court of Yearning: Poems by Lucian Blaga* (Ohio State University Press, 1989; translation of Romania's great modern poet).

1988 *A Craving for Swan, essays* (Ohio State University Press).

1987 *Monsieur Teste in America & Other Instances of Realism, stories* (Coffee House Press).

1987 *Raised by Puppets Only to Be Killed by Research* (Addison-Wesley).

1983 *In America's Shoes* (City Lights).

1983 *Selected Poems 1970–1980* (Sun Books).

1982 *Necrocorrida, poems* (Panjandrum Books).

1979 *The Lady Painter, poems* (Four Zoas Press).

1978 *For the Love of a Coat, poems* (Four Zoas Press).

1975 *The Life & Times of an Involuntary Genius* (George Braziller).

1974 *The Marriage of Insult & Injury* (Cymric Press).

1973 *The History of the Growth of Heaven, poems* (George Braziller).

1973 *A Serious Morning, poems* (Capra Press).

1971 *Why I Can't Talk on the Telephone, stories* (kingdom kum press).

1970 *License to Carry a Gun* (Big Table Award; Big Table/Follet; reprinted by Carnegie-Mellon University Press, 1998)

EDITOR/FOUNDER

Exquisite Corpse: A Journal of Books and Ideas (1983–1997)
Exquisitecorpse.org (1997–ongoing)
Exquisite Corpse Books (2004-ongoing)

ANTHOLOGIES EDITED

American Poets Say Goodbye to the 20th Century, with Laura Rosenthal. 4 Walls/8 Windows, 1996.
American Poetry Since 1970: Up Late. 4 Walls/8 Windows, 1988.
The Stiffest of the Corpse: an Exquisite Corpse Reader, 1983-1990. City Lights Books, 1990.
Thus Spake the Corpse: an Exquisite Corpse Reader 1988-1998. Volume One, Poetry and Essays, with Laura Rosenthal. Black Sparrow Press, 1999.
Thus Spake the Corpse: An Exquisite Corpse Reader 1988-1998. Volume Two, Fictions, Travels, and Translations, with Laura Rosenthal. Black Sparrow Press, 2000.

AUDIOTAPES/CD/SOLO RECORDINGS

American Life with Andrei Codrescu. Washington, DC: NPR, 1988. Two one-hour tapes.
The Blood Countess. New York: Simon & Schuster audio, 1995. Read by the author and Suzanne Bertish.
Fax Your Prayers. Los Angeles: Dove Audio, 1995.
No Tacos for Saddam. Los Angeles: Gang of Seven, BMG Distributors, 1994.
Plato Sucks. Los Angeles: Dove Audio, 1996.
The Valley of Christmas. GertTown Records, 1998.
Wakefield, audio book, CD/cassette. Highbridge, 2001.

FILM SCREENWRITER/ON CAMERA PRINCIPAL

After the Revolution, Andrei Codrescu and Christopher Hitchens in Chicago. The Lannan Foundation. Directed by Lewis MacAdams. 1991.
Battle of the Bards. The Lannan Foundation. Produced and directed by Lewis MacAdams and John Dorr. The 8th Annual World Heavyweight Poetry Championship. 1990.

Road Scholar. Public Policy Productions. Feature documentary written by and starring Andrei Codrescu, produced by Roger Weisberg, directed by Roger Weisberg and Jean de Segonzac. Winner: George Foster Peabody Award, Golden Eagle Award, Cine Festival; Chris Award, Columbus Film Festival. Best Documentary: Seattle International Film Festival; Best Documentary: San Francisco Film Festival. Distributed nationally by Samuel Goldwyn Co., 1993. Premiered on PBS, Fall 1994. Hallmark Video.

Romania: My Old Haunt. PBS/Frontline International. Written and narrated by Andrei Codrescu. Directed by Marian Marzinsky. First national PBS air date: October 31, 2002.

NATIONAL APPEARANCES

Architecture, "Stereopticon," a monthly column, contributing editor, 1997–2000.

The Baltimore Sun, biweekly columnist, 1981–1988.

Funny Times, regular contributor.

Gambit Weekly, weekly columnist.

msnbc.com, biweekly commentary, 1998–2000.

Nightline with Ted Koppel, frequent contributor, commentary.

NPR: *All Things Considered,* weekly commentary.

Appearances on *The Today Show, The Tonight Show, The David Letterman Show, The Charlie Rose Show, CNN-International Hour,* C-Span, ABC News, NBC News, CBS News. Contributed to various PBS and cable documentaries, including appearances in Ken Burns' "Statue of Liberty," Rick Burns' "Coney Island," and the series *Future Quest.* Helped write screenplays for several movies. Has published essays in *The New York Times, The Boston Globe, The Philadelphia Inquirer, The Chicago Tribune, Newsday, The Kansas City Star, Playboy, Sierra Magazine, Digital Media, Index on Censorship.* Has appeared on numerous cultural and public affairs programs on radio and television. Contributes frequently to academic publications and literary magazines. Lectures nationally and internationally.

AWARDS

1970 Big Table Poetry Award

1973 National Endowment for the Arts Fellowships for poetry, editing, radio

1984 National Endowment for the Arts Fellowships for poetry, editing, radio

1985 National Endowment for the Arts Fellowships for poetry, editing, radio
1987 National Endowment for the Arts Fellowships for poetry, editing, radio
1987 Towson State University Literature Prize
1988 General Electric Foundation Poetry Prize
1991 Honorary Member of the Romanian Writers Union
1991 National Endowment for the Arts Fellowships for poetry, editing, radio
1993 Mayor's Arts Award, New Orleans.
1995 Peabody Award for *Road Scholar*
1996 Literature Prize of the Romanian Cultural Foundation, Bucharest
1998 ACLU Freedom of Speech Award
1998 Louisiana Press Association, Best Regular Column
1998 Shenandoah University Honorary Doctorate
2000 Lowell Thomas Gold Award for Excellence in Travel Journalism
2000 MacCurdy Distinguished Professor of English, LSU
2001 Alternative Newsweekly Awards, first prize for column
2001 Decorated with the Star of Romania at the rank of Commander

REFERENCE

Andrei Codrescu: An American-Romanian or a Romanian American Writer? Doctoral Thesis by Damiana Bottaro, University of Padua, Italy. 2004.

Andrei Codrescu: A Bibliography, 1966–1990 by Daniel Lee Butcher. M.A. thesis based on the Codrescu holdings at LSU's Hill Memorial Library. 1995.

"Andrei Codrescu's Mioritic Space" by Richard Collins. *MELUS*, Volume 23, Number 3, Fall 1998.

Contemporary Authors Autobiography Series, Volume 19, Gale Research. Andrei Codrescu. 1994.

Romani in Stiinta si Cultura Occidentala, American-Romanian Academy of Arts and Sciences, Davis, 1992. Encyclopedia: Romanians in Arts & Sciences in the Western World.

Romania through the Eyes of an Exiled Transylvanian: A Story of Return, Revolution, and What Happened Afterwards: Andrei Codrescu's Journey from Romania to America and Back Again. Doctoral thesis by Roxana Maria Crisan, Lucian Blaga University, Department of British and American Studies, Sibiu, Romania. 2004.

Scriitori Din Diaspora: Andrei Codrescu by Florea Firan. Analele Universitatii din Craiova, Seria Stiinte Filologice, Literatura Romana si Universala, Nr.1-12, 1997.

"Song of My Emerging Self: The Poetry of Andrei Codrescu" by Ileana Alexandra Orlich. *MELUS*, Volume 18, No. 3, Fall 1993.

Xavier Review, Vol. 20, No.1, New Orleans. "Translating Codrescu into Romanian" by Ioana Avadani; "Andreiology" by Julian Semilian; "Codrescu Verses America: A Postmodern Turned Loose" by Tim Lehnert. 2000.

General Bibliography

Altieri, Charles. *Enlarging the Temple: New Directions in American Poetry During the 1960s.* Lewisburg, PA: Bucknell, 1979.

_____. *Canons and Consequences: Reflections on the Ethical Force of Imaginative Ideals.* Evanston: Northwestern, 1990.

Arendt, Hannah. *The Human Condition.* 1958. Chicago: The University of Chicago Press, 1998.

_____. "Introduction to Walter Benjamin," in *Illuminations.* London: Harper-Collins, 1992.

Aristotle. *Poetics.* Trans. S.H. Butcher. New York: Hill and Wang, 1961.

Augustine. *City of God.* Trans. Henry Betteman. 1467. London: Pelican, 1988.

Bachofen, Jacob. *Myth, Religion and Mother Right.* Trans. Ralph Manheim. Princeton: Princeton University Press, 1979.

Bainton, Roland. *Here I Stand: A Life of Martin Luther.* Nashville: Abingdon, 1950.

Barthes, Roland. "The Death of the Author," in *Image Music Text.* Trans. Stephen Heath. (London: Fontana, 1977).

Bataille, Georges. *Oeuvres Complètes 12 Articles 2 1950-1961.* Paris: Gallimard, 1988.

Bateson, Gregory. *Steps to an Ecology of Mind.* New York: Ballantine, 1972.

Benjamin, Lya. "The Jews in Romania," in *Romania: A Historic Perspective.* Eds. Dinu C. Giurescu and Stephen Fischer-Galati. Boulder: East European Monographs, 1998: 533–544.

Benjamin, Walter. *Illuminations.* Trans. Edmund Jephcott. New York: Schocken, 1978.

_____. *Reflections.* Ed. Peter Demetz. New York: Schocken, 1978.

Benne, Robert. *The Ethic of Democratic Capitalism.* Philadelphia: Fortress, 1981.

_____. *Ordinary Saints.* Philadelphia: Fortress, 1988.

_____. *The Paradoxical Vision.* Minneapolis: Fortress Press, 1995.

Berkeley, George. *Works on Vision.* Edited with commentary by Colin M. Turbayne. New York: Bobbs-Merrill, 1963.

Bernstein, Charles. *Content's Dream.* Los Angeles: Sun & Moon, 1986.

Bible: New International Version. Colorado Springs: International Bible Society, 1984.

Bonnet, Marguerite, ed. Adhérer au Paris Communiste? Archives du surréalisme. Sept.–Dec. 1926. Paris: Gallimard, 1992.

Breton, Andre. *La clé des champs.* Paris: 10/18, 1967.

_____. *Manifestes.* Paris: Pauvert, 1979.

_____. *Nadja.* Trans. Richard Howard. New York: Grove, 1960.

_____. *Vases Communicants.* Paris: Gallimard, 1955.

Bojtar, Endre. *East European Avant-Garde Literature.* Budapest: Akademia Kiado, 1992.

Buck-Morss, Susan. *The Dialectics of Seeing.* Boston: MIT, 1993.

Buell, Lawrence. "Introduction: In Pursuit of Ethics," in *PMLA* Vol. 114, No. 1, Jan. 1999: 7-19.

Burgin, Victor. "The City in Pieces," in *The Actuality of Walter Benjamin.* Ed. Laura Marcus and Lynda Nead, "New Formations: a Journal of Culture/Theory/Politics," 20 (1993): 33-46.

Burke, Kenneth. *Attitudes Toward History.* 1937. Berkeley: University of California Press, 1984.

_____. *The Philosophy of Literary Form.* 1941; Berkeley: University of California Press, 1984.

Butterick, Charles. *Guide to the Maximus Poems of Charles Olson.* Berkeley: University of California Press, 1980.

Cafard, Max. "The Surre(gion)alist Manifesto," *Exquisite Corpse* vol. 8, 1-4, (1993): 1, 9-10. *The Fifth Estate* vol. 28, no. 1 (Spring 1993), 15-18.

Ceausescu, Nicolae. *An Independent Foreign Policy for Peace and Cooperation.* Washington, D.C.: Acropolis Books, 1987.

_____. *Romania's International Policy of Peace, Friendship, and Cooperation with all the Peoples.* Bucharest: Meridiane, 1979.

Chénieux-Gendron, Jacqueline. *Surrealism.* Trans. Vivian Folkenflik. New York: Columbia, 1990.

_____. "Surrealists in Exile." *Poetics Today,* Vol. 17, No. 3, Fall 1996, pp. 436–451.

Cioran, E.M. *Sur les Cimes du Désespoir.* Paris: L'Herne, 1990.

Clark, Tom. *Charles Olson: The Allegory of a Poet's Life.* Berkeley, CA: North Atlantic Books, 2000.

_____. *The Great Naropa Poetry Wars.* Santa Barbara: Cadmus Editions, 1980.

_____. *Paradise Resisted.* Santa Barbara: Black Sparrow Press, 1984.

Codrescu, Andrei. *Alien Candor.* Santa Barbara: Black Sparrow, 1996.

_____. *Ay, Cuba.* New York: St. Martin's Press, 1999.

_____. *The Blood Countess.* New York: Simon & Schuster, 1995.

_____. *Casanova in Bohemia.* New York: Free Press, 2002.

_____. *Comrade Past & Mister Present.* Minneapolis: Coffee House Press, 1986.

_____. *The Disappearance of the Outside.* Reading, Massachusetts: Addison Wesley, 1990.

_____. *The Dog With a Chip In His Neck.* New York: Picador, 1996.

_____. *The Hole in the Flag.* New York: Morrow, 1991.

_____. *Hail Babylon!* New York: St. Martin's, 1998.

_____. *In America's Shoes.* San Francisco: City Lights Books, 1983.

_____. "Interview with Kay Bonetti and Walter Bargen." *The Missouri Review Vol. XXI* (1) 1989: 71-88.

_____. *The Life and Times of an Involuntary Genius.* New York: Braziller, 1975.

_____. *Messiah.* New York: Simon & Schuster, 1999.

_____. *Raised by Puppets Only to be Killed by Research.* Reading, MA: Addison Wesley, 1989.

_____. *Road Scholar.* New York: Hyperion, 1993.

_____. *Selected Poems 1970-1980.* New York: Sun Press, 1983.

Cohen, Margaret. *Profane Illumination: Walter Benjamin and the Paris of Surrealist Revolution.* Berkeley: University of California Press, 1993.

Cohen, Ted. *Jokes: Philosophical Thoughts on Joking Matters.* Chicago: University of Chicago Press, 1999.

Collins, Richard. "Interview with Andrei Codrescu." *Xavier Review* Vol. 20 (2) 2000: 13-18.

Cornis-Pope, Marcel. *The Unfinished Battles: Romanian Postmodernism Before and After 1989.* Iasi, Romania: Polirom, 1996.

Creeley, Robert. *Hello: A Journal.* New York: Marion Boyars, 1978.

Cribb, Kenneth T. *Choosing the Right College: The Whole Truth About America's Top Schools.* Grand Rapids, Michigan: Eerdman's, 2001.

Crusius, Timothy W. *Kenneth Burke and the Conversation after Philosophy.* Carbondale: Southern Illinois University Press, 1999.

Deleuze, Gilles. *Anti-Oedipus* (with Félix Guattari). Trans. Robert Hurley, et al. Minneapolis: University of Minnesota Press, 1992.

_____. *Coldness and Cruelty.* Trans. Jean McNeil. New York: Zone, 1989.

_____. *Dialogues* (with Claire Parnet). Trans. Hugh Tomlinson and Barbara Habberjam. New York: Columbia, 1987.

_____. *Difference and Repetition.* Trans. Paul Patton. New York: Columbia, 1994.

_____. *Kant's Critical Philosophy.* Trans. Hugh Tomlinson, et al. Minneapolis: University of Minnesota Press, 1984.

_____. *Nietzsche et la Philosophie.* 1962. Paris: Presses Universitaires de France, 1983.

_____. *A Thousand Plateaus* (with Félix Guattari). Trans. Brian Massumi. Minneapolis: University of Minnesota Press, 1991).

Denby, Edward. "The Thirties," in *Writing New York.* New York: Washington Square Press, 1998: 819–823.

Detienne, Marcel. *Dionysos at Large.* Trans. Arthur Goldhammer. Cambridge: Harvard UP, 1989).

Duve, Thierry de. *Kant after Duchamp*. Cambridge: MIT, 1997.

Eddy, Steve, and Hamilton, Claire. *Greek Myths*. Chicago: McGraw-Hill, 2001.

Foucault, Michel. "What is an Author?" In *Textual Strategies: Perspectives in Post-Structuralist Criticism*. Ed. Josué V. Harari. London: Methuen, 1979.

French, Peter. *Responsibility Matters*. Lawrence: University of Kansas, 1992.

Freud, Sigmund. *Jokes and Their Relation to the Unconscious*. Trans. James Strachey. New York: Norton, 1960.

Garaudy, Roger. *Pour Connaître La Pensée de Hegel*. Paris: Bordas, 1966.

Georgoudi, Stella. "Creating a Myth of Patriarchy," in *A History of Women: From Ancient Goddesses to Christian Saints*. Boston: Harvard University Press, 1992.

Girard, René. *To Double Business Bound*. Baltimore: Johns Hopkins, 1978.

_____. *Violence and the Sacred*. Trans. Patrick Gregory. Baltimore: Johns Hopkins, 1977.

Goeckel, Robert F. *The Lutheran Church and the East German State: Political Conflict Under Ulbricht and Honecker*. Ithaca, NY: Cornell University Press, 1990.

Goux, Jean-Joseph. *Oedipus, Philosopher*. Trans. Catherine Porter. Stanford, CA: Stanford University Press, 1993.

Guattari, Félix. *Chaosophy*. New York: Semiotexte, 1995.

Hall, Sir Peter. *Cities in Civilization*. New York: Pantheon, 1998.

Haraszti, Miklós. *The Velvet Prison: Artists Under State Socialism*. Trans. Katalin and Stephen Landesmann. New York: FSG, 1987.

Harrison, Jane. *Prolegomena to the Study of Greek Religion*. 1903. New York: Meridian Noonday Books, 1955.

Hawking, Stephen. *A Brief History of Time*. 1988. New York: Bantam, 1998.

Hegel, Georg. *Hegel: The Essential Writings*. Ed. Frederick W. Weiss. New York: Harper Torchbooks, 1974.

_____. *Phenomenology of Spirit*. Trans. A.V. Miller. Oxford: Oxford University Press, 1977.

Hinlicky, Paul. "On the Need for Lutheran Political Thought: An Essay in Honor of Richard Niebanck." Lutheran Forum. Pentecost 1985: 8-11.

Hochman, Jiri, ed. *Hope Dies Last: The Autobiography of Alexander Dubcek*. New York: Kodansha International, 1993.

Hollo, Anselm. *Caws and Causeries: Around Poetry and Poets*. Albuquerque: La Alameda Press, 1999.

_____. *Outlying Districts* Minneapolis: Coffee House Press, 1990.

_____. *Pick Up the House*. Minneapolis: Coffee House Press, 1986.

Hyers, Conrad. *And God Created Laughter: The Bible as Divine Comedy*. Atlanta: John Knox Press, 1987.

Ionesco, Eugene. *Hugoliad: Or the Grotesque and Tragic Life of Victor Hugo*. New York: Grove Press, 1987.

Jacobs, Jane. *The Life and Death of Great American Cities*. New York: Vintage, 1992.

Jakobsen, Erik. "Finding What We've Lost: New Urbanism, Traditional Neighborhoods, and the Christian Faith." The Cresset (Easter 2003) Vol. LXVI (4): 18-26.

Kant, Immanuel. *The Critique of Judgment.* Trans. J.H. Bernard. New York: Hafner Press, 1951.

_____. "Religion within the Limits of Reason Alone," in *Basic Writings of Kant.* Ed. Allen Wood (New York: Modern Library, 2001): 367-414.

Kaplan, Cora. *Sea Changes.* London: Verso, 1986.

Kauppi, Niilo. *Tel Quel: La Constitution Sociale D'Une Avant-Garde.* Helsinki: The Finnish Society of Arts and Letters, 1991.

Keane, John. "The Modern Democratic Revolution: Reflections on Lyotard's *The Postmodern Condition.*" In *Judging Lyotard.* Ed. Andrew Benjamin. New York: Routledge, 1992.

Kennedy, X.J. ed. *The Brief Bedford Reader.* Boston: St. Martin's, 2000.

Kerouac, Jack. *On the Road.* New York: New American Library, 1957.

Kierkegaard, Soren. *Fear and Trembling.* Trans. Walter Lowrie. Princeton: Princeton University Press, 1984.

Kjellberg, Seppo. *Urban Ecotheology.* Amsterdam: International Books, 1999.

Klossowski, Pierre. *Diana at her Bath/The Women of Rome.* Trans. Stephen Sartorelli and Sophie Hawkes. Boston: Eridanos, 1990.

_____. *La Monnaie Vivante.* 1970. Marseille: Losfeld, 1994.

_____. *Nietzsche et le Cercle Vicieux.* Paris: Mercure de France, 1969.

Kojeve, Alexandre. *Introduction to the Reading of Hegel.* Trans. James H. Nichols, Jr. Ithaca, NY: Cornell University Press, 1969.

Kundera, Milan. *Testaments Betrayed.* Trans. Linda Asher. New York: HarperPerennial, 1995.

Lacan, Jacques. "Of Structure as an Inmixing of an Otherness Prerequisite to Any Subject Whatever," in Richard Macksey and Eugenio Donato (eds.) *The Structuralist Controversy: The Languages of Criticism and the Sciences of Man,* second edition. Baltimore: Johns Hopkins University Press, 1972, 186–200.

Löwith, Karl. *Nietzsche's Philosophy of the Eternal Recurrence of the Same.* Berkeley: University of California Press, 1997.

Lynch, Kevin. *What Time Is This Place?* Boston: MIT Press, 1972.

Lyotard, Jean-François. *The Differend: Phrases in Dispute.* Minneapolis: University of Minnesota Press, 1988.

_____. *Discours, Figur.* Paris: Klinksieck, 1973.

_____. *The Hyphen Between Judaism and Christianity (with Eberhard Gruber.* Trans. Pascale-Anne Brault and Michael Naas. Amherst, NY: Humanity Books, 1999.

_____. *Just Gaming.* Trans. Wlad Godzich. Minneapolis: University of Minnesota Press, 1985.

_____. *The Inhuman.* Trans. Geoffrey Bennington and Rachel Bowlby. Stanford: Stanford University Press, 1991.

_____. *Libidinal Economy.* Trans. Hamilton Grant. Bloomington: Indiana University Press, 1993.

_____. *Political Writings*. Trans. Bill Readings and Kevin Paul Geiman. Minneapolis: University of Minnesota Press, 1993.

_____. *The Postmodern Condition*. Trans. Geoff Bennington and Brian Massumi. Minneapolis: University of Minnesota Press, 1991.

_____. *Postmodern Fables*. Trans. Georges van den Abbeele. Minneapolis: University of Minnesota Press, 1999.

_____. *Toward the Post-Modern*. Trans. Mira Kamdor, et al. New Jersey: Humanities Press, 1993.

Marx, Karl. "Theses on Feuerbach," in *Ludwig Feuerbach And the Outcome of Classical German Philosophy*, by Frederick Engels. New York: International, n.d.

May, Todd. "Is Post-Structuralist Theory Anarchist?" *Philosophy and Social Criticism* 15: 3 (1989).

_____. *The Political Philosophy of Poststructuralist Anarchism*. University Park, PA: Pennsylvania State University Press, 1994.

Morris, Tom. *If Aristotle Ran General Motors*. New York: Henry Holt, 1997.

Morreall, John. *The Philosophy of Laughter and Humor*. Albany, NY: SUNY Press, 1987.

Niebuhr, Reinhold. *The Essential Reinhold Niebuhr: Selected Essays and Addresses*. Ed. Robert McAfee Brown. New Haven: Yale University Press, 1986.

Nietzsche, Friedrich. *The Birth of Tragedy*. Trans. Francis Golffing. New York: Doubleday, 1956.

_____. *The Portable Nietzsche*. Trans. Walter Kaufman. New York: Viking, 1964.

O'Hara, Frank. *The Selected Poems of Frank O'Hara*. New York: Vintage, 1974.

Olson, Charles. *Call Me Ishmael: A Study of Melville*. San Francisco: City Lights, n.d.

_____. *The Maximus Poems*. Berkeley: University of California Press, 1983.

_____. *Selected Writings of Charles Olson*. Ed. Robert Creeley. New York: New Directions, 1966.

Olson, Kirby. "Interview with Andrei Codrescu." *Asylum*, 5 (4), 1990, 35-36.

Otto, Rudolf. *Dionysus: Myth and Cult*. Trans. Robert B. Palmer. Bloomington: Indiana University Press, 1965.

Palmer, Donald. *Looking at Philosophy: The Unbearable Heaviness of Philosophy Made Lighter*. Mountain View, CA: Mayfield, 2001.

Paz, Octavio. *On Poets and Others*. trans. Michael Schmidt. New York: Arcade Publishing, 1986.

Pearson, Keith Anselm. *Deleuze and Philosophy: The Difference Engineer*. London: Routledge, 1997.

Pelikan, Jaroslav. *Fools for Christ*. Philadelphia: Muhlenberg Press, 1955.

Poele, Ieme van der. *Une Révolution de la Pensée: Maoïsme et Feminisme à Travers Tel Quel, Les Temps Modernes, et Esprit*. Amsterdam: Rodopi, 1992.

Pound, Ezra. *The ABC of Reading*. New York: New Directions, 1960.

Price, Sir Uvedale. *An Essay on the Picturesque*. London: 1796-1798.

Readings, Bill. *Introducing Lyotard*. New York: Routledge, 1991.

_____. "Pagans, Perverts or Primitives? Experimental Justice in the Empire of Capital." In *Judging Lyotard*. Ed. Andrew Benjamin. New York: Routledge, 1992.

Reznikoff, Charles. *By the Waters of Manhattan*. New York: New Directions, 1962.

Robert, Bernard-Paul. *Antécédents du Surréalisme*. Ottawa: Less Presses Universitaires d'Ottawa, 1988.

Sa'adah, Anne. *The Shaping of Liberal Politics in Revolutionary France: A Comparative Perspective*. Princeton: Princeton University Press, 1990.

Sainsbury, R.M. *Paradoxes*. Cambridge: Cambridge University Press, 1995.

Sanders, Ed. *Fame and Love in New York*. Berkeley: Turtle Island, 1980.

_____. *The Family*. New York: Dutton, 1972.

_____. *Investigative Poetry*. San Francisco: City Lights, 1976.

_____. *1968*. Los Angeles: Black Sparrow, 1997.

_____. *The Party*. Woodstock, NY: Poetry, Crime & Culture Press, 1977.

_____. *Thirsting for Peace in a Raging Century: Selected Poems*. Minneapolis: Coffee House Press, 1987.

_____. *The Z-D Generation*. Barrytown, N.Y.: Station Hill Press, 1981.

Shakespeare, William. *Hamlet*. Ed. Harold Jenkins. London: Methuen, 1982.

Shawcross, William. *Dubcek*. New York: Simon & Schuster, 1990.

Sittler, Joseph. *The Care of the Earth and Other University Sermons*. Philadelphia: Fortress Press, 1964.

Spariosu, Mihai. *Dionysus Reborn*. Ithaca: Cornell University Press, 1989.

_____. "Exile, Play, and Intellectual Autobiography." In *Building a Profession: Autobiographical Perspectives on the Beginnings of Comparative Literature in the United States*. Ed. Lionel Grossman and Mihai Spariosu. Albany, NY: SUNY Press, 1994, 205-216.

Stalin, Joseph. *Selected Writings*. New York: International, 1942.

Stirner, Max. *The Ego and Its Own*. Trans. Steven Byington. London: Rebel Press, 1993.

Tillich, Paul. *The Dynamics of Faith*. New York: Harper Torchbooks, 1957.

_____. *The Religious Situation*. New York: Meridian, 1956.

Tinder, Glenn. *The Political Meaning of Christianity*. Baton Rouge: LSU Press, 1989.

Urmuz. *Weird Pages*. Trans. Stavros Deligiorgis. Bucharest: Cartea Romaneasca, 1985.

Vernant, Jean-Pierre. "Greek Tragedy: Problems of Interpretation." In *The Structuralist Controversy*. Ed. Richard Macksey and Eugenio Donatio. Baltimore: Johns Hopkins, 1982.

Whitman, Walt. *The Portable Walt Whitman*. New York: Penguin, 1977.

Williams, William Carlos. *Paterson*. New York: New Directions, 1963.

_____. *Selected Essays*. New York: New Directions, 1969.

Wilms, Mark. "The Rebirth of Luther's Two Kingdoms in Kant's Commonwealths." *Journal for Christian Theological Research*. http://apu.edu/~CTRF/articles/1998_articles/wilms.html, 3:1 (1998): 1–9.

Wittgenstein, Ludwig. *Culture and Value.* Ed. by Georg von Wright. Chicago: University of Chicago Press, 1982.

Wolff, Janet. "Memoirs and Micrologies." In *The Actuality of Walter Benjamin.* Ed. Laura Marcus and Lynda Nead. London: Lawrence & Wishart, 1993, 111–122.

Wurmbrand, Richard. *From Suffering to Triumph!* Grand Rapids, MI: Kregel Publications, 1991.

Yakovlev, Alexander. *The Fate of Marxism in Russia.* Trans. Catherine A. Fitzpatrick. New Haven: Yale, 1993.

Young-Bruehl, Elisabeth. "Hannah Arendt Among Feminists." In *Hannah Arendt: Twenty Years Later.* Ed. Larry May and Jerome Kohn. London: MIT, 1996.

Zhdanov, Andrei A. *Essays on Literature, Philosophy and Music.* New York: International Publishers, 1950.

Zizek, Slavoj. *The Fragile Absolute—or why is the Christian legacy worth fighting for?* London: Verso, 2000.

Index

"À Francis Ponge" 127–128, 179–180
Adams, Noah 169
Alien Candor 26, 34, 42, 156, 157–158
Altieri, Charles 35, 177
American Poets Since 1970: Up Late 26
Ancua, Titu 164–165
Anderson, Sherwood 18
Apollinaire, Guillaume 64–65
Aquinas, Saint Thomas 15, 69
Arendt, Hannah 64, 70, 142
Aristotle 47, 130, 148
Artaud, Antonin 10, 128, 148
Ashbery, John 64, 109, 113, 180
Atlantis 155
Augustine, Saint 6
Ay, Cuba! A Socio-Erotic Journey 129, 172–173

Bachofen, Johann 155
Baltimore 24–25, 50
Balzac, Honoré 36
Barthes, Roland 93
Bataille, Georges 10
Baudelaire, Charles 16, 20
Baudrillard, Jean 78, 81
Benjamin, Lya 38
Benjamin, Walter 4, 7–11, 14–17, 19–21, 64, 111, 146, 147
Bergson, Henri 15, 180
Berkeley, George 93
Bernd, Magnus 79

Berrigan, Ted 14, 26, 71, 108, 177, 180, 187
Berry, Wendell 109, 112–113
Blackburn, Paul 26, 198
Blaga, Lucian 115
The Blood Countess 139–147, 188
Bly, Robert 3, 102, 178
Bojtar, Endre 146
Bonaparte, Josephine 13
Bonaparte, Napoleon 13, 173
Bonnet, Marguerite 137
Borges, J.L. 188
Boston 36
Boswell, James 36
Brautigan, Richard 171
Breton, André 6, 10–13, 14, 136, 152, 156, 187
Brodey, Jim 113
Brodsky, Joseph 48
Broughton, James 54
Brownstein, Michael 113
Brucan, Silviu 131
Bruderhoff Community 54, 181
Bucharest 25, 57–59, 66, 69, 129–130, 168–169
Buck-Morss, Susan 8
Budapest 18–19
Bulgakov, Mihail 184
Burgin, Victor 20
Burroughs, William 18, 128
Butterick, George 105

Caragiale, Ion 162
Cardarelli, Joseph 26
Carroll, Jim 113
Casanova, Giacomo 153–155, 158, 184
Casanova in Bohemia 153–154, 188
Cassady, Neil 78, 81
Castro, Fidel 129
Ceausescu, Nicolae 57, 76, 87, 119,
    125–138, 157–158, 166–167, 169, 174
Celan, Paul 38, 115
Cervantes, Miguel 187
Chénieux-Gendron, Jacqueline 10, 12
Chicago 36, 82
Christo 177
Cincinnati 18
Cioran, E.M. 26, 40, 66, 69, 144, 171,
    174, 183, 186
Cixous, Hélène 10
Clark, Tom 5–6, 103, 106, 113, 117, 144,
    154
Coatzee, J.M. 188
Codrescu, Alice 24
Codrescu, Lucian 64–65
Cohen, Margaret 10–11
Cohen, Ted 131
Comrade Past & Mister Present 29,
    31–32, 49, 106
Cornis-Pope, Marcel 28, 127
Corso, Gregory 4, 5, 86, 106
Couliano, Ioan 26, 119
Creeley, Robert 6, 100–101, 103, 108, 154
Crisan, Roxana, Maria 159–169
Cruz, Victor Hernandez 86, 108
Curtean, Thomas 164

Danton, Georges Jacques 137
"Dear Masoch" 45–46
Deleuze, Gilles 10, 14, 16, 24, 27, 33,
    42, 45–46, 69–70, 72, 74, 76, 83,
    85–87, 91, 99, 107, 117, 128, 142–143,
    147–148, 180
Demetrescu-Buzau, Demetru 152; *see
    also* Urmuz
Denver 58
Derrida, Jacques 92
Desnos, Robert 64
Detienne, Marcel 155
Detroit 36, 55–63, 74–75, 84, 88, 110
Dionysus 33, 43, 47, 55, 69, 83, 122,
    155
DiPrima, Diane 114

Disappearance of the Outside 9, 12,
    19–20, 27–28, 30, 36–39, 43, 48, 61,
    91, 95–98, 111, 113
The Dog with a Chip in His Neck 132,
    162–163
Dorn, Edward 6, 104
Dracula 11, 16, 20, 37, 41, 43, 53, 74,
    84, 158, 187
Dragos-Munteanu, Aurel 131
Dubcek, Alexander 141
Duck, Donald 65
Dugulescu, Pastor 126

Eco, Umberto 188
Eliade, Mircea 26, 27
Emerson, Ralph Waldo 54
Eminescu, Mihai 162
Equi, Elaine 108
Evergreen State College 3
Exquisite Corpse 3, 8, 36, 112, 141, 152,
    156, 176

Fagin, Larry 113, 117
Falwell, Jerry 184
Fantomas 12
Farkas, Bolyai 106
"Fascinations" 180
Faulkner, William 18
Ferlinghetti, Lawrence 69
Feuerbach, Ludwig 17
"Fish Out Your Window" 12
Fitzgerald, F. Scott 18, 183
Fondane, Benjamin 38, 115
Ford, Henry 57, 73
Foucault, Michel 93–94
Fourier, Charles 9, 27, 49–50, 142
Franz, Kafka 177
Frege, Gottlob 93
Freud, Sigmund 11, 13, 19, 42

Gal, Robert 177
Galileo 177
Gallup, Dick 108
Gheorghiu-Dej, Gheorghe 129
Ginsberg, Allen 5, 7, 53, 74, 106
Giorno, John 108
Girard, René 121–124
Gloucester, Massachusetts 5, 105
Goeckel, Robert 140–141
Gogol, Nikolai 184
Goldmann, Lucian 129

Gombrowicz, Witold 118
Graham, David 79, 82
Gray, Darrel 71, 176
Griscom, Chris 71–72
Guattari, Félix 33, 42, 76, 94, 99, 117, 128
Gustafson, Jim 84–89, 108, 114, 180

Haiti 182
Hamann, Georg 175
Havel, Václav 138
Hawking, Stephen 47
Hawthorne, Nathaniel 184–185
Hegel, Georg 13, 35, 47, 146, 174–175
Heraclitus 79
Hirschman, Jack 114
"History" 149
Hitler, Adolf 149
The Hole in the Flag 121, 125–133, 161, 169
Hollo, Anselm 6, 100–104, 107, 108–109, 111, 113, 117–118, 154
Howe, Susan 188
Hughes, Robert 52
Hugo, Victor 40
Hume, David 80
Huxley, Aldous 64
Huysmans, Joris-Karl 186

In America's Shoes 24, 29, 36, 65–77, 82, 112
"Indecent Exposure" 19
Investigative Poetry 6, 100–120, 123, 137
Ioanid, Constantin 126
Ionesco, Eugène 40–41, 171
Isou, Isidore 41

Jacobs, Jane 58–59, 61–62
Jenkins, Harold 148
Jerusalem 144, 175
Jesus Christ 54, 115, 147, 178, 181
Jones, Bradley 114
Jones, Jim 123

Kant, Immanuel 53–54, 80, 126–127, 149
Kerouac, Jack 5, 53, 69–70, 74, 76, 81
Kicknosway, Faye 114
Kipling, Rudyard 64
Klossowski, Pierre 42, 87–89
Knott, Bill 108, 114, 179
Knudsen, Glen 71

Koch, Kenneth 64, 108, 109
Konrad, Kurt 146

Lacan, Jacques 10, 93–94
L'Amour, Louis 68
Language poetry 26, 98–99, 102
Las Vegas 68, 72–77, 82
Lenin, Vladimir 43, 140
Lewinsky, Monica 181
License to Carry a Gun 67, 170
Life and Times of an Involuntary Genius 171
Locke, John 135
London, Jack 69, 76, 78
Louis XIV, King 136
Lowell, Robert 35
Löwith, Karl 79
Loy, Mina 108
Luca, Gherasim 20, 26
Lungu, Cornel 165
Luther, Martin 139
Lynch, Kevin 18–19, 25, 80–81
Lyotard, Jean-Francois 90–95, 133–134, 142, 149

Malanga, Gerard 113
Manson, Charles 121–124, 155, 171
Marinetti, F.T. 53
Marlowe, Christopher 184
Marquez, Garcia 188
Marx, Karl 10, 17, 42, 49, 146, 149–150, 172; *Communist Manifesto* 14
Mayakovsky, Vladimir 48
Mayer, Bernadette 113
McAdams, Lewis 86
McClure, Michael 114
Meltzer, David 114
Melville, Herman 111
Merwin, W.S. 42
Messiah 144–150, 172–176, 188
Miller, Henry 69–70, 76, 78, 81
Miller, Jacques-Alain 94
Miller, Jeffrey 26, 59, 71, 85, 108, 180
"The Mind Circus Is in Town" 17
Minneapolis 18
Mioritza 96
"Model Work" 34
Monte Rio, CA 23–25, 42, 54
Morreall, John 11
"My Brush with Hollywood" 17
Myles, Eileen 108

Naropa Institute 110
National Public Radio 7, 8
Nauen, Elinor 113
"The New Gazette" 42
New Haven 53
New Jerusalem 53
New Orleans 17–18, 50, 53, 116, 144, 145, 170, 173, 175
New Rochelle 53
New York City 53, 69, 75, 116–117
New York School of Poets 27, 39, 64–65, 111, 113
Nietzsche, Friedrich 26–27, 30, 33, 40, 43, 45–46, 79, 82, 83–89, 107, 110
Norse, Harold 36, 114
Notley, Alice 113

O'Hara, Frank 28–29, 39, 64, 108, 109, 111, 116, 187
Olson, Charles 5, 104–107
Oneida Community 54
Oppenheimer, Joel 26, 108
Orpheus 187
Otto, Walter F. 33
Ovid 48, 103

Padgett, Ron 113
Palmer, Donald 80
Palmer, Robert B. 33
Paris (France) 3, 19, 25, 35, 62, 65–66, 70, 75, 77
Pauker, Ana 129
Pavlov, Ivan 49
Paz, Octavio 154
Perlmutter, Andrei 36
"A Petite Histoire of Red Fascism" 31–32
Picasso, Pablo 65
Plath, Sylvia 3
Plato 47, 70
Poe, Edgar Allan 1, 65, 111
Pollock, Jackson 109
Pound, Ezra 5, 178
Powell, Colin 60
Prague 19
Proust, Marcel 15, 147

Queneau, Raymond 188

Rabelais, Francois 187
Raised by Puppets Only to Be Killed by Research 12, 18–19, 109–110

Rakosi, Carl 54
Readings, Bill 90–91
Reagan, Ronald 187
Reich, Wilhelm 24
Rimbaud, Arthur 36, 74
Rivera, Diego 57
Rivers, Larry 109
Road Scholar 50–51, 56–63, 173, 181
Robertson, Pat 184
Rome 35
Roseman, Kenneth 164
Runnings, John 62–63

Sa'adah, Anne 134–137, 139
Sade, Marquis de 45
Sainsbury, R.M. 47
Saint-Just, Louis Antoine de 137
San Francisco 23–24, 50, 68, 74–75
Sanders, Edward 1, 6, 36, 104, 108, 110, 121–124, 154–155
Santa Fe, NM 68, 71, 74
Saussure, Ferdinand 92
Savonarola, Girolamo 182
Schelling, Friedrich Wilhelm 126–127
Schlesinger, Alex 161
Schopenhauer, Arthur 40
Seattle 12, 18, 62–63, 155, 170, 185–186
Securitate 57, 125
Segonzac, Jean de
Selected Poems 67, 111, 114
Semilian, Julian 48–49
Shakespeare, William 148
Shang, Ntozake 86
Shaviro, Steven 27
Shmuilovici, Filip 128
Sibiu, Romania 39, 69, 159–165, 186–187
Simmons, Al 86
Snyder, Gary 109, 112–113
Socrates 33, 44
Solzhenitsyn, Alexander 141
Soupault, Philippe 137
Spariosu, Mihai 127
Starr, Kenneth 182
Steinbeck, John 69, 78, 81
Sterne, Laurence 187
Stirner, Max 142
Sue, Eugène 61
Sukenick, Ron 65–66
The Superball 20
Szymborska, Wislawa 48